T0221123

Intelligent Systems for Rehabilitation Engineering

Scrivener Publishing
100 Cummings Center, Suite 541J
Beverly, MA 01915-6106

Publishers at Scrivener
Martin Scrivener (martin@scrivenerpublishing.com)
Phillip Carmical (pcarmical@scrivenerpublishing.com)

Intelligent Systems for Rehabilitation Engineering

Edited by
Roshani Raut, Pranav Pathak, Sandeep Kautish

and
Pradeep N

Scrivener
Publishing

This edition first published 2022 by John Wiley & Sons, Inc., 111 River Street, Hoboken, NJ 07030, USA
and Scrivener Publishing LLC, 100 Cummings Center, Suite 541J, Beverly, MA 01915, USA
© 2022 Scrivener Publishing LLC
For more information about Scrivener publications please visit www.scrivenerpublishing.com.

Wiley Global Headquarters
111 River Street, Hoboken, NJ 07030, USA

For details of our global editorial offices, customer services, and more information about Wiley products visit us at www.wiley.com.

Limit of Liability/Disclaimer of Warranty
While the publisher and authors have used their best efforts in preparing this work, they make no rep-
resentations or warranties with respect to the accuracy or completeness of the contents of this work and
specifically disclaim all warranties, including without limitation any implied warranties of merchant-
ability or fitness for a particular purpose. No warranty may be created or extended by sales representa-
tives, written sales materials, or promotional statements for this work. The fact that an organization,
website, or product is referred to in this work as a citation and/or potential source of further information does not mean that the publisher and authors endorse the information or services the organization, website, or product may provide or recommendations it may make. This work is sold with the
understanding that the publisher is not engaged in rendering professional services. The advice and
strategies contained herein may not be suitable for your situation. You should consult with a specialist
where appropriate. Neither the publisher nor authors shall be liable for any loss of profit or any other
commercial damages, including but not limited to special, incidental, consequential, or other damages.
Further, readers should be aware that websites listed in this work may have changed or disappeared
between when this work was written and when it is read.

Library of Congress Cataloging-in-Publication Data

ISBN 978-1-119-78566-8

Cover image: Pixabay.Com
Cover design by Russell Richardson

Contents

Preface

Rehabilitation engineering uses engineering sciences to develop technological solutions and devices to assist individuals with disabilities and also supports the rehabilitation of those who have lost their physical and cognitive functions. Systems can be designed and built to meet a wide range of needs in order to help those with impaired mobility, communication, vision, hearing and cognition. And these tools and devices assist the disabled in their daily activities such as, for example, attending school or working.

Intelligent systems have a wide range of technological developments which will enhance research in the field of rehabilitation engineering. The growing list of these developments, such as machine learning, deep learning, robotics, virtual intelligence, etc., plays an important role in rehabilitation engineering.

The material collected in this book has been edited to provide information on current research achievements and challenges in the area of rehabilitation engineering and intelligent systems. The target audience of this book includes senior and junior engineers, undergraduate and postgraduate students, researchers, and anyone else interested in the trends, developments, and opportunities of rehabilitation engineering and intelligent system concepts. Research trends in the design and development of innovative technologies are highlighted along with the techniques involved. And even though it is impossible to include all current aspects of the research being conducted in targeted areas, the book is a useful resource in terms of presenting the various possible methodologies that can be applied to achieve results in the field. Presented below is a brief description of the topics covered in the 10 chapters of the book.

– Chapter 1 discusses the different spheres of rehabilitation robotics. Robots are being widely used in medical practice to support various procedures and therapies to help people with physical and psychological limitations. A survey was conducted on rehabilitation robotics that reviews rehabilitation robots with an eye towards future applications. Many researchers have collaborated on an integrated human-robot structure with cognitive abilities; and orthotic and prosthetic devices can also benefit from rehabilitation robots. Additionally, sensing technology is being used in rehabilitation robots. Moreover, this chapter examines the use of rehabilitation robots in Europe and North America.

– Chapter 2 reviews the use of neurorehabilitation robots for an automated process for the upper limb. This chapter illustrates and defines all areas of mechanical recovery technology for novices, and captures the recent robot advances being widely used by talented scientists and clinicians. Also, a few company devices for mechanical recovery are given for a better understanding of the complete picture. The use of productive robotic methodologies promotes the recovery of motor skills. This innovation combines the outcomes of social investigations on motor learning and neurological recovery in the creation and execution of automated processes, with the approval of robot specialists who operate as ideal instructors. Human-robot collaboration assumes a leading role in creating a beneficial relationship, where the human body and the robot can benefit from each other's components.

– Chapter 3 highlights an effective affordable rehabilitation robot for nervous system disorders powered by dynamic convolutional neural network (CNN) and hidden Markov model (HMM). Neurological disorders are a frequent health concern of billions of individuals around the world. This condition is caused by malfunctioning of the central and peripheral nervous systems. For example, Alzheimer's and Parkinson's diseases are not uncommon and wreck the lives of many people. In particular, those afflicted with Parkinson's disease have impaired movement resulting in freezing of gait (FOG). The only accessible treatment option is the artificial creation of dopamine levels. Therefore, robotic rehabilitation devices have been proposed which apply vibrations to activate muscle performance. These bracelets, bands, and chains are part of the sensors which are fixed to the patient's body. For processing sensor signals and decision-making, CNN and HMM are used.

– Chapter 4 focuses on smart sensors for activity recognition. Health informatics is used to collect, store, and retrieve essential health-related data. Information and communication technologies and wireless connections lead to the creation of smarter sensors. These devices are commonly used for self-monitoring of health and well-being. Use of smart sensors could help healthcare providers monitor the daily activities of the elderly. Also addressed in this chapter is the use of machine learning (ML) techniques on smartphones and wearables to capture and model human body motions and vital signs during activities of normal living.

– Chapter 5 discusses the use of assistive technology for those who are visually impaired. Acquiring knowledge is difficult for the blind, with Braille being the most commonly utilized technique of transferring information to them. These new forms of Braille include American Literary Braille, British Braille, Computer Braille, Literary Braille, Music Braille, and so on. Traditional Braille writing employs a slate and stylus. Other forms of Braille writers and computer software, such as voice recognition software, special computer keyboards and optical scanners, have been developed. Virtual Pencil math software, Audio Exam Player, and educational chatbots are a few examples of smart education solutions for the visually impaired. This chapter presents an overview of different rehabilitation procedures.

– Chapter 6 discusses IoT-assisted smart devices for the blind. Since blind people face several challenges, a lot of effort has been put into making them less reliant on others to perform tasks. As a result, we conceptualized and constructed an intelligent blindfold. Also, a smart walking stick helps visually impaired people safely move around without assistance. Even though several walking sticks and aids currently exist, they do not feature run-time autonomous navigation, object detection, identification warnings, or voice and face recognition. The proposed stick combines IoT, echo location, image processing, artificial intelligence and navigation system technology to help the user avoid obstacles.

– Chapter 7 focuses on the use of a technology that offers mobile accessibility to people with disabilities, who face numerous physical, social, and psychological problems. In many aspects of life, cutting-edge technologies are critically important. Mobile technology revolutionized the process of communication as well as education, business and rehabilitation. Many development platforms now have accessibility features that assist developers in designing apps by leveraging machine learning and deep learning, which benefit those with disabilities. A wide range of applications are available, but they all have advantages and disadvantages. The results of investigations may help those with disabilities find new alternatives that offer substantial assistance.

– Chapter 8 presents a smart solar-powered wheelchair. Mobilization is a requirement for those with disabilities, and for those with a serious impairment a mechanical wheelchair is an adequate alternative. Because mechanical wheelchairs present a significant risk of upper limb strain and injury, electric-powered wheelchairs were invented to help reduce this risk. However, inelectric-powered wheelchairs, motors are powered by batteries and hence have limited travel range and need frequent recharging. These limits can be eliminated by adding a thin-film solar panel that can be mounted behind the wheelchair as a folding, retractable roof, which doesn't employ a fixed, large, and heavy fixed panel that cannot be dismantled. Various design options, including smart controls that use electroencephalography (EEG) signals, smart navigation systems, and data acquisition via the IoT are also being considered.

– Chapter 9 discusses hand-talk assistive technology. For those who are deaf, enabling their ability to communicate requires creative technology. Therefore, many technologies may be employed for communication. Since their major form of communication is gestures, a non-signing individual is unable to comprehend hand motions; therefore, a sign language-to-audible voice conversion technique is required in order for a person with "normal" hearing to be able to understand what is being said. This chapter discusses the technology that allows the deaf to converse with the general population by employing special sensor gloves. As the speech-and-hearing impaired person moves, their moving hand uses sign language, and the technology will intercept the movement and transform it into sound so that the person with "normal" hearing can easily hear it. For those that are speech-and-hearing impaired, speech recognition systems using EEG signals, smart navigation systems, and data collection via the IoT are also described in this chapter.

– Chapter 10 discusses assistive technology for hearing-impaired children. Appropriate educational services are critical for children with hearing impairment (CwHI) due to diseases or accidents. Current research reveals that using assistive technology (AT) to communicate fully with others in an inclusive educational settingis highly beneficial for these children. Assistive technology has a strong influence on integrating these children in schools. Additionally, self-motivation is another benefit of using AT for CwHI. Assistive technology is the use of any communication device used to raise, expand, or enhance the experiences of a CwHI. It promotes the concept of beautiful individuality and works toward the aim of inclusive education by helping students manage their own needs. An inclusive education model studied CwHI, and the results of many trials, methodologies, and facilities are discussed in this study. Also described are various techniques that enhance capabilities and resources to ensure that the AT can provide an inclusive classroom environment.

To summarize, innovation has played an essential part in rehabilitating individuals with disabilities over the ages by introducing new helpful devices and techniques. While it is still possible to improve both user satisfaction and healthcare expenses, society's happiness and wealth can also be affected. Most importantly, these rehabilitation and assistive technologies and strategies help people recover by improving cognitive function and other capabilities.

The Editors
November 2021

Different Spheres of Rehabilitation Robotics: A Brief Survey Over the Past Three Decades

Saumyadip Hazra, Abhimanyu Kumar, Yashonidhi Srivastava
and Souvik Ganguli*

*Department of Electrical and Instrumentation Engineering, Thapar Institute of
Engineering and Technology, Punjab, India*

Abstract

Robots have been widely applied in the medical field to aid various surgeries and different therapies, to assist movement for patients with physical disabilities, etc. Although some review works have been carried out, trends and applications deliberated, and future of rehabilitation robotics has been forecasted, yet a consolidated survey was missing in the literature. The objective of this survey is to present a review of the rehabilitation robots, which will also open the reader to understand futuristic applications in this domain. Several researchers worked on the integrated architecture of human beings and robots with cognitive skills. The application of rehabilitation robots in orthotics and prosthetics has also been significant. The use of sensing technology in rehabilitation robots has also been addressed. Further, the scenario of rehabilitation robotics in Europe and the northern part of America is also highlighted in this work.

Keywords: Rehabilitation robotics, assistance robots, neurological disorders, prosthetics, exo-skeleton, smart robotics

1.1 Introduction

Several researchers have contributed [1] to robotics applications in surgery, rehabilitation [2, 3], neurological disorders [4], prosthetics/exoskeleton

---

Corresponding author: souvik.ganguli@thapar.edu

Roshani Raut, Pranav Pathak, Sandeep Kautish and Pradeep N (eds.) Intelligent Systems for Rehabilitation Engineering, (1–18) © 2022 Scrivener Publishing LLC

[5, 6], assistance [7], etc. The usefulness and development of rehabilitation robotics have been sufficiently emphasized in literature [8, 9]. The guidelines issued by the European Commission for robotics in healthcare were examined, and areas in rehabilitation robotics where the development is required are highlighted in [10]. The optimal approach for the iterative learning control for the robotic systems was described with its application in [11]. The research done in the field of exoskeleton robotic system was overviewed, and its applications were provided [12]. A novel method was presented for the development of a device for patients who suffered from sprained ankles and was able to track the activity of ankle [13]. The design, control, and application of Gentle/G system were presented for the patients who were recovering from brain injury [14]. The control algorithms and use of AI were overviewed, and ongoing trends, issues, and future trends were discussed in [15]. The overview of the therapeutic robotic systems and its applications areas have been explored earlier [16]. A robotic workstation was constructed using a manipulator and was tested on spinal cord injury patients [17]. For the neuroprosthetics of spinal cord injury patients, an effective FES system was developed [18].

A robotic ontology, called RehabRobo-Onto, was developed that displayed the information of rehabilitation. A software RehabRobo-Query for facilitating the ontology was presented [19]. fMRI compatible rehabilitation robotic glove was introduced for hand therapy and was equipped with a pneumatic actuator that generated motion [20]. RehabRobo-Onto, which was robotic ontology, was equipped with a method that answered natural language queries [21]. The estimation of force between joint position and joint actuation was done using an extended state observer (ESO) [22]. The process of recovery of upper limbs stroke patients was reviewed [23]. With the help of Virtual Gait Rehabilitation Robotics (ViGRR), a new concept of rehabilitation was introduced that did not require any therapist [24]. The properties of the exoskeleton robotic system were studied, and predictions regarding their benefit in coordination movements were done [25]. A design of the exoskeleton robotic system was proposed for the knee orthosis of poliomyelitis patients [26]. The previous reviews of such works can be found in [27, 28]. Work has also been conducted on the development of FCE using machine learning for rehabilitation robotics [29]. The applications of disturbance observer for rehabilitation and the challenges faced by them are presented in [30].

In this chapter, a thorough review of the various applications of robotics in rehabilitation has been conducted. The applications of robotics in neurology, cognitive science, stroke, biomechanical, machine interface, assistive, motion detection, limb injury, etc. are considered in this chapter. The chapter is organized as follows. Section 1.2 gives an overview of robotics for medical applications. Section 1.3 presents the relevant discussion and future scope in this direction. Finally, the chapter is concluded in Section 1.4.

1.2   An Overview of Robotics for Medical Applications

1.2.1   Neurological and Cognitive

Behavioral approaches have been proved effective in many cases for the treatment of patients with different injuries. A multidisciplinary behavioral approach was made for patients who had movement issues [31]. Neurological disorders have been faced by many patients due to some or other reasons. In [32], a pneumatic muscle actuated orthosis system was developed, and in [33], VR technologies were used with rehabilitation robotics for curing of neurologically disordered patients. The overview of the tools used for the rehabilitation of patients with weak limbs due to neurological disorders was presented [34].

1.2.2   Stroke Patients

Stroke is a medical emergency that needs immediate treatment. A large number of cases around the world are witnessed every year. For disabled stroke patients, the key approaches used for treatment using MANUS robotic system were presented in [35]. A novel algorithm was developed based on performance-based-progressive theory for rehabilitation, and an algorithm was developed for triggering the recovery of stroke patients [36]. The approaches made in human-centered robotic systems were presented and consisted of patient-cooperative abilities that did not impose any predefined movement on stroke patients [37]. ARKOD device for knee rehabilitation was presented, which had damping closed-loop control and an electro-rheological fluid for effective flexion of knee movement [38]. Virtual Gait Rehabilitation Robot (ViGRR) for providing gait motion, training, and motivation to the stroke patients was designed and prototyped [39]. The wearable inflatable robot was designed for stroke patients and showed less cardiac activity for the therapist [40]. Table 1.1 enlists some of the published work with the proposed solution(s) for the stroke patients employing rehabilitation robotics.

Table 1.1 Summary of certain articles related to the use of robotics for stroke patients.

Ref. number	Area of rehabilitation robotics explored	Remarks
[35]	MANUS robotic systems	Different approaches used for treating disabled people and the main areas where MANUS system had significant effects were presented.
[36]	Assistance using a performance-based-progressive theory	A novel method for assistance was developed for stroke patients, and the assistance was based on speed, time, or EMG limits.
[37]	Human-centered robotic systems	The system was applied for the rehabilitation of the impaired stroke patients, and patient-cooperative system, which produced actions based on the actions of the patient, was presented.
[38]	Knee rehabilitation device AKROD	A device was designed particularly for stroke patients and consisted of damped closed-loop control and electro-rheological fluid.
[39]	Haptic-based rehabilitation robot	Virtual Gait Rehabilitation Robot (ViGRR) was designed for stroke patients, and its prototype was also presented. It provided gait motion, training, and motivation.
[40]	Inflatable wearable robot	The device was tested on stroke patients and showed less cardiac and muscular activity by the therapist.

1.2.3 Biomechanical or Mechatronic Robotic Systems

A systems approach, mechatronics, mobility sensors, cost/benefit ratio, and softness were discussed for rehabilitation robotics [41]. An exoskeleton robot WOTAS was introduced and was loaded with control strategies that were based on biomechanical loading [42]. The analysis and applications of MEMS technology were tested by applying it to exoskeleton-based bio-mechatronic robotic systems [43]. Based on EMG signals, the torque produced by the muscles was determined using a biomechanical model, and it was predicted whether the proposed model was feasible or not [44]. An ankle rehabilitation robotic device was built, and its mechanical performance was tested [45].

1.2.4 Human–Machine Interfacing

Human–machine integration includes the tactics incorporated for better communication between machines and humans. The structure and implementation of CURL language, MUSIIC, RoboGlyph, and multitasking operator robotic system were presented [46]. The architecture of ARCHIN was produced whose task was to integrate machines with humans, and its performance was evaluated [47]. The perspective of human–machine interaction was presented, which included the issues faced by it and the solution to them [48].

1.2.5 Smart Robotics

A 2D vision-based localization system was illustrated, which could identify the light-emitting markers. It was equipped with a web camera and human–machine interaction interface [49]. An attempt was made for bridging the gap between assistive robotic systems and smart homes. Robotic system

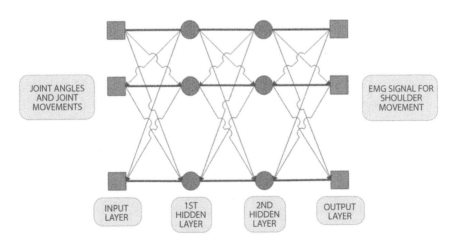

Figure 1.1 The architecture of the feed-forward neural network (FFNN) to obtain EMG signals from shoulder muscles.

Table 1.2 Summary of certain studies which explored smart robotics for rehabilitation.

Ref. number	Area of rehabilitation robotics explored	Remarks
[49]	2D vision-based localization system	The illustrated system could identify the light-emitting markers. The system was equipped with a web camera along with a human–machine interaction interface.
[50]	Assistive rehabilitation robotics and smart homes	The proposed methodology bridged the gap between these two aspects. The robotic systems extended the movement of patients and smart homes accessed their requirements and made necessary changes in itself.
[51]	A novel algorithm for impaired patients' therapy	The proposed algorithm exploited the similarities between motor recovery and motor learning, which adopted with the patients as they recovered.
[52]	Feed-forward neural network (FFNN)	FFNN was used for predicting the EMG signals from eight shoulder muscles of patients.
[53]	VR strategies	VR was integrated with multimodal displays, which enhanced the performance and also provided feedback information to the patient and motivated the patients using additional audiovisual features.
[54]	Neural networking-based facial emotion interpreter	Thermal images of persons who suffered from speech disorder were prepared, and then using a confusion matrix, its performance was evaluated.
[55]	Decision-making ability	Task-oriented robots were studied and were tested on BAXTER to check whether it was able to assist the person for training or not.

assisted the patient and smart home adjusted as per the requirements of the patient [50]. An algorithm was proposed for the therapy of impaired patients, which adopted with the patients as they recovered [51]. The feed-forward neural network (FFNN) was used for the determination of EMG signals from eight shoulder muscles [52]. A diagram representing the architecture of the feed-forward neural network (FFNN) to obtain the EMG signal from the different shoulder muscles is shown in Figure 1.1.

VR technology was integrated with multimodal displays, which provided feedback information to the patient and motivated him [53]. The facial emotions were determined using the thermal images for speech disorder patients using a confusion matrix [54]. The decision-making ability of task-oriented rehabilitation robot was tested on BAXTER robot, and its feasibility was determined [55]. A synopsis of the above discussion on the smart robotics being employed for rehabilitation purposes is deliberated in Table 1.2.

Table 1.2 summarizes some of the work that presented smart robotics for rehabilitation purposes. The work done in VR and NN technologies will instigate future research in this field.

1.2.6   Control and Stability Analysis of Robotic Systems

The stability of teaching-in method was estimated by applying it to rehabilitation robotics where it is the least error and fastest settling force was also calculated [56]. The prototype of device that enabled humans to feel and visualize synthetic objectives was designed [57]. Development of pneumatic controlled orthosis was described for stroke patients, and it was capable of position control of the robotic arm [58]. Design and interfacing of active leg exoskeleton (ALEX) were described for patients with impairment in which active force-field controller was used [59]. The complex nature of bio-cooperative rehabilitation systems and its control strategies was discussed. The probable solution to these problems was also described [60]. The stability analysis of rehabilitation robotics was presented, which consisted of the design of a controller to suppress the unintended movements [61]. An admittance control algorithm was applied on an underdevelopment rehabilitation robotics, and its preliminary report was generated [62]. The summary of the control aspects and the stability issues are presented in Table 1.3.

Thus, Table 1.3 enlists some of the work done in the field of control theory and stability analysis associated with robotics employed for rehabilitation purposes.

Table 1.3 Summary of certain articles on the control and stability analysis.

Ref. number	Area of rehabilitation robotics explored	Remarks
[56]	Stability of teaching-in method	The stability was analyzed applying it to rehabilitation robotics. The least error and fastest settling force were also calculated, and analysis was done on the elasticity of force sensor.
[57]	Devices that allowed humans to visualize and feel	The prototype required motor control and the ability to learn about human motor tasks and capability to adapt to different situations.
[58]	Pneumatic actuated orthosis	The system was developed for stroke patients. The system was capable of performing position control of the robotic arm and learning from the movement and storing it for movement the next time.
[59]	Design and interfacing of active leg exoskeleton (ALEX)	The device included a force-field controller for applying forces for proper movement, and the experimental results based on it were also presented.
[60]	Importance of psychological factors in rehabilitation	The article described challenges faced while using the closed-loop control of bio-cooperative rehabilitation systems.
[61]	Method for the stability analysis	The method consisted of the ability to customize as per the recovery rate of the patient and had a controller to suppress the unintended movements.
[62]	Admittance control algorithm on hand rehabilitation	The system consisted of a single degree of freedom. The robot was under development, and a preliminary report was generated, which showed positive results.

1.2.7 Assistive Robotic Systems

The importance of socially assistive robots was presented, which entertained the patients socially whenever they required [63]. For motivating, monitoring, and reminding stroke patients, an assistive robotic system was described, which also tracked the arm activity of the patient [64]. The cognitive strategy was extended with rehabilitation robotics by testing the Active Learning Program for Stroke (ALPS) [65]. Socially assistive robotics (SAR) was tested, and their kinematic and temporal features, which were related to fatigue, were determined [66].

1.2.8 Limb Injury

Importance of development of rehabilitation robotics for the patients who suffered from upper limbs impairment was highlighted [67]. An application of wireless sensing technology in rehabilitation robotics was presented for patients who had upper limb injury due to stroke [68]. For the rehabilitation of upper limb injury patients, a task-oriented robotic system ADAPT was designed, and its performance was evaluated [69].

1.2.9 Motion Detection

Patients who suffer from any kind of impairment are not able to produce proper movement. The robotic systems may help in determining their intention of motion and aid it by helping them to move. Production of torque in the desired direction and compensation of kinetic and breakaway friction was presented [70]. Investigation of support vector machine (SVM) identified the sEMG signals from the muscles and produced motion in that

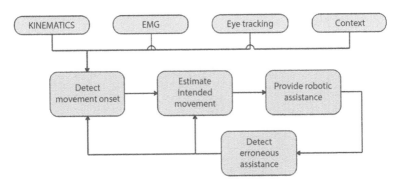

Figure 1.2 Block diagram representation of the intention estimation algorithm.

direction [71]. A method enhancing the degree of freedom of the patient and supporting the motion was developed. It was tested on ARM in III robotic system [72]. Based on the EMG signals produced by muscles, the torque and intention of motion were determined [73]. The visualization for the intention estimation algorithm is denoted by Figure 1.2 for inquisitive readers.

The intended motion of hand for hemiparetic hand patients was done using sEMG signals. It was introduced in the form of a soft glove [74].

1.3   Discussions and Future Scope of Work

The research focusing on workstation adaptations of rehabilitation robotics is mentioned in [75]. Rehabilitation game was integrated with robotics based on reinforcement learning method and depending on the skills of the player. The difficulty level of the game was increased gradually as per the skills of player [76]. A system was designed for adjusting the difficulty of game based on the score produced by the player [77]. A diagrammatic representation of the difficulty adjustment in games as per the flow model is provided with the help of Figure 1.3.

The works carried out then in Europe on rehabilitation robotics were summarized, and historical aspects and EU's different funded and active projects were also summarized [78]. The projects that were carried out on rehabilitation robotics in North America were described, and they were

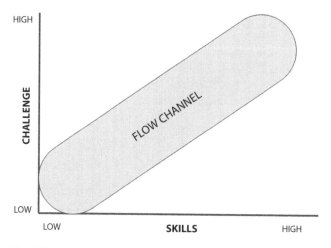

Figure 1.3 The difficulty adjustment in games according to the flow model.

Table 1.4 List of some works done in areas with potential future.

Ref. number	Area of rehabilitation robotics explored	Remarks
[14]	Gentle/G system for patients with brain injury	The design, control, and application of an experimental setup were presented for the rehabilitation. The robot had six active and three passive degrees of freedom.
[24]	Virtual Gait Rehabilitation Robotics (ViGRR)	A novel concept for rehabilitation robotics; its insights were based on ViGRR and did not require any therapist.
[33]	VR in rehabilitation robotics	Approaches made to cure neurologically disordered patients, and the importance of exercises by clinical robots was presented.
[41]	Mechatronic rehabilitation robotics	A systems approach, mobility sensors, cost/benefit ratio, and softness were discussed. The importance of softness was also discussed and was considered as an important factor.
[65]	Robotic-assisted therapy	Active Learning Program for Stroke (ALPS) was designed, and testing was done on patients for a while and was found successful in extending cognitive strategies.
[66]	Socially assistive robotics (SAR)	SAR was tested, and kinematic and temporal features related to fatigue were determined. The test was done for a sit-to-stand test and concluded that three kinematic features had a relation with fatigue.
[71]	Support vector machine (SVM)	The feasibility of SVM for the identification of the locomotion from sEMG signals produced by the muscles for rehabilitation robotics was calculated.

judged as success or failure [79]. A summary of the project carried out jointly by VA and Stanford University was examined, and all the pros and cons of the project were listed [80]. Table 1.4 showcases a list of certain areas that have the potential future scope as well.

Application of virtual reality, SVMs, etc. still requires innovative thinking and ingenuity. Robots with multiple degrees of freedom and robotic-assisted therapy have constantly been a subject of research. The readers interested in pursuing this field could consider the above topics for their study.

1.4 Conclusion

This chapter presents a review of the progress of rehabilitation robotics. Robots have found application in neurology, cognitive science, stroke, bio-mechanical, machine interface, assistive, motion detection, limb injury, etc. They have been used to aid surgeries and therapies, to take care of neurological disorders of patients, assisting patients for movement, etc. Adaptive robotics has been developed catering to patient needs and abilities. Moreover, the application of robots in orthotics, prosthetics, and neuro-rehabilitation has been intriguing. This chapter also presents the scenario of rehabilitation robotics in Europe and the northern part of America. The scope of research lies in the exploration of virtual reality, neural networks, and SVM, and application to robotics. The use of sensing technology in the rehabilitation robots with various degrees of freedom is also worthy of attention. The readers are encouraged to pursue this line of research.

References

1. Speich, J.E. and Rosen, J., Medical robotics, in: *Encyclopedia of biomaterials and biomedical engineering*, vol. *983*, p. 993, 2004.
2. Loureiro, R.C., Harwin, W.S., Nagai, K., Johnson, M., Advances in upper limb stroke rehabilitation: a technology push. *Med. Biol. Eng. Comput.*, *49*, 10, 1103, 2011.
3. Yue, Z., Zhang, X., Wang, J., Hand rehabilitation robotics on post-stroke motor recovery. *Behav. Neurol.*, *2017*, 2017. 3908135.://doi.org/10.1155/2017/3908135
4. Tefertiller, C., Pharo, B., Evans, N., Winchester, P., Efficacy of rehabilitation robotics for walking training in neurological disorders: A review. *J. Rehabil. Res. Dev.*, *48*, 4, 387–416, 2011.

5. Nef, T., Guidali, M., Klamroth-Marganska, V., Riener, R., ARM in-exoskeleton robot for stroke rehabilitation, in: *World Congress on Medical Physics and Biomedical Engineering*, Munich, Germany, September 7-12, 2009, Springer, Berlin, Heidelberg, pp. 127–130, 2009.

6. Cardona, M., Destarac, M., Cena, C.G., Robotics for Rehabilitation: A State of the Ar, in: *Exoskeleton Robots for Rehabilitation and Healthcare Devices*, pp. 1–11, Springer, Singapore, 2020.

7. Pignolo, L., Robotics in neuro-rehabilitation. *J. Rehabil. Med.*, *41*, 12, 955–960, 2009.

8. Krebs, H.I., Rehabilitation robotics: an academic engineer perspective, in: *2011 Annual International Conference of the IEEE Engineering in Medicine and Biology Society*, 2011, August, IEEE, pp. 6709–6712.

9. Yakub, F., Khudzari, A.Z.M., Mori, Y., Recent trends for practical rehabilitation robotics, current challenges and the future. *Int. J. Rehabil. Res.*, *37*, 1, 9–21, 2014.

10. Gelderblom, G.J., De Wilt, M., Cremers, G., Rensma, A., Rehabilitation robotics in robotics for healthcare; a roadmap study for the European Commission, in: *2009 IEEE International Conference on Rehabilitation Robotics*, 2009, June, IEEE, pp. 834–838.

11. Rogers, E., Owens, D.H., Werner, H., Freeman, C.T., Lewin, P.L., Kichhoff, S., Lichtenberg, G., Norm optimal iterative learning control with application to problems in accelerator based free electron lasers and rehabilitation robotics. *Eur. J. Control*, *16*, 5, 497–524, 2010.

12. Pons, J.L., Rehabilitation exoskeletal robotics. *IEEE Eng. Med. Biol. Mag.*, *29*, 3, 57–63, 2010.

13. Dai, J.S., Zhao, T., Nester, C., Sprained ankle physiotherapy based mechanism synthesis and stiffness analysis of a robotic rehabilitation device. *Auton. Robots*, *16*, 2, 207–218, 2004.

14. Loureiro, R.C. and Harwin, W.S., Reach & grasp therapy: design and control of a 9-DOF robotic neuro-rehabilitation system, in: *2007 IEEE 10th International Conference on Rehabilitation Robotics*, 2007, June, IEEE, pp. 757–763.

15. Novak, D. and Riener, R., Control strategies and artificial intelligence in rehabilitation robotics. *Ai Mag.*, *36*, 4, 23–33, 2015.

16. Krebs, H.I., *et al.*, A paradigm shift for rehabilitation robotics. *IEEE Eng. Med. Biol. Mag.*, *27*, 4, 61–70, 2008.

17. Hillman, M.R., Pullin, G.M., Gammie, A.R., Stammers, C.W., Orpwood, R.D., Clinical experience in rehabilitation robotics. *J. Biomed. Eng.*, *13*, 3, 239–243, 1991.

18. Brunetti, F., Garay, A., Moreno, J.C., Pons, J.L., Enhancing functional electrical stimulation for emerging rehabilitation robotics in the framework of hyper project, in: *2011 IEEE International Conference on Rehabilitation Robotics*, 2011, June, IEEE, pp. 1–6.

19. Dogmus, Z., Papantoniou, A., Kilinc, M., Yildirim, S.A., Erdem, E., Patoglu, V., Rehabilitation robotics ontology on the cloud, in: *2013 IEEE 13th International Conference on Rehabilitation Robotics (ICORR)*, 2013, June, IEEE, pp. 1–6.

20. Yap, H.K., Lim, J.H., Nasrallah, F., Low, F.Z., Goh, J.C., Yeow, R.C., MRC-glove: A fMRI compatible soft robotic glove for hand rehabilitation application, in: *2015 IEEE International Conference on Rehabilitation Robotics (ICORR)*, 2015, August, IEEE, pp. 735–740.

21. Dogmus, Z., Erdem, E., Patoglu, V., RehabRobo-Query: Answering natural language queries about rehabilitation robotics ontology on the cloud. *Semant. Web*, 10, 3, 605–629, 2019.

22. Sebastian, G., Li, Z., Crocher, V., Kremers, D., Tan, Y., Oetomo, D., Interaction Force Estimation Using Extended State Observers: An Application to Impedance-Based Assistive and Rehabilitation Robotics. *IEEE Robot. Autom. Lett.*, 4, 2, 1156–1161, 2019.

23. Krebs, H.I., Volpe, B., Hogan, N., A working model of stroke recovery from rehabilitation robotics practitioners. *J. Neuroeng. Rehabil.*, 6, 1, 6, 2009.

24. Berezny, N., Dowlatshahi, D., Ahmadi, M., Novel Concept of a Lower-limb Rehabilitation Robot Targeting Bed-bound Acute Stroke Patients. *CMBES Proceedings*, vol. 42, 2019.

25. Penalver-Andres, J., Duarte, J., Vallery, H., Klamroth-Marganska, V., Riener, R., Marchal-Crespo, L., Rauter, G., Do we need complex rehabilitation robots for training complex tasks?, in: *2019 IEEE 16th International Conference on Rehabilitation Robotics (ICORR)*, 2019, June, IEEE, pp. 1085–1090.

26. Yu, K.P., Yeung, L.F., Ng, S.W., Tong, K.Y., Bionic robotics for post polio walking, in: *Intelligent Biomechatronics in Neurorehabilitation*, pp. 83–109, Cambridge, Massachusetts, Academic Press, 2020.

27. Tejima, N., Rehabilitation robotics: a review. *Adv. Rob.*, 14, 7, 551–564, 2001.

28. Hillman, M., 2 rehabilitation robotics from past to present–a historical perspective, in: *Advances in Rehabilitation Robotics*, pp. 25–44, Springer, Berlin, Heidelberg, 2004.

29. Fong, J., Ocampo, R., Gross, D.P., Tavakoli, M., Intelligent Robotics Incorporating Machine Learning Algorithms for Improving Functional Capacity Evaluation and Occupational Rehabilitation. *J. Occup. Rehabil.*, 30, 3, 362–370, 2020.

30. Mohammadi, A. and Dallali, H., Disturbance observer applications in rehabilitation robotics: an overview, in: *Powered Prostheses*, pp. 113–133, Cambridge, Massachusetts, Academic Press, 2020.

31. van Vliet, P. and Wing, A.M., A new challenge—robotics in the rehabilitation of the neurologically motor impaired. *Phys. Ther.*, 71, 1, 39–47, 1991.

32. Knestel, M., Hofer, E.P., Barillas, S.K., Rupp, R., The artificial muscle as an innovative actuator in rehabilitation robotics. *IFAC Proc. Volumes*, 41, 2, 773–778, 2008.

33. Munih, M. and Bajd, T., Rehabilitation robotics. *Technol. Healthcare*, *19*, 6, 483–495, 2011.
34. Krebs, H.I., and Volpe, B.T., Rehabilitation robotics, in: *Handbook of clinical neurology*, vol. 110, pp. 283–294, Amsterdam, Elsevier, 2013.
35. Rosier, J.C. *et al.*, Rehabilitation robotics: The MANUS concept, in: *Fifth International Conference on Advanced Robotics' Robots in Unstructured Environments*, 1991, June, IEEE, pp. 893–898.
36. Krebs, H.I., Palazzolo, J.J., Dipietro, L., Ferraro, M., Krol, J., Rannekleiv, K., Hogan, N., Rehabilitation robotics: Performance-based progressive robot-assisted therapy. *Auton. Robots*, *15*, 1, 7–20, 2003.
37. Riener, R., Frey, M., Bernhardt, M., Nef, T., Colombo, G., Human-centered rehabilitation robotics, in: *9th International Conference on Rehabilitation Robotics, 2005. ICORR 2005*, 2005, June, IEEE, pp. 319–322.
38. Weinberg, B., Nikitczuk, J., Patel, S., Patritti, B., Mavroidis, C., Bonato, P., Canavan, P., Design, control and human testing of an active knee rehabilitation orthotic device, in: *Proceedings 2007 IEEE International Conference on Robotics and Automation*, 2007, April, IEEE, pp. 4126–4133.
39. Chisholm, K.J., Klumper, K., Mullins, A., Ahmadi, M., A task oriented haptic gait rehabilitation robot. *Mechatronics*, *24*, 8, 1083–1091, 2014.
40. O'Neill, C. *et al.*, Inflatable soft wearable robot for reducing therapist fatigue during upper extremity rehabilitation in severe stroke. *IEEE Rob. Autom. Lett.*, *5*, 3, 3899–3906, 2020.
41. Kwee, H.H., Rehabilitation robotics-softening the hardware. *IEEE Eng. Med. Biol. Mag.*, *14*, 3, 330–335, 1995.
42. Rocon, E., Belda-Lois, J.M., Ruiz, A.F., Manto, M., Moreno, J.C., Pons, J.L., Design and validation of a rehabilitation robotic exoskeleton for tremor assessment and suppression. *IEEE Trans. Neural Syst. Rehabil. Eng.*, *15*, 3, 367–378, 2007.
43. Rocon, E., Moreno, J.C., Ruiz, A.F., Brunetti, F., Miranda, J.A., Pons, J.L., Application of inertial sensors in rehabilitation robotics, in: *2007 IEEE 10th International Conference on Rehabilitation Robotics*, 2007, June, IEEE, pp. 145–150.
44. Sartori, M., Reggiani, M., Mezzato, C., Pagello, E., A lower limb EMG-driven biomechanical model for applications in rehabilitation robotics, in: *2009 International Conference on Advanced Robotics*, 2009, June, IEEE, pp. 1–7.
45. Guo, K., Zha, S., Liu, Y., Liu, B., Yang, H., Li, Z., Experimental Study On Wearable Ankle Rehabilitation Device, in: *2019 International Conference on Mathematics, Big Data Analysis and Simulation and Modelling (MBDASM 2019)*, 2019, October, Atlantis Press.
46. Harwin, W.S., Gosine, R.G., Kazi, Z., Lees, D.S., Dallaway, J.L., A comparison of rehabilitation robotics languages and software. *Robotica*, *15*, 2, 133–151, 1997.
47. Galindo, C., Gonzalez, J., Fernández-Madrigal, J.A., An architecture for cognitive human-robot integration. Application to rehabilitation robotics, in:

IEEE International Conference Mechatronics and Automation, 2005, 2005, July, vol. 1, IEEE, pp. 329–334.

48. Beckerle, P., Salvietti, G., Unal, R., Prattichizzo, D., Rossi, S., Castellini, C., Mastrogiovanni, F., A human–robot interaction perspective on assistive and rehabilitation robotics. *Front. Neurorob.*, *11*, 24, 2017.

49. Sabatini, A.M., Genovese, V., Maini, E.S., Toward low-cost vision-based 2D localisation systems for applications in rehabilitation robotics, in: *IEEE/RSJ International Conference on Intelligent Robots and Systems*, 2002, October, vol. 2, IEEE, pp. 1355–1360.

50. Mokhtari, M., Abdulrazak, B., Feki, M.A., Rodriguez, R., Grandjean, B., Integration of rehabilitation robotics in the context of smart homes: Application to assistive robotics. *Int. J. Human-friendly Welfare Robot. Syst. (HWRSERS)*, *4*, 2, 29–32, 2003.

51. Buerger, S.P., Palazzolo, J.J., Krebs, H.I., Hogan, N., Rehabilitation robotics: adapting robot behavior to suit patient needs and abilities, in: *Proceedings of the 2004 American Control Conference*, 2004, June, vol. 4, IEEE, pp. 3239–3244.

52. Rittenhouse, D.M., Abdullah, H.A., Runciman, R.J., Basir, O., A neural network model for reconstructing EMG signals from eight shoulder muscles: Consequences for rehabilitation robotics and biofeedback. *J. Biomech.*, *39*, 10, 1924–1932, 2006.

53. Riener, R., Wellner, M., Nef, T., Von Zitzewitz, J., Duschau-Wicke, A., Colombo, G., Lunenburger, L., A view on VR-enhanced rehabilitation robotics, in: *2006 International Workshop on Virtual Rehabilitation*, 2006, August, IEEE, pp. 149–154.

54. Appel, V.C., Belini, V.L., Jong, D.H., Magalhães, D.V., Caurin, G.A., Classifying emotions in rehabilitation robotics based on facial skin temperature, in: *5th IEEE RAS/EMBS International Conference on Biomedical Robotics and Biomechatronics*, 2014, August, IEEE, pp. 276–280.

55. Wang, W.S., Mendonca, R., Kording, K., Avery, M., Johnson, M.J., Towards Data-Driven Autonomous Robot-Assisted Physical Rehabilitation Therapy, in: *2019 IEEE 16th International Conference on Rehabilitation Robotics (ICORR)*, 2019, June, IEEE, pp. 34–39.

56. Kovács, L.L. and Stépán, G., Dynamics of digital force control applied in rehabilitation robotics. *Meccanica*, *38*, 2, 213–226, 2003.

57. Patton, J.L., Dawe, G., Scharver, C., Mussa-Ivaldi, F.A., Kenyon, R., Robotics and virtual reality: the development of a life-sized 3-D system for the rehabilitation of motor function, in: *The 26th Annual International Conference of the IEEE Engineering in Medicine and Biology Society*, 2004, September, vol. 2, IEEE, pp. 4840–4843.

58. Wolbrecht, E.T., Leavitt, J., Reinkensmeyer, D.J., Bobrow, J.E., Control of a pneumatic orthosis for upper extremity stroke rehabilitation, in: *2006 International Conference of the IEEE Engineering in Medicine and Biology Society*, 2006, August, IEEE, pp. 2687–2693.

59. Banala, S.K., Agrawal, S.K., Scholz, J.P., Active Leg Exoskeleton (ALEX) for gait rehabilitation of motor-impaired patients, in: *2007 IEEE 10th International Conference on Rehabilitation Robotics*, 2007, June, IEEE, pp. 401–407.

60. Mihelj, M., Novak, D., Ziherl, J., Olenšek, A., Munih, M., Challenges in bio-cooperative rehabilitation robotics, in: *2011 IEEE International Conference on Rehabilitation Robotics*, 2011, June, IEEE, pp. 1–6.

61. Zhang, J., Cheah, C.C., Collins, S.H., Stable human-robot interaction control for upper-limb rehabilitation robotics, in: *2013 IEEE International Conference on Robotics and Automation*, 2013, May, IEEE, pp. 2201–2206.

62. Koçak, M., Ayar, O., Gezgın, E., Preliminary Study on the Admittance Control of a Hand Rehabilitation System, in: *2019 Medical Technologies Congress (TIPTEKNO)*, 2019, October, IEEE, pp. 1–4.

63. Feil-Seifer, D. and Mataric, M.J., Defining socially assistive robotics, in: *9th International Conference on Rehabilitation Robotics, 2005. ICORR 2005*, 2005, June, IEEE, pp. 465–468.

64. Matarić, M.J., Eriksson, J., Feil-Seifer, D.J., Winstein, C.J., Socially assistive robotics for post-stroke rehabilitation. *J. NeuroEng. Rehabil.*, 4, 1, 5, 2007.

65. Fasoli, S.E. and Adans-Dester, C.P., A Paradigm Shift: Rehabilitation Robotics, Cognitive Skills Training and Function after Stroke. *Front. Neurol.*, 10, 1088, 2019.

66. Aguirre, A., Casas, J., Céspedes, N., Múnera, M., Rincon-Roncancio, M., Cuesta-Vargas, A., Cifuentes, C.A., Feasibility study: Towards Estimation of Fatigue Level in Robot-Assisted Exercise for Cardiac Rehabilitation, in: *2019 IEEE 16th International Conference on Rehabilitation Robotics (ICORR)*, 2019, June, IEEE, pp. 911–916.

67. Masiero, S., Carraro, E., Ferraro, C., Gallina, P., Rossi, A., Rosati, G., Upper limb rehabilitation robotics after stroke: a perspective from the University of Padua, Italy. *J. Rehabil. Med.*, 41, 12, 981–985, 2009.

68. Schweighofer, N., Choi, Y., Winstein, C., Gordon, J., Task-oriented rehabilitation robotics. *Am. J. Phys. Med. Rehabil.*, 91, 11, S270–S279, 2012.

69. Cifuentes, C., Braidot, A., Rodríguez, L., Frisoli, M., Santiago, A., Frizera, A., Development of a wearable ZigBee sensor system for upper limb rehabilitation robotics, in: *2012 4th IEEE RAS & EMBS International Conference on Biomedical Robotics and Biomechatronics (BioRob)*, 2012, June, IEEE, pp. 1989–1994.

70. Nef, T. and Lum, P., Improving backdrivability in geared rehabilitation robots. *Med. Biol. Eng. Comput.*, 47, 4, 441–447, 2009.

71. Ceseracciu, E., Reggiani, M., Sawacha, Z., Sartori, M., Spolaor, F., Cobelli, C., Pagello, E., SVM classification of locomotion modes using surface electromyography for applications in rehabilitation robotics, in: *19th International Symposium in Robot and Human Interactive Communication*, 2010, September, IEEE, pp. 165–170.

72. Novak, D. and Riener, R., Enhancing patient freedom in rehabilitation robotics using gaze-based intention detection, in: *2013 IEEE 13th International Conference on Rehabilitation Robotics (ICORR)*, 2013, June, IEEE, pp. 1–6.
73. Ai, Q., Ding, B., Liu, Q., Meng, W., A subject-specific EMG-driven musculoskeletal model for applications in lower-limb rehabilitation robotics. *Int. J. Humanoid Rob.*, 13, 03, 1650005, 2016.
74. Wang, L., Peng, G., Yao, W., Biggar, S., Hu, C., Yin, X., Fan, Y., Soft robotics for hand rehabilitation, in: *Intelligent Biomechatronics in Neurorehabilitation*, pp. 167–176, Cambridge, Massachusetts, Academic Press, 2020.
75. Neveryd, H., Eftring, H., Bolmsjö, G., The swedish experience of rehabilitation robotics, in: *Proc. of Rehabilitation Robotics Workshop*, 1999.
76. Andrade, K.D.O., Fernandes, G., Caurin, G.A., Siqueira, A.A., Romero, R.A., Pereira, R.D.L., Dynamic player modelling in serious games applied to rehabilitation robotics, in: *2014 Joint Conference on Robotics: SBR-LARS Robotics Symposium and Robocontrol*, 2014, October, IEEE, pp. 211–216.
77. Andrade, K.D.O., Pasqual, T.B., Caurin, G.A., Crocomo, M.K., Dynamic difficulty adjustment with Evolutionary Algorithm in games for rehabilitation robotics, in: *2016 IEEE International Conference on Serious Games and Applications for Health (SeGAH)*, 2016, May, IEEE, pp. 1–8.
78. Dallaway, J.L., Jackson, R.D., Timmers, P.H., Rehabilitation robotics in Europe. *IEEE Trans. Rehabil. Eng.*, 3, 1, 35–45, 1995.
79. Harwin, W.S., Rahman, T., Foulds, R.A., A review of design issues in rehabilitation robotics with reference to North American research. *IEEE Trans. Rehabil. Eng.*, 3, 1, 3–13, 1995.
80. Van der Loos, H.M., VA/Stanford rehabilitation robotics research and development program: lessons learned in the application of robotics technology to the field of rehabilitation. *IEEE Trans. Rehabil. Eng.*, 3, 1, 46–55, 1995.

Neurorehabilitation Robots Review: Towards a Mechanized Process for Upper Limb

Yogini Dilip Borole*[1] and Roshani Raut[2]

*[1]Department of E&TC, G H Raisoni Institute of Engineering and Technology,
SPPU, Pune University, Pune, India
[2]Department of Information Technology, Pimpari Chinchwad College of
Engineering, SPPU, Pune University, Pune, India*

Abstract

Restoration Robotics gives a presentation and outline of all zones of recovery mechanical technology, ideal for anybody new to the field. It likewise sums up accessible robot advancements and their application to various pathologies for talented scientists and clinicians. A few business gadgets for mechanical recovery have empowered to build up the ability and skill important to manage those looking for complete comprehension of the point. The usage of productive robot methodologies encourages the re-securing of engine abilities. This innovation fuses the results of social examinations on engine learning, and its neural relates into the plan, execution, and approval of robot specialists that act as "ideal" coaches, effectively abusing the construction and versatility of the human sensorimotor frameworks. In this specific situation, human–robot cooperation assumes a principal part, at both the physical and intellectual levels, toward accomplishing an advantageous connection where the human body and the robot can profit by one another's elements.

Keywords: Exoskeleton, electromyograph, rehabilitation robots, stroke

2.1 Introduction

The proportion of adolescent patients with functional impairment of the upper appendages brought on by stroke has increased rapidly, as influenced

*Corresponding author:

Roshani Raut, Pranav Pathak, Sandeep Kautish and Pradeep N (eds.) Intelligent Systems for Rehabilitation Engineering, (19–56) © 2022 Scrivener Publishing LLC

by the speed of life, unhealthy lifestyle, and environmental factors [1, 2]. The issue of appendix development, brought on by hemiplegia after a stroke, not only reduces patient satisfaction but also carries excruciating pain in education and scientific expertise. Strong restorative adjustment can improve patients' sensory function and maintain a level of joint action, and prevents reunion and improves patients' "final recovery rate."

The engine operates basically [3]. The most common remedy for recovery is moderate exercise of patients by a specialist. This strategy is difficult to build a compulsory treatment plan and is largely well managed [4]. With the advancement of robotic rehabilitation and drug rehabilitation, the regenerative robot has become a new therapeutic sensory therapy. It is very important to abuse the introduction of robots in order to recover the supplemental dose of patients with stroke [5]. Common treatment strategies, based on expert clinical knowledge, have problems with high staff utilization, long recovery cycles, side effects of restricted boundaries, etc. for the successful rehabilitation of clinical assets, and to improve personal satisfaction of patients with stroke [6, 7]. The advanced add-on robot can be divided into two types according to the original design: the last foot and the type of exoskeleton. The latter type actually provides a return that prepares for flight development. In addition, the exoskeleton type expands the range of retrieval adjustments from the plane to the third-dimensional (3D) space, which can help the affected appendix to complete the adjusted restoration in 3D space. The exoskeleton retrieval robot for the most part conducts the development of patient placement with the aid gadget (otherwise called the mechanical exoskeleton structure). The design of the auxiliary gadget is similar to the bone structure of a human implant. During the preparation, the patient appendages and comparing parts of the assistant gadget are merged together, and the merger bar of the auxiliary gadget rotates the associated member in order to deliver moving additions. It can make the appendages be trained especially in a variety of situations by controlling the gadget's auxiliary power indicators. Currently, the basic strategy of the exoskeleton robot repositioning model is one of the hottest problems in robotic retrieval tests. Contributing to the construction of various equipment and recovery levels, various land reclamation robots are developed, e.g., unique exoskeleton ADEN-7 robot with 7 degrees [8], ARMIN robot with six levels of chance (four dynamic and two active) semi-exoskeleton structure [9], an ARMEO robot that provides arm weight depletion network that supports emotional preparation, enhancement of installation, and test instruments [10], etc. In addition, the air muscles are used as a pilot to receive four levels of stimulus potential for the RUPERT movement robot [11], a LIMPACT water-based robot [12], and a CAREX cord-based robot [13]. Since then, scientists have recreated and designed a superficial regenerative robot based on pneumatic muscle drive [2], a superficial regenerative retrieval robot, an over-the-top rescue robot, and a half-drive and under the upper exoskeleton drive retrieval robot [14–22]. The reciprocal robot takes care of the problem of controlling the adequacy of movement and the summary of each human body during the recovery time spent repairing and overcomes the burden of ultimately redirecting recovered robot, which can only make basic adjustment (direct or circular movement) enough for minimal movement. Currently a protected and productive robotic retrieval building available for different applications. In any case, in the system of exoskeleton prostheses, the integration of mechanical joint movement pivot and human joint movement hub is important. The exoskeleton produces a surprising effect on the patient's joint under a deformed condition, which not only promotes pain associated with the patient's injury but also further prevents the developmental space of the patient's placement, and reduces the impact of prepared recovery. In line with these lines, the pivot of each travel pair is directed and focused on the reversal of each joint of the human body in the same way as can be considered in the external regenerative device system. The movement of each integration of the foreign exchange gadget is basically accepted by modifying or moving the couple, and obtained positive results [23, 24]. Compared with non-invasive treatment, the robotic rehabilitation framework has the advantages of high preparation, easy-to-measure performance measurement, and long-term systematic treatment of patient rehabilitation.

To meet the need for rehabilitation of patients with augmentation [21, 25] problem, a robotic over-the-counter replacement robot is being developed, primarily a powerful recovery and rehabilitation gadget for patients with stroke. The basic renewal process is shown in Figure 2.1.

Because of the understanding of common rehabilitation barriers and displays of regenerative robots, combined with the upper body appendage of vital signs structures and parameters, we determine the arm development for each integrated range from all bones and upper limbs to improve extension features; this document proposes a robotic regenerative robot design system. It is an over-the-top acquisition robot used for therapeutic restorative therapy for hemiplegic supplementation to maintain the range of motion of the appendix, prevent muscle degeneration of the appendix, improve system muscle strength, and promote functional recovery. As a result, it can provide a powerful recovery gear for patients with high appendage hemiplegia brought on by stroke [31, 47].

In this article, due to the investigation of life structures, the movement of metal, and the range of motion of the upper human appendix, the movement area of each joint is determined by the human arm, and part of the machine

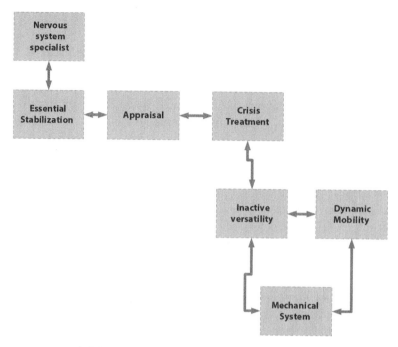

Figure 2.1 Basic rehabilitation process.

all levels designed. First, set the location link between each moving part and the ultimate high return robot wear; then model the navigation system set up on the Denavit-Hartenberg (DH) boundary plan, and the movement space is set up for an advanced wearable high-speed acquisition robot. The kinematics test is used to disperse the movement of the over-the-top wearable robot. Alternatively, to check if the return robot designed for top wear is able to understand the top assistant adjustable adjustment, working space is allocated to an over-the-counter wearable robot. Third, to investigate the harvesting potential of a more advanced retrieval robot, a powerful simulation of the robot has been completed. In conclusion, it is planned to control the robots for the acquisition of high-quality wearable, which received the following results of the adjustment of the robotic reversal.

It also ensures the ingenuity of the return robot design for high wear. The main commitments for this article are summarized as follows:

(1) Due to the speculative health features, partial movements, and scope of additional human appendages, a retrieval robot mounted with a pressure gauge is located directly on the fixed bat, then re-examined, interrupted by the above appendix depending on the patient relying on flexible transmission during recovery to prepare the scale. A

joint operated by specially designed joints intended for the elbow/wrist and shoulder joint is driven by a dental band. All engines connected to the link have been reversed to achieve greater distance transmission and reduce driving delays for the last members. The material belt is rigged to drive the members of the return robot designed for high wear, which authorizes high balance.

The design of an obsolete durable adhesive robot promotes the restoration of integration, adequately reduces the volume, weight, and delay of the actuators, and achieves a lightweight design of the standard design.

(2) In addition, the paper proposes a parallel design for the wrist-operated. With a rope and kept in a spring pressure. With a rope and kept in a spring pressure, the fixed base and the moving base of the additional decorative return robot are connected to the three wires and the spring pressure involved. The fixed base and the moving base of the additional decorative return robot are connected to the three wires and the spring pressure involved. The springs are designed to mimic the human wrist and support the versatile section to complete the growth of the wrist, while the wires are formed by regenerating the wrist muscles to control the wearable retrieval robot. In this paper, the system approach will contribute to the ongoing investigation of equal instruments with flexible members. The results will play an important role in reversing the development of the human wrist and further in improving the retrieval robot, the cord that creates the drive.

(3) The kinematics and performance of the retrieval robot designed for high wear are also confirmed, decreasing according to the DH plan and the Monte Carlo process. It shows that a removable retrieval robot that can be worn can meet recovery needs by preparing for kinematics/element investigations as well as prepared tests. In this way, it also looks at the availability and adequacy of the planning strategy, which provides an important strategy for improving the robot recovery tool.

2.2   Recovery and the Robotics

The accompanying issues have consistently existed in recovery [1]:

- Operational and useful redesign from a cerebral perspective and engine recuperation appear to require treatments that require a significant utilization of the appendage related with an imaginative kind of learning as well as capacity concerning new engine abilities.

- Based on the past thought, it is apparent that straightforward developments do not lead to greatest recuperation of the restored appendage.
- Based on the primary thought, it is additionally certain that even the utilization of uninvolved activities does not prompt ideal recuperation of the influenced appendage.

Thus, the thinking prompted the beginning and the first utilization of mechanical technology as commonsense and viable restoration devices [2, 3] in light of the fact that they can permit organization of recovery treatments that include:

1. Rousing and drawing in recovery work out.
2. Preparing that both upgrades and amplifies the usefulness of the appendage.
3. A climate brimming with rousing improvements.

Recovery upheld by the utilization of automated frameworks can have various points of interest [4]. Specifically, it permits more escalation and is custom-fitted to the patient recovery exercises and administrations (expanding the sum and nature of treatment that can be regulated); what's more, it permits all the elaborate entertainers in the group (e.g., physiotherapists, doctors, bioengineers, and different figures) to set and deal with some work boundaries to make the recovery explicit and ideal for the patient (the kind of activity, the degree of help from the robot, the power and the kinematic that the patient should apply, following the exercise).

2.2.1   Automated Technological Tools Used in Rehabilitation

There are two distinct sorts of mechanical innovative instrument (RTT) in restoration for both the lower and upper appendages. The first depends on exoskeletal instruments. The second is of the end-effector type.

2.2.1.1   Exoskeletal-Type RTT

The exoskeletal robot, regardless of whether it is for the lower [5] or upper appendages [6], totally covers the appendage, following and imitating its anthropometric attributes and hence managing each portion associated with the recovery practice. The exoskeletons are frameworks with a combination of mechanical and electronic segments that comprise a mechatronic mechanical assembly that is worn and that plays out a similar sort of kinematic/dynamic action rehearsed by the patient who wears it. These frameworks cover the influenced appendage, or if nothing else the piece of the appendage influenced by the clinical viewpoints from a restoration perspective. In these frameworks, the quantity of levels of opportunity is equivalent to that of the joints on which the restoration treatment should mediate depending on the targets. As to recovery of the lower appendages [4], we allude to class 1 exoskeletal frameworks regarding nonportable mechanical frameworks. Class 1 has a place with those nonportable automated frameworks comprising of a mechanical exoskeleton. At times, there is likewise a body weight uphold (BWS) [4] type framework circulated over the entire body for weight alleviation, a transport line, and a control data framework including biofeedback reaction frameworks dependent on augmented experience. These frameworks are normally utilized uniquely in the facility and halfway establish a development of unadulterated BWS frameworks. We explicitly allude to Class 2 exoskeletal frameworks with explicit reference to versatile frameworks that can likewise be utilized remotely to the restoration clinical climate.

2.2.1.2 End-Effector-Type RTT

In a mechanical end-effector gadget, the contribution for completing the restoration work out comes straightforwardly from the distal piece of the appendage, permitting the characteristic kinematic initiation of the development without unnatural requirements. These frameworks are utilized for both lower [7] and also upper appendage [8, 9] restoration. The robot with the end-effector interconnects to the appendage in a solitary point, for the most part a handle or a grasp point for the restoration of the upper appendage or a pedal-like apparatus for the restoration of the lower appendages. As regard the restoration of the upper appendages regarding end-effector frameworks, now and again we talk about Cartesian frameworks because of certain imperatives that can be forced in the directions additionally joined with explicit activities (likewise gamified) given by programming.

2.2.2 Benefits of the RTTs

Both the two RTTs produce persistent advantages [4–9]. It is currently grounded that for the lower appendages, the RTT produces different advantages, counting:

Improved trunk control.

Improvement of the rest wake cadence and decrease of apparent weariness in conveying our everyday life exercises.

Pain alleviation.

Improvement in the condition of emotional well-being.

Improvement of general anthropometric attributes (decrease of fat mass, increment of lean mass).

Improvement of intestinal and bladder work.

A portion of these advantages are additionally gotten because of the blending with explicit programming additionally dependent on computer-generated simulation (VR) as well as enlarged reality (AR), and furthermore in characterized secured vivid virtual conditions where the recovery situations called Cave Programmed Virtual Environment (better known with the abbreviation CAVE) occur.

It is presently grounded that for the upper appendages, the utilization of an RTT shows a few benefits, including:

- Neuromata improvement of appendage work.
- Pain alleviation.
- Improvement in the condition of psychological well-being
- Improvement of general anthropometric attributes (decrease of fat mass, increment of lean mass).
- Improvement of psychological capacities.

A portion of these advantages are additionally acquired thanks to blending with explicit programming that, for the most part, offers spurring GAME and as of late, at times, is likewise dependent on computer-generated reality or potentially enlarged reality.

2.3 New Directions to Explore and Open Problems: Aims of the Editorial

2.3.1 New Directions of Research and Development and First Aim of the Editorial

As of now, advanced mechanics for recovery are pushing a great deal of innovative work; what's more, various new fascinating headings are opening both straightforwardly associated with the automated apparatuses referenced above and on the side of a considerably more extensive restoration measure.

A portion of these headings that all the more straightforwardly relate with movement recovery [4, 10, 11] are:

1. To evaluate the impacts of utilizing robots at various periods of recuperation.
2. To create wearable robots simple and viable to wear and eliminate.
3. To diminish the expenses likewise by methods for new models of care.
4. To improve and reevaluate the models of care dependent on advanced mechanics.
5. To engage the cooperative energy and coordinated effort between experts of the recovery group and architects through shared and appropriately planned undertakings.
6. To make computer-generated reality, expanded reality, at home advancements, exoskeleton, and counterfeit insight accessible for the treatment of psychological as well as degenerative conditions.

Different bearings, more engaged to mental help, in a more extensive way to deal with recovery measure are the accompanying [12]:

1. To put resources into social robots explicitly intended to help during the recovery stages (concerning model being taken care of by the older).
2. To put resources into social robots explicitly planned as social middle people to help during correspondence/treatment movement (as being taken care of by the chemical imbalance).
3. To deal with the issue of the sympathy in mechanical technology particularly according to communication with the social robots. Considering the abovementioned, the publication intends to invigorate researchers to report their encounters identifying with different parts of advancement on the turn of events and utilization of mechanical technology in recovery both from a mechanical and clinical perspective.

2.3.2 Open Problems and Second Aim of the Editorial

In spite of the incredible improvement of advanced mechanics in the restoration field, we are helping to a few unique methodologies in the utilization and in the pertinent models of care. For instance, both the recovery treatments and the results in the global display are frequently evaluated in an alternate manner. As in different areas, for example, telemedicine, mechanical technology is regularly utilized exceptionally restricted to direct as well as examination projects. Much the same as in telemedicine, all angles that can fortify the utilization of mechanical technology in routine clinical exercises should be tended to in the global display with solid committed activities. Through this methodology, restoration advanced mechanics will actually want to be important for the arrangement of proposed medical care offers in each state with an unmistakable repayment of the demonstrated administrations. Considering the abovementioned, the article points likewise to animate researchers to report their encounters identified with these different parts of the utilization of mechanical advances utilized in the recovery habitats and research facilities. From this assortment acquired with heterogeneous strategies, which probably will go from the audit to the mass overview, we hope to have significant reactions and boosts for the global academic local area.

2.4   Overview

As the findings regarding the Global Activity on Neurology and Public Health developed by the World Health Organization, a large number of vascular disorders continue and are reversible, contain a global medical issue [1], and have a particular impact on individual adults. Also, a high future makes society of more than 60 people progressively higher [2]. Persistent gatherings for rehabilitation administrators in the Commonwealth are designed for neurological disorders, as outlined in the general view [3]. 70% of respondents provided recovery management for people with stroke, multiple sclerosis, severe cerebrum injury, neurological disorders, and, in addition, other neuromuscular conditions. The different treatments mentioned were those that provided recovery for people with a single brain injury (10%), spinal cord injury (9%), amputees (5%), muscle paralysis (4%), learning disabilities (1%), and suffering (1%). In Spain, a similar situation appears where muscle and bone failure (half), neurological disorders (15%), severe injuries (29%), and others (6%) are treated in the management of recovery [4]. The current situation, along with the need for further recovery, assistance for people with disabilities, means that automatic care and rehabilitation can play a significant role in the long run. Nowadays, research on the use of automated frameworks in various fields identified by healthcare is extensive [5–7].

In the field of recovery, logical writing demonstrates the different order of such structures as indicated by their level of communication [8], the most important points treated [9–12], the release of rescue robots [13, 14], control strategies [15, 16], and therapeutic efficacy [17–20]. In any case, no experiments were performed on the method of appropriate recovery, and the commitment of mechanical technology to the various stages of the recovery or communication cycle was not examined. In this article, an efficient writing survey is directed to distinguish the commitment of mechanical technology for upper appendage neuro rehabilitation featuring its connection with the restoration cycle and to explain the planned examination headings in the advancement of a self-sufficient recovery measure.

2.5   Renewal Process

A World Disability Report by WHO and the World Bank [21] provides the definition of recovery: "a number of measures that help people who experience, or are likely to experience, inability to achieve and continue to function effectively in communication with their surroundings." in various definitions in a world characterized by social diversity. UMeyer *et al.* [22] provided the calculated visual recovery:

"The social process is based on the WHO integration model of performance, inefficiency and efficiency, with the aim of empowering people with medical problems they experience or tend to cope with inability to achieve and maintain good co-operation with the climate" of the patient's well-being throughout the recovery cycle. These interactions include tangible evidence of human problems and needs, related to issues in human priorities and climate, setting goals for recovery, planning and action, and impact assessments [21]. This approach is called the recovery cycle (see Figure 2.1), adapted from the World Report on Disability [21], and recently developed by Stucki and Sangha [23] and modified by Steiner *et al.* [24].

By the way it works, the recovery cycle consists of four steps: testing, operation, mediation, and testing. The interaction occurs at two levels: the first is about the direction given by the continuation of care, and the second is about the provision of specific care [25]. From a practical point of view, the test program contains an ID of individual issues and needs, an investigation of the ability to rescue and guess, a description of the assistance provided, and the objectives of the plea program. Work refers to the placement of a person in the most appropriate intercession assistance program in treating their needs. From the direction of the guide, no decisions appear on the roll. Assessment refers to the help and accomplishment of the purpose of intercession. From the point of view of providing specific assistance, the assessment includes tangible evidence of issues, audits, and expected changes in assistance or mediation program objectives, a description of the main objectives of the recovery cycle, and objectives to address. The action phase refers to the professional side, and social advocacy is essential to achieving the goals of mediation. Dependence includes the determination of methods, measures, and a description of the target measures to be achieved within a predetermined timeframe. Ultimately, testing determines spatial achievements related to specific symptoms, recovery cycle objectives, and, finally, the goals of the mediation program. It also includes selections in relation to the requirement for another mediation cycle based on other tests.

2.5.1 Renovation Team

Rehabilitation requires the management of many medical care providers with novel skills, preparation, and skills that are used to fully restore patients' strengths and their positive recovery in all areas of life [26]. Rehabilitation experts have chosen the concept of "continuous focused treatment." This is not intended to alleviate the needs of the patient but rather to strengthen the patient as the head and judge of the mediation as indicated by the wishes implanted by the patient [27]. The inclusion of different clinical approaches can be done with three functional models [26, 28]: (a) a multigroup model—in which colleagues interact and transmit between them, knowing that they are composed of all components and provide testing and equal but free operation; (b) a multisectoral group model—in which group members share a common source of information (intended to encourage the advancement of nonfiction), and selections are made in one or a few general circuits (hence, drugs developed by independent experts); and (c) a multidisciplinary team model—not only promoting communication within the group but also gaining information from other related scholars and joining them in training [29]. Since the segmentation model is specific to promote early communication, it is extremely appropriate for retrieval groups [28].

2.5.2 Renewal Methods and Results

Recovery techniques are a myriad of recovery activities that reflect more physical strength, structure, exercise and coordination, natural flexibility, and other factors. The effects of restorative benefits and changes in human performance over the long term cannot be measured by a single measure or set of measures [30]. These results can be tested in three terms measurements of the Worldwide Classification of Functioning, Disability and Wellbeing (ICF) [31]: body capacities and designs, exercises, and, furthermore, interest.

2.6 Neurological Rehabilitation

One example of recovery points to the treatment of neurological problems that affect the nervous system and the neuromuscular system, known as neuro regeneration. These types of problems can bring about mental or physical disability or recurrence of both and persist or may change again. Rehabilitation can be seen as a cycle that aims to improve one's social cohesion in the public eye and a sense of prosperity. This description includes a few highlights: recovery is by no means a form of mediation; emphasis is placed on the patient himself; objectives indicate social functioning, as well as welfare or prosperity; and nothing but a closed cycle in patients who can recover, especially or completely, but applies to all remaining patients with long-term withdrawal problems [32]. This will be followed by shortages, travel limits, and investment restrictions, which include a comprehensive approach to assistance [33].

The complexity of the issues brought on by traumatic brain injury underscores the need for a team working on its own treatment, a model of the most widely used multidisciplinary framework [34]. The organization of a multifaceted group in the renewal of the neuro is not entirely clear, but there is agreement on the key people who should be in the group. According to the Union of European Clinical Specialists (UEMS), the multidisciplinary team must include complementary medical professionals: real-time specialists, returning paramedics, rehabilitation doctors, terminology counselors, speech therapists, therapists, social workers, muscle therapists, and specialists diet [35].

The recovery cycle that appears in Figure 2.2 works in the case of the emotional recovery of some of the underlying substances examined below.

2.6.1 Evaluation

The recovery interaction begins with gathering information from the patient and others to set up the issues; the reasons for, and factors affecting, every issue; and, furthermore, the desires and assumptions for every invested individual. It is also important to consider expectations that depend on analysis, general history, broadcast, and autonomy and the nature of impedance, as well as other individual, social, and environmental factors [36].

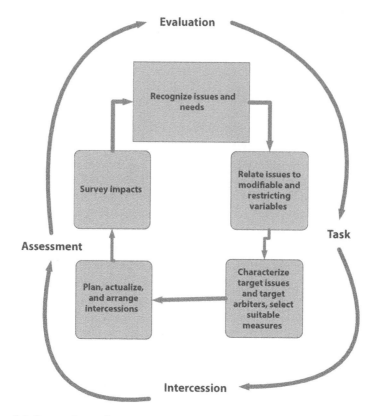

Figure 2.2 Restoration cycle.

To date, the development of targeted scales has been developed to assess the level of freedom of patients. Three basic ICF sites can be used at this point as a clinical device [37, 38].

(i)   Disability: The general physical functions that need to be assessed in a neurosurgeon are those identified by genetic makeup, muscle, development, and hearing and cognitive ability.

After that, the few most important growths are muscle, developmental size, concentration, memory, and balance.

There are traditional scales included at this level similar to the Beck Depression Inventory, Behavioral Disruption Test, Canadian Neurological Scale, Clock Drawing Test, French Aphasia Test, Fugl-Meyer Trial Recovery after Stroke, General Health Questionnaire-28, Geriatric Depression Scale and

Despondency Anxiety Scale, Mini-Mental State Examination, Altered Ashworth Scale, Montreal Visual Comprehension Test, Invisible Visual Vision Test, Community Health Center Stroke Scale, and Orrington Prognostic Scale.

(ii) Function: while evaluating a patient's exercise, the specialist will check whether they are competent as it was the assignment yet and the quality with which it is performed. According to a study by Lennon [39], one of the most widely used scales in the recovery process was the Barthel Index, followed by the Rivermead Motor Assessment and Useful Independence Measuring. More than a quarter of counselors (28%) used the results tools they were pregnant with, which could not be tested for static quality or legitimacy. The various types of scales at this level are: Test Action Test, Berg Balance Scale, Box and Square Test, Chedoke-McMaster Stroke Assessment Scale, Variety of Clinical Outcomes, Active Activity Phases, Country Renewal Revealing System, Frenchay Activities Index, Modified Rankin Handicap Scale, Motor Assessment Scale, Nine-Hole Peg Test, Rivermead Mobility File, Timed "Up and Go" Test, and the Wolf Motor Capacity Test.

(iii) Participation: this is a more complex concept than the challenges and exercise, but it is the key in understanding patients and their health and helping to plan treatment. Collaborative physiotherapy testing thus focuses on exercise or activities and when patients participate in them, patients are excluded, and patients wish to cut more than that, which can be improved and will definitely be weakened. The standard scales used are the following:

Canadian Performance Measure, EuroQol Quality of Life Scale, London Handicap Scale, Medical Results Short Form 36, Nottingham Health Profile, General Health Index Recovery, Stroke Impact Scale Profile, Stroke Impact Scale, and Stroke Specific Quality of Life Scale.

2.6.2   Treatment Planning

As indicated by the pathology, the rescue team plans specific arrangements based on the conclusion (issuing ID) and the patient's inability. It is important to note the clear terms identified for usage issues. Restoration purposes often follow SMART standard as it should be clear, measurable, feasible, efficient, and time-limited [32]. There are three key areas in which restorative communication is divided: (1) it moves towards that disability reduction; (2) methods aimed at acquiring new skills and programs, which will enhance action; and (3) is approaching that assistance to address the climate, physical, and social, and therefore inefficiency transmits a series of minor setbacks. The design of a sensory recovery program should take into account the previous three approaches, including SMART level.

2.6.3   Mediation

Specific Methods. Explicit restoration mediations incorporate those identified with actual medication, word-related treatment, discourse and language treatment, dysphagia, the executives, neurophysiological mediations, mental evaluation and intercessions, healthful treatment, and, furthermore, different intercessions [25]. A wide scope of explicit methods is utilized in the act of recovery [40]. These strategies are used to treat various patients who differ extensively across various topographical areas.

As of now, the proof recommends that to be powerful, restoration requires the act of exercises in the most important potential conditions, as opposed to undertaking logical activities pointed toward changing weaknesses [41]. This is once in a while alluded to as assignment that is explicit to the preparation. Notwithstanding, different methodologies are referred to like help procedures (like Bobath idea, Brunnstrom strategy, Kabat strategy, or Rood strategy), present-day procedures (such as treadmill preparing with body weight uphold, requirement induced development treatment, or useful electrical incitement), or, on the other hand, remuneration procedures.

2.6.4   Assessment

In this stage, the state of being of the tolerant is reconsidered to decide the adequacy of the treatment, in view of the SMART goals [32] at first raised. The contemplations for release on account of the neurological patient are extremely differed, since the clinician should decide if the improvement accomplished is adequate from the clinical perspective of the patient (patient-centered practice). Past quantitative examinations and contextual analyses have shown that the utilization of patient-focused objective arranged with grown-ups going through neurological restoration can improve self-saw and noticed objective execution and fulfillment [42]. A patient-focused methodology includes objectives that are set by the patients based on their own definition of the issues. This methodology empowers a more noteworthy self-determination; what's more, it controls and upgrades the individual's latent capacity for dynamic investment.

Furthermore, one should consider the basic obsessive cycle, the constant idea of specific pathologies, the requirement for oversight as well as the congruity in the nonappearance of an expressive up close and personal restoration treatment, or, on the other hand, the degenerative and reformist character of a few neurological pathologies [44, 45], like Parkinson's illness, different sclerosis, or Alzheimer's illness.

2.7   State-of-the-Art Healthcare Equipment

2.7.1   Neuro Renewal of Upper Limb

In this phase, this test will include parts of the recovery cycle used to regenerate the high neuro appendage created with the help of any type of repair framework. The robot system for the upper limb regeneration is shown in Figure 2.3.

2.7.1.1   *Things and Method*

2.7.1.1.1   Methods of Search
The creators welcomed the October 2017 writing review on the discovery of high-resolution neurotransmitter robots using visual terms such as robot, emotions, recovery, high, augmentation, point of resilience, arm, hand, neuro regeneration, mediation, medical aid, treatment program, and different combinations. The data sets were from Brain, Science Direct, PubMed/Medline, and IEEE. Only papers written in English were considered to the pursuit that stretches all the details of the information. Studies are included for the following reasons: (1) high-quality (direct) add-on frames; (2) frames depend on the end user and exoskeleton gadgets (economically available or not); (3) clinical communication was led; and (4) the effects of robotic-assisted treatment were evaluated.

2.7.2   Advanced Equipment for Neuro Revival of the Upper Limb

In line with the Strategic Research Agenda for Robotics in Europe [43], medical services are considered to be a combination of three domains:

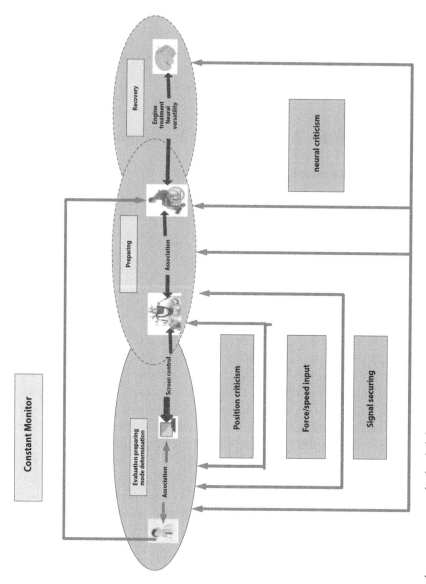

Figure 2.3 Robot system: upper limb rehabilitation.

(1) high-quality clinical equipment—care support structures (determination) and remedial measures (medical procedure); (2) recovery—which includes postoperative care or post-traumatic stress disorder where direct contact with the robot's frame will promote recovery or continue as a exchange of lost energy; and (3) assistive technology—incorporating various components of operational technology within the range of medical care where the essential capacity of the service delivery framework is either to provide assistive care or services or directly to patients in a medical clinic or specialist research office.

In this way, gadgets [61–70] that need to be prepared (robotic-assisted treatments), supportive (exoskeletons), or implanted (prosthesis) disability tests or, on the other hand, impaired physical strength and construction are limited to restoring high-quality equipment. Therefore, robots are included as an important tool in the recovery cycle in neurological therapy.

Such structures are effective and help the professional to perform a high recovery rate. However, it is unclear how long the default entities provide this assistance in the recovery cycle. To improve the type of assistance provided, it should be divided into how the guide is administered and when.

2.7.2.1   Methods of Testing

As recently shown, the first and final part of the recovery cycle is an active test. It is important to note that most of the tests performed by mechanical components are not functional tests (indicated on the bench and in the follow-up treatment categories), and their results provided indications for patient presentation. Currently, useful tests are performed with custom tests and scales given by experts. The basic highlights of the robotic-assisted study framework relating to the experimental cycle are as follows:

(1) Test Mode. Patient demonstration tests can be completed in two ways: scheduled or nonscheduled. Scheduled mode compares the online information test, that is, during the turn of events or at the end of a meeting. In fact, the nondefault mode compares to a broken information investigation (after the end of the meeting). Progress data are available for the entire work group, as indicated by the segmentation model. Data management is one of the boring activities that promote the flexibility of the consultant. As of now, there are a number of systems for the electronic clinical recording (EMR) system for patient information management [46], including by looking at man-made assumptions [47]. After all, one of the useful features integrated into the robotic aided structures is the organization, and the power of knowledge as a result allows for years of renewable energy reports.

The results of the study show that an additional 45% of entities (business) offer some form of assistance in expanding treatment. The most popular help is by offering a wide range of activities, games (REOGO, DIEGO, and ARMEO), or medical meetings (INMOTION framework) that can be developed or coordinated by a consultant. The other framework (REHAROB) similarly allows for the selection of practices based on the most commonly used coping strategies in real recovery, such as the Bobath or Kabat strategy. Then again, the internal and external investigation of the record-based treatment of robotic aids, as it allows for rapid deployment testing, fills in as a selection aid tool to determine patient discharge. The INMOTION [71–80] framework allows the release sites to be built based on a five-test exhibition that registers kinematics knowledge and energy knowledge. To the creators' information, there are no business frameworks ready to naturally produce a total recovery procedure from the underlying practical evaluation information, and along these lines, the advisor actually needs to appropriately distinguish the patient's issues by methods for a dependable analysis and the correct decision of clinical measures to assess the adequacy of the treatment.

2.7.2.2 Renewal Methods and Results

Normally, rehabilitation takes place over a period of time but may involve one or more individual interventions delivered by a person or, on the other hand, a team of rehabilitation staff and may be required from a strong or early stage immediately following admission of illness in post-acute condition and final stages. Recovery reduces the effect of a wide range of diseases. In addition, neuro regeneration often relies on expert control, competing between different ways of thinking and exposing the greatest risk to what the neuro regenerative robot should do [48].

The robotic aided structures allow for the repair of a disabled appendage in many assemblies and effectively, without loss of functionality. In the case of a targeted treatment district, the number of members in the appropriate treatment unit has been indicated. No gadgets covering the construction of all the upper appendage members were found, i.e., shoulder, elbow, wrist, and hand (including finger joints). ARMEOSPRING, INMOTION, and ARMEOPOWER structures learn how to connect the joints of the shoulder and elbow and in addition prepare for the expansion of the flexo wrist and hand grip, without the finger joints.

The therapeutic performance of specific tasks prepared for prayer assisted by robots is demonstrated. It is therefore reasonable that 86% of audit entities look at this approach. It is evident that the structures have more than one mode of operation (pride, flexibility, strong support, or strong restraint). This speaks to the amazing preferred position when considering treatment options in a flexible and well-planned way for the type of injury. A few frameworks are developing robotic applications, which can provide assistance in the development or remuneration of gravity through transmissions based on connectors or pneumatic actuator components.

The pneumatic actuator [81, 90, 98] frames offer the advantage of building high power with low weight added to the gadget, while the transmission modes have more stunting input, perfection, and greater flexibility in their input by members.

Finally, all of the restorative components of the tested technology can detect and naturally maintain biomechanical measurements during treatment. To each set of machines, one is able to measure workplace, levels of shared development, more energy expenditure, such as quality in terms of greater accuracy, and completeness of directions. Various steps were obtained in the past at a given speed to perform and fulfill assignments, and as response times. The security and power of these parameters are accelerated due to the natural sensitivity of the automatic frame (encoders, power sensors, current sensors, etc.). These are paid records due to the physical properties of the equipment.

2.8 Towards Autonomous Restoration Processes?

The advancement of independent frameworks is a functioning line in mechanical technology by and large, and with expanding presence in medical services applications, it is as of now producing valuable outcomes as it has done in industry [49]. That is the situation of careful robots in insignificantly intrusive systems for executing independently straightforward careful assignments, in view of the exactness of robot developments, picture handling calculations, and psychological frameworks [82–89].

There are numerous different models than careful advanced mechanics of translational exploration applied to medical care. The regular comprehension in the mechanical local area is that the objective of automated restoration gadgets ought to be to help specialists in playing out the sorts of exercises and practices they accept to give their patients the most obvious opportunity with regards to a useful recuperation. Be that as it may, a few boundaries have been recognized, for the specific instance of recovery advanced mechanics. The first recognized hindrance is the absence of viable correspondence in the arranging phase of planning mechanical technology helps, between engineers and also specialists. Second, large numbers of gadgets are extraordinarily confounded, from both a designing and an ease of use perspective. Indeed, "easy to-utilize" gadgets are more probable to be embraced by the clinical local area than those that have since quite a while ago been set up on occasions or require numerous advisors and additionally help to utilize [50]. Other major obstacles are the cost and accessibility, its relevance and adequacy of treatment, and the duration of mechanical therapy. Many works address these issues. The back models are those of Acosta *et al.*, which show that while computer games can provide a convincing interface, it is much better whenever it is intended to identify obvious weaknesses [51]. Burgar *et al.* incorporate the importance of providing high administrative power (long duration of treatment each day) in a powerful side study using the MIME robot [52]. Telemedicine and telephone rehabilitation are promising features for remote construction for a superficial, easy-to-use restorative framework that can allow for patient counseling work at home. Real games and tangible portable gadgets are emerging as the most inspiring devices to break this limit. The last limit, however not the smallest one in the view of the creators, is the lack of equipment, which greatly creates the total cost of medicine. Is there a great deal of power to capture medical interactions?

To incorporate this method of mechanization to deal with the rate of retrieval, it is first important to differentiate how connections are created and to classify the ones that are less useful. Computer programming, such as the needs and controls to achieving this goal.

In the literature review presented in this document, we have divided the three main regions into a recovery cycle in which key technicians add to the use of equipment: treatment planning conferences, mediation, and evaluation of therapeutic efficacy. This cycle of recovery, from Figure 2.1, has been transformed into a computerized cycle as shown in Figure 2.2. In this figure, entertainers (patient and professional) are supported by a few computer resources, as will be explained below.

2.8.1 Default Renewal Cycle

This document suggests the formation of a continuous cycle of recovery that is more explicit as to which components of interaction will be installed on a computer, just as the processors and components are installed. The autonomous cycle will be constructed in this way with five elements directly related to the squares of the first cycle. In line with this trend, three forms of entertainment have been categorized: client, clinic (grouped), and computer systems. Although a few frames with robots can be accessed, as shown in Figure 2.2, we expect that the ones used are better suited for each case. Proper joint effort between the medical team and the robotic structures is essential in achieving a well-established recovery rate.

The association between the three members during the mechanical rehabilitation process will be shown in Figure 2.4. Initially, a basic examination (performed by a meeting and investigation) is performed by a physician to distinguish the patient's issues and needs and select the most appropriate treatment options. Similarly, appropriate scales for practical testing are taken to measure the impedance level of usefulness

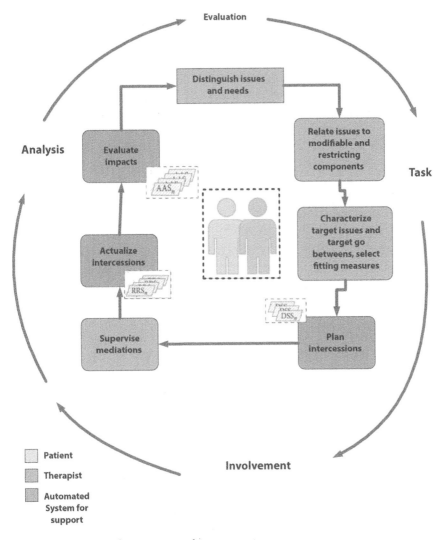

Figure 2.4 Automated restoration cycle.

brought on by nerve injury. Here, where the first robotic-to-robin framework is present, the standardized test framework plays a practical test using the same clinically approved scales. The results obtained with AAS are naturally renewed in the patient's clinical history. Moreover, these effects are effective as a limitation of knowledge in the second structured framework, a network of spiritual selection. DSS [91–96] aims to organize the most appropriate treatment session for the patient, creating specific interventions. This figure is based on the requirements identified in the recently launched writing survey.

The specialist talks about the patient to evaluate and change goals, choosing which treatment plans proposed by the DSS will be available. At that point, automated rescue agencies play communication. After pleading with RRS, a feasibility test similar to the one below was performed, measuring the adequacy of the recovery measures. With this, AAS is also used. Finally, when all identified issues are considered to have been resolved or accepted by both physicians and the patient, the recovery cycle is over. Alternatively, important cycles will be made to try to deal with excessive problems.

It can be well documented that the proposed mechanical frameworks operate independently and freely but that they are naturally related and dependent on each other for productive work, with concerted effort by the clinic and the patient. Strategies for issuing measurements and providing them and their level of acceptance by both clients and social workers should be supported and evaluated, such as the right to achieve computer use. Planning to help recovery frameworks, although it is emphasized that no obligation is to be met, it is important to plan for the understanding of the requirements requested by counselors to enable easy reconciliation of innovation in their daily activities [53].

By making it easier and easier to access resources to make this cycle of recovery, the power to extend the recovery cycle can be expanded not only as a permanent action but also in addition as a fixed recovery, for example, finding appropriate energy-saving treatment in destructive cases.

In this way, in the test of the creators, the requirements for the components of the recovery cycle be met in order to be self-sufficient are depicted next.

2.8.1.1 Computerized Testing Programs

With the discovery of experimental strategies in neuro regeneration [97–111], the use of a standard engine and practical scales is a key approach to determining the adequacy of the reversal rate. Therefore, the development of strategies based on the standard commonly used test and known expert in retrieval is one of the research lines developed to achieve a self-sufficient cycle.

There is now an investigation into this work, looking at two structures: process and measurement. In terms of techniques, controlled experiments without direct consultation with a specialist are best suited for robotics. With respect to measurements, it is important to examine which provides the most important and least disruptive data for the study to be evaluated [54].

It is commonly seen that FMA may be the most widely used scales used in engine testing in early clinical trials for this included study. It therefore makes sense that these types of experimental strategies may be explored. The use of RGB-D sensors, internal balance sensors, and various sensors allows beating a piece of FMA to be made into a robot [55]. Besides, perhaps the biggest problem related to testing using a culture test is the time they take the counselor to control us.

The address of the various activities sets out the design of the test strategies, for example, the BBT model [56]. All assumptions, a large number of scales, and a combination of strategies (based on sensors, global positioning frames, PC based, etc.) make the topic of computerized testing a promising line of testing.

In this regard, writing in addition reveals a few activities that focus on using machines on a very high level and "advanced" scale. As cultural scales are widely used in clinical preliminaries in retrieval, as found in this article, and since the experimental organization is tedious, it seems reasonable that robotization of these species of assessment strategies be considered. There is a significant difference in focus between clinical evaluation and evaluation. Custom scales include a few things.

However, the estimates are based on feature tests and a few investigations [57], which show that multi-item measures require fewer selectively selected products to produce reliable and legal standards.

Following the recovery cycle model, most of the tested components (depending on the end result or exoskeletons) are clearly found within the mediation stages of the recovery cycle. In any case, their level (46% of final performance, more than 43% exoskeleton) adjusted the test phase, based on the estimates available for use.

These tests complement as a "quick test" procedure to assist the counselor and educate the patient about the effectiveness of recovery interactions; however, there are not many activities that report near trials or clinical initiatives for acknowledging nonclinical ratings.

2.8.1.2   Choice Support System

Choice emotionally supportive networks in view of computerized reasoning (AI-fueled DSS) are quite possibly the most dynamic fields as of late, and it is normal that they will before long add to the dynamic measure. In medical services, an assortment of programming for EMR, the board is as of now accessible to help the specialist in dynamic. Notwithstanding, the conclusion of infections still presents genuine restrictions. We can discover various cell phone applications that permit an online determination, yet the dependability of the finding is not yet predictable with that of a specialist [58]. Plus, scientists in the man-made brainpower local area have begun to plan robot-helped recovery gadgets that execute man-made reasoning strategies to enhance the dynamic help procedures found in Section 2.2. Clinical choices are a significant part of the restoration cycle, since they include the assurance of the goals and plan of the restoration treatment. As can be found in this survey, the help given via mechanized frameworks for this sort of errand is through more solid target data about the engine execution of the client during the mediation, just as permitting the execution of various sorts of mediation techniques that can be designed by the clinician.

With respect to the task phase of the recovery cycle, there are two stages that could be robotized by utilizing computerized reasoning procedures: the arranging of mediation medicines and the task of fitting RRS for intercession.

Identified by the classification of antibodies, the age of these conferences depends on the various components depending on the type of wound and what it means in the evolution of events of exercise for the daily life of the patient. Many interventions are designed to manage a particular effect (strong measures of obvious problems); however, there is no reason to accept that good treatment.

In addition, meeting planning should consider the resources available to hold such a meeting to remove the appropriate RRS from the type of injury (e.g., hand injuries cannot be repaired by a elbow designed gadget).

In this way, we have identified a number of requirements that must be met to establish strategic frameworks for treatment planning: (1) the enjoyment between outcome measures and standardized approaches, with the aim of ending innovative-based interventions and critical thinking processes; (2) classify these measures according to the level of impact (mild, moderate, and sensitive); (3) by looking at the models, distinguishing the boundaries that reflect the sufficiency of the socio-economic status of the patient and the sound profiles; (4) having the opportunity to measure the client's status against a reliable government assistance model; and (5) create a meeting that can be used with accessible mediation structures.

These requirements suggest that the integration of DSS-controlled intelligence into a computer cycle is required as the information affects the results of the testing frameworks (AAS) and, as a result, introduces an advanced medical conference that can be used by structured communication frameworks (RRS). This is why unconventional considerations are expected in the development of strategies that allow for integration and social inclination in the manufacture of these mechanical structures.

2.8.1.3   *Mechanical Rehabilitation Systems*

The evolution of events in the medical technology fields and the RRS are areas that have aroused great interest in research in mechanical technology. Because of the rapid interaction in the communication phase, the various strategies used for recovery (work planning, motivation demand, etc.), and the understanding of these most involved, appropriate treatment can be a powerful topic for testing [59].

Two key issues have been identified: the RRS's ability to obtain a variety of patient performance information during the turn of events and that from this information a patient's performance assessment is obtained, or for the same type of points as cultural scales.

However, the type and amount of data available depend largely on the framework of the default framework (end-to-end or otherwise exoskeleton) and physical visual framework. In addition, the parameters obtained in the measurement, such as value marks (precision, completeness, etc.), may vary significantly. In this way, the key issue is to integrate the ratings obtained by the RRS, so they provide as much data as possible for a quick test by a consultant and not just raw data. In line with this, among these types of measurements, we have compliance: scope of improvement, speed, accuracy, and efficiency.

The level of patient activity and the level of robot activity, and the level of consideration in the delivery of items should be absolutely equal. All the experimental activities are related to the acquisition of kinematic information; however, they do not look for important level marks, for example, robot levels and patient activity (other than NeRe-Bot offers you as a level) or level of consideration.

Another important issue is to promote client adherence to treatment. It is important to provide adequate input to convince the patient. Using realms that are unpopular with consumers is the most widely used answer for this reason. However, it is important not just how the current criticism is given in addition to the data provided to the client. In this sense, counselors agree that a visual input that informs the client of the possibility of improving his or her score during treatment may be helpful. Other markers at an undeniable level, for example, robot and patient activity levels, control signal, or additional kinematic information, may be helpful to the client if they are likely to help show the importance of patient development.

RRS-type structures are currently integrated into the recovery cycle due to their proximity to mediation; in any case, looking at the questions mentioned earlier will allow the rest of the computer components shown in this article (AAS and DSS) to use the specified data obtained through RRS.

2.9   Conclusion

Another segment of PC recovery is proposed depending on a composed review of computerized recuperation modes for cutting-edge treatment, which incorporates its connection with the recuperation cycle. This construction has been acquainted in connection with the utilization of a specific free reclamation strategy. Three mechanical parts are shown to frame the proposed framework: mechanized testing frameworks, discretionary assistance structures, and computerized recuperation systems. The advancement of AAS ought to be founded on standard demonstrative methods, since standard scales are right now the "best quality" for estimating results and deciding treatment ampleness. Furthermore, the outcomes given by AAS are acquired in an objective scoring way, creating extra information on customer execution.

Those systems ought to be enhanced with DSS books to help with clinical arranging and treatment arranging. The board is right now inclined to use patient information for the utilization of unequivocal frameworks dependent on verifiable levels and notwithstanding man-made abilities. Progressed treatment meetings adjusted to the patient's condition rely upon them being made normally by the DSS. Hence, AI is presently a promising device. Dealing with an assortment of goals in picking insightful arranging and supporting learning measurements [60] may consider fitting gatherings to be built. Along these lines, treatment gatherings may require just approval or change by the facility. Taking everything into account, the execution of the proposed plan should address a couple of issues summed up as follows:

(i)   For the advancement of instruments to consider further correspondence, socialization of these PC frameworks is required. One should have thought of data pertinent to administrators to permit AAS and DSS to focus on information acquired through RRS. In accordance with these lines, a book channel, for example, the different segments of PC parts will be empowered.

(ii) For the situation of the advancement of AAS, the arranged testing association ought to be thought of and not simply a replication of results. Customer data are similarly just about as significant as system usage, on the grounds that without the customer's collaboration and endorsement, structure may not work.

(iii) The seriousness of the neurological issues and their impact regularly lead to extra illnesses at the same time with a huge issue (comorbidity) that may thwart the patient's recuperation.

(iv) The disclosure of utilizing AI to create positive remedial gatherings is as yet youthful; anyway, considering these non-logical advances as of now being created, it is feasible to add to the proposed utilization of DSS to engage you.

(v) Clinical meetings are affirmed by the act of randomized controlled preliminaries when countless patients get a similar treatment. Accordingly, more significant models ought to be selected RCTs that evaluate the immediate impact of characteristic neurological issues. Robots are at present seen as forefront gadgets under the direction of an advisor. Regardless, the utilization of the previously mentioned structures can make an ever increasing number of free, sharp cycles in neuro recovery.

References

1. Janca, A., Aarli, J.A., Prilipko, L., Dua, T., Saxena, S., Saraceno, B., WHO/WFN survey of neurological services: a worldwide perspective. *J. Neurol. Sci.*, 247, 1, 29–34, 2006.

2. United Nations, World Population Ageing 2017 Report, 2017, October, 2017 http://www.un.org/en/development/desa/population/publications/index.html.

3. Holliday, R.C., Antoun, M., Play ford, E.D., A survey of goal-setting methods used in rehabilitation. *Neuro Rehabil. Neural Repair*, 19, 3, 227–231, 2005, 16093413.

4. Climent Barbera, J. and Sanchez-Paya, J., Indicadores desalud y medicina de rehabilitacion: estimadores de incapacidad en la poblacion. *Rehabilitacion*, 30, 277–286, 1996.

5. Chua, K.S.G. and Kuah, C.W.K., Innovating with rehabilitation technology in the real world: promises, potentials, and perspectives. *Am. J. Phys. Med. Rehabil.*, 96, 10, S150–S156, 2017.

6. Van der Loos, H.M., Reinkensmeyer, D.J., Guglielmelli, E., Rehabilitation and healthcare robotics, in: *Springer Handbook of Robotics*, B. Siciliano and O. Khatib (Eds.), pp. 1685–1728, Springer International Publishing, Cham, 2016.

7. Gomes, P., Surgical robotics: reviewing the past, analyzing the present, imagining the future. *Robot. Comput.- Integr. Manuf.*, 27, 2, 261–266, 2011, Translational Research – Where Engineering Meets Medicine.

8. Huang, H., Wolf, S.L., He, J., Recent developments in biofeedback for neuro motor rehabilitation. *J. Neuro Eng. Rehabil.*, 3, 1, 11, 2006.

9. Poli, P., Morone, G., Rosati, G., Masiero, S., Robotic technologies and rehabilitation: new tools for stroke patients' therapy. *BioMed. Res. Int.*, 2013, 8 pages, 2013.

10. Timmermans, A.A., Seelen, H.A., Willmann, R.D., Kingman, H., Technology-assisted training of arm-hand skills in stroke: concepts on reacquisition of motor control and therapist guidelines for rehabilitation technology design. *J. Neuro Eng. Rehabil.*, 6, 1, 1, 2009.

11. Diaz, I., Gil, J.J., Sanchez, E., Lower-limb robotic rehabilitation: literature review and challenges. *J. Rob.*, 2011, Article ID 759764, 11 pages, 2011.

12. Lv, X. and Wu, Z., Review of robot-assisted gait rehabilitation after stroke. *J. Rehabil. Robot.*, 2013, 3–8, 2013.

13. Qian, Z. and Bi, Z., Recent development of rehabilitation robots. *Adv. Mech. Eng.*, 7, 2, 14–23, Article ID 563062, 2014.

14. Rodriguez-Prunotto, L., Cano-de la Cuerda, R., Cuesta- Gomez, A., Alguacil-Diego, I.M., Molina-Rueda, F., Terapia robótica para la rehabilitation del miembro superior en patología neurological. *Rehabilitation*, 48, 2, 104–128, 2014.

15. Marchal-Crespo, L. and Reinkensmeyer, D.J., Review of control strategies for robotic movement training after neurologic injury. *J. Neuro Eng. Rehabil.*, 6, 1, 20, 2009.

16. Yan, T., Cempini, M., Oddo, C.M., Vitiello, N., Review of assistive strategies in powered lower-limb orthoses and exoskeletons. *Rob. Auton. Syst.*, 64, 120–136, 2015.

17. Please note that Figures 2.4 and 2.3 citation was unsequence thus change it to be in sequence. Edit OK? Note that figures should be cited sequentially.

18. Kwakkel, G., Kollen, B.J., Krebs, H.I., Effects of robot-assisted therapy on upper limb recovery after stroke: a systematic review. *Neuro Rehabil. Neural Repair*, 22, 2, 111–121, 2008.

19. Norouzi-Gheidari, N., Archambault, P.S., Fung, J., Effects of robot-assisted therapy on stroke rehabilitation in upper limbs: systematic review and meta-analysis of the literature. *J. Rehabil. Res. Dev.*, 49, 4, 479–496, 2012.

20. Veerbeek, J.M., Langbroek-Amersfoort, A.C., van Wegen, E.E.H., Meskers, C.G.M., Kwakkel, G., Effects of robot-assisted therapy for the upper limb after stroke: a systematic review and meta-analysis. *Neuro Rehabil. Neural Repair*, 31, 2, 107–121, 2017.

21. World Health Organization, *World Report on Disability*, 2011, October 2017, http://www.who.int/en/.
22. Meyer, T., Gutenbrunner, C., Bickenbach, J., Cieza, A., Melvin, J., Stucki, G., Towards a conceptual description of rehabilitation as a health strategy. *J. Rehabil. Med.*, 43, 769, 765–769, 2011.
23. Stucki, G. and Sangha, O., Principles of rehabilitation. *Rheumatology*, 1, 517–530, 1998.
24. Steiner, W.A., Ryser, L., Huber, E., Uebelhart, D., Aeschlimann, A., Stucki, G., Use of the icf model as a clinical problem-solving tool in physical therapy and rehabilitation medicine. *Phys. Ther.*, 82, 111, 1098–1107, 2002.
25. World Health Organization, Neurological Disorders: Public Health Challenges, 2006, October 2017, http://www.who.int/ mental_health/neurology/neurodiso/en/.
26. King, J., Nelson, T., Blankenship, K., Turturro, T., Beck, A., *Rehabilitation Team Function and Prescriptions, Referrals, and Order Writing, Rehabilitation Medicine: Principles and Practice*, 4th edition, J.A. Delisa (Ed.), Lippincott Williams & Wilkins, Philadelphia, PA, USA, 2005.
27. McColl, M., Gerein, N., Valentine, F., Meeting the challenges of disability: models for enabling function and wellbeing, in: *Occupational Therapy: Enabling Function and Well-Being*, pp. 509–528, Slack, Thorofare, NJ, USA, 1997.
28. Ramiro-Gonzalez, M. and Gonzalez Alted, C., El equipo de trabajo en neurorehabilitacion, in: *Neurorehabilitacion*, R. Cano-de la Cuerda and S. Collado Vazquez (Eds.), pp. 61–72, Medica Panamericana, Madrid, Spain, 2012.
29. Reilly, C., Transdisciplinary approach: an atypical strategy for improving outcomes in rehabilitative and long-term acute care settings. *Rehabil. Nurs.*, 26, 6, 216–244, 2001.
30. Finch, E., *Physical Rehabilitation Outcome Measures: A Guide to Enhanced Clinical Decision Making*, 2nd edition, Canadian Physiotherapy Association, Hamilton, ON, Canada, 2002.
31. World Health Organization, *International Classification of Functioning, Disability and Health (ICF)*, 2001, October 2017, http://www.who.int/classifications/icf/en/.
32. Barnes, M.P., Principles of neurological rehabilitation. *J. Neurol. Eurosurg. Psychiatry*, 74, 90004, 3iv–3iv7, 2003.
33. Thompson, A.J., Neurological rehabilitation: from mechanisms to management. *J. Neurol. Neurosurg. Psychiatry*, 69, 6, 718–722, 2000.
34. Miller, E.L., Murray, L., Richards, L. *et al.*, Comprehensive overview of nursing and interdisciplinary rehabilitation care of the stroke patient: a scientific statement from the American Heart Association. *Stroke*, 41, 10, 2402–2448, 2010.
35. Neumann, V., Gutenbrunner, C., Fialka-Moser, V. *et al.*, Interdisciplinary team working in physical and rehabilitation medicine. *J. Rehabil. Med.*, 42, 1, 4–8, 2010.

36. Katz, D., Mills, V., Cassidy, J., Neurological rehabilitation: a guide to diagnosis, prognosis and treatment planning, in: *The Neurological Rehabilitation Model in Clinical Practice*, pp. 1–27, Blackwell Science, Oxford, UK, 2018.

37. Kersten, P., Principles of physiotherapy assessment and outcome measures, in: *Physical Management in Neurological Rehabilitation*, vol. 2, pp. 29–46, 2004.

38. Salter, K., Campbell, N., Richardson, M. *et al.*, Outcome measures in stroke rehabilitation, in: *Evidence-Based Review of Stroke Rehabilitation, Heart and Stroke Foundation*, Canadian Partnership for Stroke Recovery, Ontario, Canada, 2014.

39. Lennon, S., Physiotherapy practice in stroke rehabilitation: a survey. *Disabil. Rehabil.*, 25, 9, 455–461, 2003, 12745940.

40. Pomeroy, V., Aglioti, S.M., Mark, V.W. *et al.*, Neurological principles and rehabilitation of action disorders: rehabilitation interventions. *Neuro Rehabil. Neural Repair*, 25, 5, 33S–43S, 2011.

41. Donaghy, M., Principles of neurological rehabilitation, in: *Brain's Diseases of the Nervous System*, 12 editions, M. Donaghy (Ed.), pp. 165–179, Oxford University Press, Oxford, UK, 2011.

42. Doig, E., Fleming, J., Cornwell, P.L., Kuipers, P., Qualitative exploration of a client-centered, goal-directed approach to community-based occupational therapy for adults with traumatic brain injury. *Am. J. Occup. Ther.*, 63, 5, 559–568, 2009.

43. The Partnership for Robotics in Europe SPARC, *Robotics 2020 Multi Annual Roadmap, Call 2 ICT24 (2015) – Horizon 2020*, Hindawi Publication, Brussels, Belgium, 2015.

44. Davis, A., Davis, S., Moss, N. *et al.*, First steps towards an interdisciplinary approach to rehabilitation. *Clin. Rehabil.*, 6, 3, 237–244, 1992.

45. Bosecker, C., Dipietro, L., Volpe, B., Krebs, H.I., Kinematic robot-based evaluation scales and clinical counterparts to measure upper limb motor performance in patients with chronic stroke. *Neurorehabil. Neural Repair*, 24, 1, 62–69, 2010, 19684304.

46. Capterra, 1999, January 2018, https://www.capterra.com/ electronic-medical-records-software/.

47. The medical futurist, 2018, January 2018, http://medical futurist.com/ top-artificial-intelligence-companies-in-healthcare/.

48. Iosa, M., Morone, G., Cherubini, A., Paolucci, S., The three laws of neuro-robotics: a review on what neurorehabilitation robots should do for patients and clinicians. *J. Med. Biol. Eng.*, 36, 1, 1–11, 2016.

49. Muradore, R., Fiorini, P., Akgun, G. *et al.*, Development of a cognitive robotic system for simple surgical tasks. *Int. J. Adv. Rob. Syst.*, 12, 4, 37, 2015.

50. Hidler, J. and Lum, P.S., The road ahead for rehabilitation robotics. *J. Rehabil. Res. Dev.*, 48, 4, vii–vix, 2011.

51. Acosta, A.M., Dewald, H.A., Dewald, J.P., Pilot study to test effectiveness of video game on reaching performance in stroke. *J. Rehabil. Res. Dev.*, 48, 4, 431–444, 2011.

52. Burgar, C.G., Garber, S.L., Van der Loos, H.M., PhD, O., Deborah Kenney, M.S., Shor, P., Robot-assisted upper limb therapy in acute rehabilitation setting following stroke: department of veterans affairs multisite clinical trial. *J. Rehabil. Res. Dev.*, 48, 4, 445–458, 2011.

53. Saborowski, M. and Kollak, I., How do you care for technology?" – care professionals' experiences with assistive technology in care of the elderly. *Technol. Forecasting Soc. Change*, 93, 133–140, 2015, Science, Technology and the "Grand Challenge" of Ageing.

54. Coster, W.J., Making the best match: selecting outcome measures for clinical trials and outcome studies. *Am. J. Occup. Ther.*, 67, 2, 162–170, 2013.

55. Otten, P., Kim, J., Son, S.H., A framework to automate assessment of upper-limb motor function impairment: a feasibility study. *Sensors*, 15, 12, 20097–20114, 2015.

56. Oña, E.D., Jardón, A., Balaguer, C., The automated box and blocks test an autonomous assessment method of gross manual dexterity in stroke rehabilitation, in: *Towards Autonomous Robotic Systems, Lecture Notes in Computer Science*, Y. Gao, S. Fallah, Y. Jin, C. Lekakou (Eds.), pp. 101–114, Springer, Cham, 2017.

57. Hobart, J., Lamping, D., Freeman, J. *et al.*, Evidence-based measurement which disability scale for neurologic rehabilitation? *Neurology*, 57, 4, 639–644, 2001.

58. Semigran, H.L., Levine, D.M., Nundy, S., Mehrotra, A., Comparison of physician and computer diagnostic accuracy. *JAMA Intern. Med.*, 176, 12, 1860–1861, 2016.

59. Krebs, H.I., Palazzolo, J.J., Dipietro, L. *et al.*, Rehabilitation robotics: performance-based progressive robot-assisted therapy. *Auton. Robots*, 15, 1, 7–20, 2003.

60. Roijers, D.M. and Whiteson, S., Multi-objective decision making. *Synth. Lect. Artif. Intell. Mach. Learn.*, 11, 1, 1–129, 2017.

61. Ellis, M.D., Sukal-Moulton, T.M., Dewald, J., Impairment-based 3-D robotic intervention improves upper extremity work area in chronic stroke: targeting abnormal joint torque coupling with progressive shoulder abduction loading. *IEEE Trans. Rob.*, 25, 3, 549–555, 2009.

62. Kahn, L.E., Zygman, M.L., Rymer, W.Z., Reinkensmeyer, D.J., Robot assisted reaching exercise promotes arm movement recovery in chronic hemiparetic stroke: a randomized controlled pilot study. *J. Neuro Eng. Rehabil.*, 3, 1, 12, 2006.

63. Reinkensmeyer, D.J., Kahn, L.E., Averbuch, M., McKenna- Cole, A., Schmit, B.D., Rymer, W.Z., Understanding and treating arm movement impairment after chronic brain injury: progress with the arm guide. *J. Rehabil. Res. Dev.*, 37, 653, 2000.

64. Casadio, M., Sanguineti, V., Morasso, P.G., Arrichiello, V., Braccio di ferro: a new aptic workstation for neuromotor rehabilitation. *Technol. Healthcare*, 14, 3, 123–142, 2006.

65. Vergaro, E., Casadio, M., Squeri, V., Giannoni, P., Morasso, P., Sanguineti, V., Self-adaptive robot training of strokesurvivors for continuous tracking movements. *J. Neuroeng. Rehabil.*, 7, 1, 13, 2010.

66. Loureiro, R., Amirabdollahian, F., Topping, M., Driessen, B., Harwin, W., Upper limb robot mediated stroke therapy— gentle/s approach. *Auton. Robots*, 15, 1, 35–51, 2003.

67. Coote, S., Murphy, B., Harwin, W., Stokes, E., The effect of the gentle/s robot-mediated therapy system on arm function after stroke. *Clin. Rehabil.*, 22, 5, 395–405, 2008.

68. Bionik Laboratories Corp, 2010, October 2017, https://www.bioniklabs.com/.

69. Jackson, A.E., Culmer, P.R., Levesley, M.C., Makower, S.G., Cozens, J.A., Bhakta, B.B., Effector force requirements to enable robotic systems to provide assisted exercise in people with upper limb impairment after stroke, in: *2011IEEE International Conference on Rehabilitation Robotics*, Zurich, Switzerland, pp. 1–6, 2011.

70. Jackson, A., Culmer, P., Makower, S. *et al.*, Initial patient testing of ipam a robotic system for stroke rehabilitation, in: *2007 IEEE 10th International Conference on Rehabilitation Robotics*, Noordwijk, Netherlands, pp. 250–256, 2007.

71. Micera, S., Sergi, P.N., Zaccone, F. *et al.*, A low-cost biomechatronic system for the restoration and assessment of upper limb motor function in hemiparetic subjects, in: *2006 The First IEEE/RAS-EMBS International Conference on Biomedical Robotics and Bio mechatronics*, BioRob, Pisa, Italy, pp. 25–30, 2006.

72. Colombo, R., Pisano, F., Micera, S. *et al.*, Robotic techniques for upper limb evaluation and rehabilitation of stroke patients. *IEEE Trans. Neural Syst. Rehabil. Eng.*, 13, 3, 311–324, 2005.

73. Lum, P.S., Burgar, C.G., Van der Loos, M., Shor, P.C., Majmundar, M., Yap, R., Mime robotic device for upper-limb neurorehabilitation in subacute stroke subjects: a follow-up study. *J. Rehabil. Res. Dev.*, 43, 5, 631–642, 2006.

74. Masiero, S., Armani, M., Rosati, G., Upper-limb robotassisted therapy in rehabilitation of acute stroke patients: focused review and results of new randomized controlled trial. *J. Rehabil. Res. Dev.*, 48, 4, 355–366, 2011.

75. Masiero, S., Armani, M., Ferlini, G., Rosati, G., Rossi, A., Randomized trial of a robotic assistive device for the upper extremity during early inpatient stroke rehabilitation. *Neurorehabil. Neural Repair*, 28, 4, 377–386, 2014, 24316679.

76. Toth, A., Fazekas, G., Arz, G., Jurak, M., Horvath, M., Passive robotic movement therapy of the spastic hemiparetic arm with reharob: report of the first clinical test and the follow-up system improvement, in: *2005 9th International Conference on Rehabilitation Robotics*, ICORR, Chicago, IL, USA, pp. 127–130, 2005.

77. Fazekas, G., Horvath, M., Troznai, T., Toth, A., Robot mediated upper limb physiotherapy for patients with spastic hemiparesis: a preliminary study. *J. Rehabil. Med.*, 39, 7, 580–582, 2007.

78. Tyro motion gmbh, 2007, October 2017, http://tyromotion.com/.

79. Sale, P., Lombardi, V., Franceschini, M., Hand robotics rehabilitation: feasibility and preliminary results of a robotic treatment in patients with hemiparesis. *Stroke Res. Treat.*, 2012, 5 pages, 2012.

80. Hwang, C.H., Seong, J.W., Son, D.-S., Individual finger synchronized robot-assisted hand rehabilitation in subacute to chronic stroke: a prospective randomized clinical trial of efficacy. *Clin. Rehabil.*, 26, 8, 696–704, 2012.

81. Hesse, S., Schulte-Tigges, G., Konrad, M., Bardeleben, A., Werner, C., Robot-assisted arm trainer for the passive and active practice of bilateral forearm and wrist movements in hemiparetic subjects. *Arch. Phys. Med. Rehabil.*, 84, 6, 915–920, 2003.

82. Schmidt, H., Hesse, S., Werner, C., Bardeleben, A., Upper and lower extremity robotic devices to promote motor recovery after stroke -recent developments, in: *2004 26th Annual International Conference of the IEEE Engineering in Medicine and Biology Society*, San Francisco, CA, USA, vol. 2, pp. 4825–4828, 2004.

83. Takahashi, C.D., Der-Yeghiaian, L., Le, V.H., Cramer, S.C., A robotic device for hand motor therapy after stroke, in: *2005 9th International Conference on Rehabilitation Robotics*, ICORR, Chicago, IL, USA, pp. 17–20, 2005.

84. Takahashi, C.D., Der-Yeghiaian, L., Le, V., Motiwala, R.R., Cramer, S.C., Robot-based hand motor therapy after stroke. *Brain*, 131, 2, 425–437, 2008.

85. Motorika medical ltd, 2004, October 2017, http://motorika.com/.

86. Treger, I., Faran, S., Ring, H., Robot-assisted therapy for neuromuscular training of sub-acute stroke patients. A feasibility study. *Eur. J. Phys. Rehabil. Med.*, 44, 4, 431–435, 2008.

87. Meyer-Rachner, P., Passon, A., Klauer, C., Schauer, T., Compensating the effects of fes-induced muscle fatigue by rehabilitation robotics during arm weight support. *Curr. Dir. Biomed. Eng.*, 3, 31–34, 2017.

88. Montagner, A., Frisoli, A., Borelli, L. *et al.*, A pilot clinical study on robotic assisted rehabilitation in vr with an arm exoskeleton device, in: *2007 Virtual Rehabilitation*, Venice, Italy, pp. 57–64.

89. Myomo, inc, 2017, October 2017, http://myomo.com/.

90. Page, S.J., Hill, V., White, S., Portable upper extremity robotics is as efficacious as upper extremity rehabilitative therapy: a randomized controlled pilot trial. *Clin. Rehabil.*, 27, 6, 494–503, 2013.

91. Kim, G.J., Rivera, L., Stein, J., Combined clinic-home approach for upper limb robotic therapy after stroke: a pilot study. *Arch. Phys. Med. Rehabil.*, 96, 12, 2243–2248, 2015.

92. Rahman, T., Sample, W., Jayakumar, S. *et al.*, Passive exoskeletons for assisting limb movement. *J. Rehabil. Res. Dev.*, 43, 5, 583–590, 2006.

93. Hocoma, 1996, October 2017, https://www.hocoma.com/.
94. Gijbels, D., Lamers, I., Kerkhofs, L., Alders, G., Knippenberg, E., Feys, P., The armeo spring as training tool to improve upper limb functionality in multiple sclerosis: a pilot study. *J. Neuroeng. Rehabil.*, 8, 1, 5, 2011.
95. Sanchez, R.J., Liu, J., Rao, S. *et al.*, Automating arm movement training following severe stroke: functional exercises with quantitative feedback in a gravity-reduced environment. *IEEE Trans. Neural Syst. Rehabil. Eng.*, 14, 3, 378–389, 2006.
96. Motus nova, 2016, October 2017, http://motusnova.com/.
97. Kutner, N.G., Zhang, R., Butler, A.J., Wolf, S.L., Alberts, J.L., Quality-of-life change associated with robotic assisted therapy to improve hand motor function in patients with subacute stroke: a randomized clinical trial. *Phys. Ther.*, 90, 4, 493–504, 2010.
98. Koeneman, E.J., Schultz, R.S., Wolf, S.L., Herring, D.E., Koeneman, J.B., A pneumatic muscle hand therapy device, in: *2004 The 26th Annual International Conference of the IEEE Engineering in Medicine and Biology Society*, San Francisco, CA, USA, vol. 1, pp. 2711–2713, 2004.
99. Schabowsky, C.N., Godfrey, S.B., Holley, R.J., Lum, P.S., Development and pilot testing of hexorr: hand exoskeleton rehabilitation robot. *J. Neuroeng. Rehabil.*, 7, 1, 36, 2010.
100. Bouzit, M., Burdea, G., Popescu, G., Boian, R., The Rutgers master ii-new design force-feedback glove. *IEEE/ASME Trans. Mechatron.*, 7, 2, 256–263, 2002.
101. Merians, A., Jack, D., Boian, R. *et al.*, Virtual reality augmented rehabilitation for patients following stroke. *Phys. Ther.*, 82, 898–915, 2002.
102. Allington, J., Spencer, S.J., Klein, J., Buell, M., Reinkensmeyer, D.J., Bobrow, J., Supinator extender (sue): a pneumatically actuated robot for forearm/wrist rehabilitation after stroke, in: *2011 Annual International Conference of the IEEE Engineering in Medicine and Biology Society*, Boston, MA, USA, pp. 1579–1582, 2011.
103. Sanchez, R., Reinkensmeyer, D., Shah, P. *et al.*, Monitoring functional arm movement for home-based therapy after stroke, in: *2004 The 26th Annual International Conference of the IEEE Engineering in Medicine and Biology Society*, San Francisco, CA, USA, vol. 2, pp. 4787–4790, 2004.
104. Rocon, E., Belda-Lois, J.M., Ruiz, A.F., Monto, M., Moreno, J.C., Pons, J.L., Design and validation of a rehabilitation robotic exoskeleton for tremor assessment and suppression. *IEEE Trans. Neural Syst. Rehabil. Eng.*, 15, 3, 367–378, 2007.
105. Nef, T. and Riener, R., Shoulder actuation mechanisms for arm rehabilitation exoskeletons, in: *2008 2nd IEEE RAS EMBS International Conference on Biomedical Robotics and Bio mechatronics*, Scottsdale, AZ, USA, pp. 862–868, 2008.
106. Guidali, M., Duschau-Wicke, A., Broggi, S., Klamroth-Marganska, V., Nef, T., Riener, R., A robotic system to train activities of daily living in a virtual environment. *Med. Biol. Eng. Comput.*, 49, 10, 1213–1223, 2011.

107. Nef, T., Mihelj, M., Colombo, G., Riener, R., Armin – robot for rehabilitation of the upper extremities, in: *Proceedings 2006 IEEE International Conference on Robotics and Automation*, Orlando, FL, USA, pp. 3152–3157, 2006.

108. Nef, T., Mihelj, M., Riener, R., Armin: a robot for patient cooperative arm therapy. *Med. Biol. Eng. Comput.*, 45, 9, 887–900, 2007.

109. Loureiro, R.C.V. and Harwin, W.S., Reach & grasp therapy: Design and control of a 9-dof robotic neuro-rehabilitation system, in: *2007 IEEE 10th International Conference on Rehabilitation Robotics*, Noordwijk, Netherlands, pp. 757–763, 2007.

110. Huang, J., Tu, X., He, J., Design and evaluation of the Rupert wearable upper extremity exoskeleton robot for clinical and in-home therapies. *IEEE Trans. Syst. Man Cybern.: Syst.*, 46, 7, 926–935, 2016.

111. Balasubramanian, S., Wei, R., Perez, M. *et al.*, Rupert: an exoskeleton robot for assisting rehabilitation of arm functions, in: *2008 Virtual Rehabilitation*, Vancouver, Canada, pp. 163–167, 2008.

3

Competent and Affordable Rehabilitation Robots for Nervous System Disorders Powered with Dynamic CNN and HMM

Sundaresan Sabapathy[1]*, Surendar Maruthu[1], Suresh Kumar Krishnadhas[2], Ananth Kumar Tamilarasan[2] and Nishanth Raghavan[3]

[1]Department of ECE, National Institute of Technology Puducherry, Karaikal, India
[2]Department of ECE, IFET College of Engineering, Villupuram, India
[3]Cochin University College of Engineering Kuttanad, CUSAT, Kerala, India

Abstract

Neurological disorder is one of the common health issues that affect billions of people in and around the world. This disease is caused by the malfunctioning of central nerve system and the peripheral nerve system. Few of such disorders like the Alzheimer's disease and Parkinson's disease are much difficult to live with and ruined life of many people. In particular, the Parkinson's disease affected patients who experience complications due to the Gait Freezing (GF) symptoms that create specific movement inabilities. The only rehabilitation mechanism available is the artificial generation of the dopamine levels. A rehabilitation mechanism robot is proposed, which triggers the exercises automatically by inducing certain vibration to the affected. It comprises of two parts, viz., a fixed actuator mechanism at the bed/chairs and the other is a wearable sensor and is fixed in the patient's hands/legs/neck as bracelets, bands, or chains. Here, convolutional neural networks (CNN) and hidden Markov model (HMM) are used for the processing of sensor signals and decision-making. Thus, the proposed sensor-based robot paves way for an affordable and efficient rehabilitation mechanics to person in need, powered with dynamic CNN techniques that keep them motivated and feel comfortable without help of a skilled person.

Keywords: Parkinson's disease, dynamic CNN, HMM, deep learning, rehabilitation

*Corresponding author: sundaresanece91@gmail.com

Roshani Raut, Pranav Pathak, Sandeep Kautish and Pradeep N (eds.) Intelligent Systems for Rehabilitation Engineering, (57–94) © 2022 Scrivener Publishing LLC

3.1   Introduction

Huge increase in population all around the globe demands for enhanced medical facilities, and the quality of life is now becoming the greatest concern in the underdeveloped countries. A lot of people are suffering from various disabilities, which might be due to injuries that occurred during accidents and some are due to severe illness. This kind of illness may result in the negative impact of the health conditions and weakness in the nerve and limbs, which will create suffering in their day-to-day activities [1]. There is no therapy suggested for training the muscles, which gets affected with such disabilities. The effective strategies followed for training the affected muscles will require some assistance and correction mechanisms. The rehabilitation technology is now acting as a motivating factor for the generation of rehabilitation robots to enhance the life quality. There exists some discrepancy in the technology due to its cost and availability. The low cost and easily affordable devices have some features related to stiffness, which is used in robotic therapy. The familiar way to reach the stiffness variation is by means of controlling the bandwidth [2], which in turn reduces the cost of implementation.

The rehabilitation device that uses power to drive itself is ruling the world. It is popularly used in many medical fields, since there is a need for the amplification in order to increase the strength in the leg and arm while doing any work [3]. The single device that combines robots and humans will provide notable chances for producing novel techniques that will assist the disabled and even normal people. The movement is controlled by the algorithms generated by the humans, and controlling of the arms and leg movement is done by considering the muscle strength. This makes an improvement in the development of automated device that induces a mechanism that supports rehabilitation of patients.

On the other hand, many people are affected with some disabilities because of major diseases and some due to accidents. But many people are affected with nerve-related diseases, especially Parkinson's disease. If a person is affected with Parkinson's disease, then he may suffer from gait scarcity problem and weakening of health. Because of the gait scarcity issue, the speed of the person gets reduced, and this will affect the day-to-day activities of the patient. The advanced stage may lead to freezing of the gait problem [4]. This problem related to freezing of the gait is one of the main issues in Parkinson's disease [5]. The affected persons cannot engage themselves in their routine activities because of the non-coordination of the nerves. Hence, there is a need of training method that uses rehabilitation mechanisms in order to alternate the existing method of training. Nowadays, smart wearable robots are used for the treatment of hemiplegia-affected patients [6]. The same method can also be utilized here in case of Parkinson's disease. The robots used for rehabilitation will endorse the improvement of medical field and the equipment's intended for medical applications. This shows a fast recovery of patients' health conditions. So for doing certain nerve coordination exercises, Exercise Therapy (ET) is also being preferred. It is an alternate method for treatment, which is aiming for treating and reducing the wrong postures caused at the time of pregnancy [7]. It is one of the best methods for patients affected by severe injuries and nerve diseases. Most of the nerve diseases are treated with the help of physical rehabilitation methods, as ET will provide healthy joints and muscles [8]. Normally persons with nerve disability find difficulties in doing an exercise on their own. Hence, rehabilitation robots that are used for various domains are being introduced. These robots provide assistance to people who are in need of doing exercises.

3.2   Related Works

Rehabilitation exercise is deliberated as a major treatment for neurological disorders like Parkinson's disease. It will enhance the ability of a person by means of his functioning capability and reduces the complications caused by secondary factors. Normally the ET constitutes a realistic understanding about a patient's health condition [9]. The ET makes some enhancement in the strengthening of muscles, enables nerve transmission, and improves the coordination of nerve tissues. This will control the patient's nerve movements and pressurize the muscle texture. Learning through machines may help to treat the Parkinson's-affected patients, but effectiveness is not as better as normal controls. Nevertheless, the situation can be made easy and somewhat effective. At present, the gait analysis is considered as an important phenomenon that found the stiffness in the gait, and it helps to trace out the stroking area of patients. The therapy done by inhibiting exercise thus will enhance the mobilization of the muscles and improves muscle strength by stretching of the muscles [10].

3.2.1   Rehabilitation Robot for Lower Limbs

Rehabilitation exercises will make the persons regain their original life activities. The therapy done using exercises is much important to enhance the movement of joints and helps to maintain the joints balance. The immobilized joints will cause severe damage to the persons, and it is found difficult to recover. Hence, a novel rehabilitation model is developed that permits the movements for the lower part of the limb [11]. The rehabilitation mechanisms used in the lower limbs are much needed to sustain the flexibility of muscles and maximum range of motion [13]. If the same exercise is performed manually depending on skilled labor, the timing is limited and it depends on the availability of skilled people's assistance often. So the rehabilitation robots are introduced to replace the exercise aided by skilled persons [14]. The new device is implemented for rehabilitation that is highly assessable, and it can extend for a long period of time. Especially for the lower limbs, this rehabilitation mechanism is cast off. Normally lower limb is an essential part of humans, which is responsible for flexibility and movement. This rehabilitation robot will generate a coordination of nerves and the related muscles in lower limbs, which the therapists find difficult to provide treatment.

There are excessive numbers of chance to proceed forward with rehabilitation mechanism. Initially the response of system is obtained through dynamic analysis. Then the device is controlled by using a control strategy, which is controlled by Artificial Intelligence (AI) algorithm and also voice command feature. The experience of the physiotherapist is not equal to machines, but it can facilitate the therapy [12]. The simulation for the musculoskeletal region is utilized for identifying and analyzing the possessions of support and the weight of the human body. The simulations dependability is checked by means of the robot, which is wearable. The relation between the robot weight and the dependability is calculated from the conditions of the hip joint handling wearable robots [15].

3.2.2   Rehabilitation Using Hip Bot

The rehabilitation robot used for the hip joint is the Hip Bot [16]. The strongest joint in the human body is the hip, and abnormal movement and accidents can create damage to the hip. The rehabilitation robots used for the treatment have latent to minimize the manual rehabilitation workload and repetition is improved. The simple Hip Bot is designed for performing the joined actions of adduction or abduction in addition to extension or flexion. These kinds of robots are utilized because of the unpredicted disturbances that occur in the systems, which is much difficult to estimate. The memory space of the Hip Bot is maximized by 120/20 in flexion/extension in addition to 45/45 in abduction/adduction. The Hip Bot that already existed contains a mechanism that can rehabilitate the patient to a maximum limit, and the capacity it can hold is up to 150 kg. These kinds of robots can be used separately for both legs. According to patient size and dimensions, the system developed can be extensible [16]. This will focus on the hip joints for various degrees of movements. The device drivers consist of a bridge circuit along with a pulse width modulation device to control the motors. The graphical user interface is used to get the inputs as patient data and to store the results. Considering the workload of the persons, these rehabilitation robots are performing a lot in assignments of making the limbs to function effectively. The adaptive control mechanisms are implemented in the Hip Bot, which is based on the GPI (Generalized Proportional Integral) based controller. The enactment of the control robot is calculated by using the simulation results based on various conditions [17].

3.2.3   Rehabilitation Wrist Robot Using MRI Compatibility

Wrist robot is designed for the treatment of defected persons due to wrist damage. The possibility of MRI-based wrist device is restored for the rehabilitation analysis. This robot was signified on the basis of the quality of the image. The robot setup consists of a control room and scanner room. The scanner room containing magnetic resonance imaging (MRI) device must contain the interfacing of sensors and actuators. The digital units are assembled in robots including electric circuit, control unit, power unit, potential meters, etc. The hydraulic parts are placed at the one end of the room. On the other hand, the wrist device contains the laser unit and 3D printing capable units. It consists of an actuator that is using a compressed air setup, and it is for rotatory motion and holding [18]. Also, this wrist device consists of a pressure sensor, pressure regulator, and microcontroller-based acquisition device. Figure 3.1 shows the components used for design of wrist robot, and Figure 3.2 displays the control room setup.

Figure 3.1 Components of wrist robot.

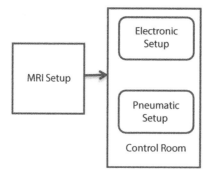

Figure 3.2 Control room setup.

3.2.4 Rehabilitation Robot for Gait Training

The stroke-affected patients will require rehabilitation after the recovery, and their anatomy is changed due to the effect of disorder, which in turn their behavior also will be changing. Hence, there is a need of a rehabilitation mechanism that will be suitable forpsychological movements and well-being of the affected patients. The number of stroke-affected patients is involved in the examination, and treatment is given by using the rehabilitation robot that might lead to the major enhancements in functioning of the cognitive mood and day-to-day activities. This significant improvement will develop the flexibility and improve the quality of life regardless of physical and mental conditions [19].

The gait training assisted through rehabilitation robot by keeping track of the acute stroke will allow affected patients to obtain a heavy prescription and concentration of the gait training when compared to the normal traditional physiotherapy. In fact, the data given for gauging the efficiency of the limb performance are limited. The Hybrid Assistive Limb (HAL) is a training method that emphasizes the acute stroke-affected patients who need an aid for walking. For the rehabilitation treatment, patients are treated with normal manual therapy method or the HAL method. Age is not a constraint for the patients who were undergoing HAL treatment for the gait rehabilitation [20]. Another approach in the gait training is intended to focus the control in dynamic equilibrium for the children with physical therapy. Here the impact of rehabilitation robot used for the gait training is based on the biomedical constraints. Due to this, the children who are undergoing such training may adopt some novel dynamic approaches of the gait subsequently following the rehabilitation [21]. These rehabilitation mechanisms will be beneficial for improving the gait performance in the children using physical therapy. The rehabilitation treatment for the stroke patients like the gait training will yield better results when compared to the traditional training. The usage of the integrated electromechanical robot for the training of the gait in accordance with the electrical stimulations produces many benefits to the patients. The result shows that the effect of the robot will provide better positive results in stroke rehabilitation process [22]. Considering the patients suffering from the hemiplegia because of the injuries in spinal cord or stroke, the rehabilitation robots are aiding much in an effective manner for the recovery of the limbs that are affected. The therapeutic outcome results primarily from amalgamation of increase in the patient's independence, and thus, it reduces physical burden of the therapist. For stroke patients, the gait rehabilitation robots might have the potential for increasing the patient's independence at the time of rehabilitation process without compromising the patient's safety [23]. The ground gait training and treadmill-based training are compared, and the performance is noted, which shows that the treadmill training performs better for the stroke-affected patients. The free displacement mode of rehabilitation is not limited to the usage of treadmill. It involves the amalgamation of the central nervous system addicted to various physical therapies. The rehabilitation involves body posture control and partial weight of the body that supports individuals by causing severe disorders. This approach is based on the assistance expected, and here locomotion strategy is used, which is based on laser sensor [24].

3.3 Solutions and Methods for the Rehabilitation Process

A lot of methods are introduced for the rehabilitation of the patients affected by Parkinson's disease. Some of such methods are discussed below.

3.3.1 Gait Analysis

The gait analysis is accomplished by applying a 3D motion-based analysis device, which will record the details by considering a sample frequency of about 100 Hz. Large numbers of reflective markers are fixed on the anatomical benchmarks for observing the model based on full body. The verification is done at the time of medication cycle regardless of the clinical-based testing. The motion of the robot is fixed to 360 degrees turning trials as discussed in the article [25]. A couple of researchers are seeking for the freezing of gait score, and it seems to be detecting the entire Freezing of Gait (FOG) serials. The value of FOG is denoted as the beginning of knee flexibility, and it is identified by the visual perception of the angle of knee in association with 3D images. These gait cycles are not encompassed in the FOG serials [26]. The total set of data is divided into a couple of groups. The freezing event is marked as freezing trials, and the non-freezing event is marked as functional gait trials. In all two models, one side of the events will be physically interpreted depending upon the visual perception marked by the coordinates of 3D marker. If the variations of two data become high, then the FOG event obtained in case of estimation is terminated.

3.3.2   Methods Based on Deep Learning

In the model prescribed on deep learning method, the most important concept to be considered is the Recurrent Neural Network (RNN). The RNN is basically connected with the sequential data modeling, and the architectures based on RNN are used to solve the learning model based on sequence-to-sequence training by using the equation shown below [27].

$$A_x = SD(T_x M^{tn} + n_{x-1} M^{nn}) \tag{3.1}$$

$$L_x = n_x M^{nL} \tag{3.2}$$

The matrices corresponding to the weights are indicated by M that is having the superscripts represented to and from relationships. The terms T_x and L_x are considered as inputs, and output is taken at the duration x. Computing the whole gradient is done by unfurling over long chronological arrangements that can lead to vanishing or to exploring the gradient [28]. The extension of the RNN along with the memory cells without considering the recurrent units is done by using the long short-term memory [29].

3.3.3   Use of Convolutional Neural Networks

The combination of the convolutional neural network (CNN) and the Recurrent Neural Network (RNN) provides a common relation for the evolution of the sequence modeling systematically. Here CNN is considered as the starting point of the sequence modeling [30], and compared to RNN, CNN performs better. The working module is based on two restrictions:

the input sequence X(x1…xn) produces the output sequence Y(y1…yn), and the value of Y depends only on the value of X with 1D CNN being used [31]. The input sequence length and the hidden layers are modified to become same length. The casual convolutions are being used by the CNN, following the batch normalization. The CNN is used for the easy identification of the gait feature. The trial-and-error method is used for the novel identification of the gait analysis using the tool called MatConvNet [32]. The analysis of the deep CNN depends upon the supervised based learning algorithm through which corresponding parameter is also obtained. Initially the periodic output consistency is represented by the loss function, and the value is calculated from the initial to end layer within the propagation manner, which is focusing forward. The loss error is being reduced, and the layer parameter is modified through SGD (Stochastic Gradient Descent) algorithm in combination with the back propagation chain rule [33]. The forward and the backward propagation processes are uninterruptedly implemented till the essential quantity of periods or supplementary discontinuing standards remain encountered. For receiving the optical performance, a cluster of deep learning details needs to be identified. In the CNN layers, the initial three sections might realize some feature extraction techniques at various measures with various kernel sizes. The individual layer might undergo the convolution operation. Due to the convolution operation, the Rectified Linear Unit (ReLU) is configured after the activation.

3.4 Proposed System

In the proposed system, a smart robot mechanism is designed to provide rehabilitation treatment to the Parkinson's disease affected patients. The people affected by neurological disorders like Parkinson's disease might undergo the ambulatory gait exploration, as it is mandatory for them to provide rehabilitation mechanism. The Parkinson's disease is described by motor malfunctions like tremors resting, getting slow in the movements, difficulty in the gait, and rigidness in the limbs. The gait analysis is one of the important and needed methods for diagnosing Parkinson's disease reliably. Nowadays, the device using wearable sensor is developed for the measurement of the gait nature from the patients affected by Parkinson's disease. This will provide detailed information about the severity of the disease. Also, the phase discrimination of gait and the monitoring methods using gait, which are using the wearable sensors, are designed for the detection and identification of Parkinson's disease. Mostly the locomotion capacities of the patients are obtained for the recovery of the mobility by providing rehabilitation to the gait. The automatic identification of parameters for the gait is done by an ambulatory gait analysis method.

One of the most advanced techniques to enhance the rehabilitation process is concentrating on the gait feature. The gait region is the most sensational region to be noticed. Hence, the analysis based on the gait region seeks more attention. The gait kinematics results in the body moments and identification of the forces to be applied. Normally the Ground Reaction Force (GRF) value and the kinetic value are measured from the body segments. The measurement that is focused by sensing the forces in between the ground and feet is the kinetic measurement, as it depends upon the solicitation of the adaptive force sensors. For analysis of the kinetics, the needed joint moment is calculated by an efficient and proper method. This is considered as an important unit of evaluation of the healthcare and diagnosing of medical issues in consideration with daily activities of the patient. Many researchers suggest that the number of stationary systems like the force plates and treadmill devices is used for measuring the GRF [34]. The various sensors placed in the stationary force plates will be responsible for the measurement of the GRF value. In the treadmill, a couple of force plates are placed underneath and it is suggested to come up with certain limitations like using distributed plates for measuring the GRF values. Basically, humans can walk in a periodic motion related to the body segments that may include the monotonous motions. The whole walking duration is described by the gait posture, and it is noted that the heel of the patient affected with paralysis syndrome may not touch the ground. Hence, the analysis is made to the waking pattern of humans by considering different duration and phases. Various gait phases need to be considered in the analysis. The robot will analyze the various phases, and accordingly, the vibration mode of pressurization is given to the affected regions. Initially, the motion across various phases is detected, and the rehabilitation mechanism is allotted for those different phases.

3.4.1 Detection of Motion and Rehabilitation Mechanism

Here in our proposed system, the wearable sensors are used to detect the gait moments. The wearable sensors for the gait kinematics used in this rehabilitation mechanism can be fixed at the patient's bed, patient's shoes [35], treadmills [36], and even clothes (as e-clothes). The wearable sensors unit consists of gyroscope sensor, accelerometer, magnetometer, strain sensor, fiber optic sensor, electromyography (EMG), and flex sensor. All these sensors are fixed in the clothes of the patient, which would be wearable. In spite of few sensors implanted in treadmills, the proposed system includes features like sensing of the body parameters, and it is made comfortable to be fixed in clothes too.

The gyroscope sensor is normally a micro machine, and it works on the principle of measurement of the coriolis force, which is the evident power corresponding to the precise pace of revolution in a pivoting reference outline [37]. The coriolis effort provides a way to detect the linear motion by accomplishing the combination of the signal from gyroscope and thus can obtain the angular rate. The gyroscope is used to measure the gesture and position of human's body segments that are involved in analysis of the gait in order to measure the angular rate. If the gyroscope is attached to the legs of humans, the angle value [38, 39] is determined for the gait and realization is possible for the same. All types of gyroscopes used in the gait analysis will have a combination with accelerometer in order to construct a whole first sensing system.

The accelerometer [40] is considered as an inertial sensor that can be used to measure the acceleration along with sensitive axis. The most common principle operation of the accelerometer will depend upon the sensing element that uses mechanical setup comprising a mass fixed to the suspension system based on the reference frame. Measuring the action of muscles is necessary in the human gait. Electromyography (EMG) [41] is used indirectly to measure the activity of muscles by using the electrodes placed in clothes. Figure 3.3 displays the block diagram of proposed methodology in which raspberry pi plays a vital role.

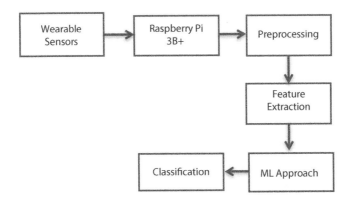

Figure 3.3 Block diagram of proposed methodology for the identification of proper locomotion activity in human.

3.4.2   Data Collection Using Wearable Sensors

The monitoring of the gait kinetics is done through wearable sensors. Multiple sensors are employed and integrated typically to a network of sensors. For the same purpose, the body sensor networks are used in earlier days. Here in the proposed system, whole sensor units are fixed at the e-clothes or band type, and sensors for various purposes are fixed at various positions. The sensors that are placed at the leg area might focus the position at the region of gait positions like foot, calf, and thigh. For hands, the sensors are placed at the shoulder region, elbow region, and wrist. Most of the persons affected with usual symptoms are benefited by above-mentioned locations, and for persons with abnormalities, the position of sensors might be placed at the back bone region that includes cervical region, mid spinal cord region, and lower cord region. For fetching the medical data using the sensors for the Parkinson's affected patients, the lower extremity movement estimation is mandatory [42]; hence, a sensor placed at the thigh region is involved in the estimation of the value. Depending on the values, the severity of the disorder can be found. The wearable sensors are used in many critical cases for the identification of abnormalities in the gait. The obtained gait information is needed for safe detection of the abnormalities in walking posture. The threshold level for each sensor is programmed in raspberry pi for monitoring activity and to provide rehabilitation as needed [43].

3.4.3   Raspberry Pi

The raspberry pi 3B+ is the controller unit that is used to sense the medical data in real time via sensors placed in patient's body, and it fetches mostly the sensitive data. Raspberry pi is casted off due to its fast computation, compact size, easy interfacing with multiple sensors, low power consumption, and easy programmability. Some information is collected through wireless units for remote access. Once the data are sensed by sensors, they will be transferred to controller, and further, they are manipulated for identification of abnormal activities. The collection of the data is succeeded by using the accelerometers positioned on the e-clothes.

3.4.4   Pre-Processing of the Data

The data gathered from sensors and camera by raspberry pi are subjected to preprocessing. The preprocessing of the data is carried out in two stages.

Initially the noise is being removed from the data and is filtered before segmentation. The signals obtained from the sensors are noisy, especially EMG signals; hence, noise removal and filtration process is carried out. The band pass filter is used for the filtering of the accelerometer and EMG signals. The removal of the AC interference is done using notch filter [44]. The segments are measured by using a single trail and utilized for the extraction of the feature.

3.5   Analysis of the Data

The sensors placed at various regions help to observe the movements. The capturing of leg movements plays a vital role in the analysis of leg position, where the treatment is to be provided. The Internal or the inertial measurement unit (IMV) is calculated from the values obtained from sensors placed. The combinations of the translational and rotational movements are bagged. Then the hand movements are calculated either in 3D motions or in 2D motions. The gestures involved in this are hand and wrist movements. For obtaining the 3D values, the movements captured are from eating, clenching, and pouring motions. The 2D motions are obtained from the circle, waving, and shape motions. The Fugl-Meyer Clinical (FMA) values are obtained from the sensor values [45] through an algorithm developed for the estimation of FMA value. Then the Functional Ability Scales (FAS) are determined from the data, and the improvement from the values of FMA provides a clinical approach to multiple joint problems. The selective movements are taken more into consideration by providing a flexion-extension approach.

3.5.1   Feature Extraction

The sensor values are gathered from the wearable device and are fed to microcontroller for storing purpose. The stored information is fed back to the preprocessing unit, and the separation of gait movement-related data is being clustered out. The features corresponding to various tasks are taken out separately and imported for exploratory analysis. The relief feature selection algorithm [46] is used for selecting various features. The attributes are rankedbased on the importance and considering their ability to increase the split-up process, which is connected with the dissimilar medical values. Here the clustered k-means algorithm is used for the feature selection, which yields maximum efficiency.

3.5.2   Machine Learning Approach

The information needed for gait movement is obtained from the data set after processing. The obtained information is then fed to the machine learning approach especially the supervised machine learning approach. The classifiers are used for classification of the type of signals for identification of the disorder types, as a specific gesture on the gait represents severity of the disorder. Here kernels are casted for classifying the category of disorder. Normally the kernel algorithms are utilized for analyzing the pattern, and one of the most familiar kernel methods is support vector machine (SVM) [47]. Initially the various patterns are implicit, and the relations are predicted by considering data sets. The kernel methods are adopted as they require a similarity function from the whole data sets. For more prediction-based learning, HMM is casted off to produce sequence of output with available data set. Also, it can be used for classification of data with likelihood of each model.

The locomotion of patient is analyzed using the above methods, and information about the patients' health condition is monitored, through which it provides valuable details to physiotherapists about the abnormalities in human locomotion. The usage of the wearable sensors will provide accessibility over patients' behavior as the process of rehabilitation happens in their day-to-day activities. This system also provides some useful data to the doctors or caretakers about the patient's health conditions. The reason for the difficulty is analyzed properly, and recovery rate is maximized accordingly. The Wireless Body Area Network (WBAN) is used for replacing the old techniques used in the healthcare systems. This is implemented by initiating periodical monitoring of the patients and providing rehabilitation to them as needed. The wearable sensors for detecting human locomotion will investigate the original position of sensors, and they will compare the measured signals with state-of-the-art provided. Numerous values are predicted by extracting the features from signals with HMM. The statistical data are obtained from accelerometer signals, and the time domain features are collected from EMG signals. The machine learning classifiers will be used for automatic detection of the disease.

After performing classification using SVM, the disorder is predicted and classified. For this, the segregated part is considered as the target data and is fed to decision maker. The decision maker will compare the obtained value with already existing standard data. After comparison, the output from decision device is fed to raspberry pi unit. The raspberry pi after obtaining the data analyzes the severity from the compared information by decision device, and it will initiate actuators for providing an artificial vibration to

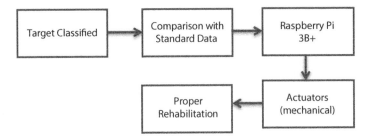

Figure 3.4 Rehabilitation in case of nerve disorder.

the affected or stroked region. The actuator is a mechanical device that will control the movements and initiate the vibration process by inducing a mechanical motion. Thus, a proper rehabilitation mechanism is provided to the affected patients in suitable area. Figure 3.4 displays the block diagram of rehabilitation mechanism in case of nerve disorder.

3.5.3   Remote Rehabilitation Mode

For the monitoring of patients' health condition remotely and for providing rehabilitation in remote-based method, the wireless body area network is used. The gateways provide a proper connectivity to the Internet. This enables devices to get connected in a network and act as smart devices (IoT). The data and computed information that are gathered from the wearable sensors are transmitted through WBAN to the responsible persons for the patients. Along with sensor data, temperature, pressure, and heartbeat are measured and are transmitted to remote caretaker or to the hospitals directly. Figure 3.5 shows the block diagram for remote monitoring and rehabilitation mechanism through IoT. Hence, the urgency or the emergency conditions of the patients are noticed periodically, and the situation is tackled effectively, which in turn connected to rehabilitation mechanism.

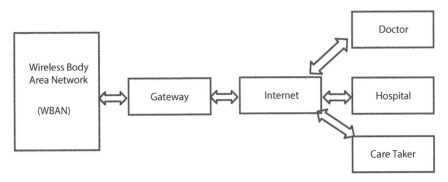

Figure 3.5 Remote monitoring and rehabilitation (IoT).

3.6 Results and Discussion

In the proposed system, the robot mechanism is used for providing rehabilitation to the Parkinson's disease affected patients. The combination of EMG data and the accelerometer data is discriminated in between the affected patients through Parkinson's disease tremors. The regularity and frequency of the gait movements distinguish the disease-affected patients from the normal patients. Studies conducted from various patients reveal that the motor function variation makes the researchers know more about the importance of Parkinson's disease. The estimation of parameters of the proposed system like accuracy, sensitivity, and specificity is carried out by this approach. The observed parameters are true positive, true negative, false positive, and false negative.

Table 3.1 Acceleration value of a healthy test person.

Acceleration (g)	Time (ms)	Acceleration (g)	Time (ms)
0.10374	14.1159	0.109593	990.342
0.108943	45.3195	0.0673171	1003.71
0.0647154	67.6077	0.0780488	1199.85
0.106016	125.557	0.105691	1248.89
0.0952846	236.999	0.108293	1315.75
0.0985366	281.575	0.108293	1480.68
0.106016	308.321	0.102439	1507.43
0.114472	379.643	0.064065	1641.16
0.0699187	401.932	0.120976	1734.77
0.114472	486.627	0.102764	1792.72
0.111545	557.949	0.107967	1837.3
0.0952846	678.306	0.105691	1868.5
0.107967	713.967	0.0627642	1953.19
0.099187	874.443	0.115447	2042.35
0.116748	936.85	0.0926829	2742.2

The result proves that the accelerometer data of the Parkinson's disease affected patients have longer amplitude when compared to the ordinary person. The predicted values of the normal person and Parkinson's disease affected person are recorded below, which shows reasonable difference between normal and disease affected persons. Table 3.1 records the acceleration values for a normal person, and Table 3.2 indicates the Parkinson's disease affected patient's acceleration values.

Next the key parameter to decide the locomotion is EMG value. EMG data, which are obtained from the sensors placed at the arm, foot, and thighs of the Parkinson's disease affected patients, are manipulated. These EMG values are the output of hands and legs movement. These EMG values are compared and classified with normal persons using HMM and dynamic CNN models through which abnormalities are identified and proper rehabilitation is provided according to the need of the patients.

Table 3.2 Acceleration value of a Parkinson disease affected person.

Acceleration (g)	Time (ms)	Acceleration (g)	Time (ms)
0.000877	42.3083	0.013787	759.309
0.060540	57.5527	-0.011612	804.784
-0.021885	93.8095	0.006841	841.093
0.007967	124.916	-0.025524	944.868
0.008870	154.324	-0.066713	989.416
0.028200	190.683	0.028968	1065.48
0.006285	207.009	0.016800	1193.93
0.011620	289.514	-0.017402	1203.66
-0.007653	317.737	0.016970	1387.68
0.014335	383.607	0.000348	1439.54
-0.000558	406.216	0.011979	1698.54
0.002146	488.567	0.016407	1745.76
0.032865	507.983	0.033280	1981.59
0.044310	555.621	-0.013162	2037.57
-0.018789	622.367	0.038449	2874.26

Table 3.3 EMG value of the arm signal from a normal person.

Signal amplitude (UV)	Time (ms)	Signal amplitude (UV)	Time (ms)	Signal amplitude (UV)	Time (ms)	Signal amplitude (UV)	Time (ms)
-16.9432	63.0748	-5.90168	1177.11	-17.441	2096.88	-6.45444	3993.69
9.8957	76.7754	9.94122	1256.54	10.8064	2173.98	13.4209	4001.21
-8.67782	211.34	-9.67337	1278.94	-11.335	2215.58	-7.05414	4124.89
9.31497	282.877	8.32227	1361.71	11.4819	2342.4	14.7265	4158.27
-9.66863	297.668	-9.01868	1364.96	-4.31639	2438.99	-13.9893	4231.06
7.82924	414.241	14.4122	1416.75	11.1477	2522.23	12.2471	4364.72
-9.89333	410.069	-10.2683	1428.87	-5.26737	2682.61	-7.9909	4424.69
4.30881	508.533	6.8337	1481.84	8.04684	2773.75	11.0174	4507.28
-4.55627	491.467	-8.34787	1514.65	-7.36892	2881.51	-10.7139	4668.65
4.71698	620.816	5.21001	1568.29	5.57979	3028.89	9.79425	4676.05
-3.51522	603.631	-7.43624	1615.6	-10.2261	3095.52	-42.7046	4805.73
3.72144	688.419	6.88395	1680.34	5.3712	3204.96	27.3044	4841.31
-4.4899	753.627	-9.93932	1728.43	-9.14715	3357.5	-14.1652	5036.34

(Continued)

Table 3.3 EMG value of the arm signal from a normal person. (*Continued*)

Signal amplitude (UV)	Time (ms)	Signal amplitude (UV)	Time (ms)	Signal amplitude (UV)	Time (ms)	Signal amplitude (UV)	Time (ms)
2.86574	808.429	33.7532	1813.88	6.72514	3553.02	7.12525	5133.47
-5.09624	858.609	-25.7443	1798.81	-6.554	3600.46	-9.70466	5155.35
3.78496	939.343	38.5773	1869.16	8.91486	3702.43	9.33867	5376.51
-5.95667	959.894	-52.9421	1867.57	-8.8153	3668.29	-8.3839	5372.33
1.27714	1033.45	29.3448	1900.85	30.4518	3773.3	39.7502	5501.9
-6.3127	1053.59	-47.8506	1978.98	-40.6841	3786.62	-28.8466	5544.7
1.94131	1156.92	29.7549	2020.62	7.71072	3946.1	36.6379	5708.47

Table 3.4 EMG value of the arm signal from a Parkinson's disease affected person.

Signal amplitude (UV)	Time (ms)	Signal amplitude (UV)	Time (ms)	Signal amplitude (UV)	Time (ms)	Signal amplitude (UV)	Time (ms)
-65.9659	-11.1754	172.827	600.041	43.1841	1210.67	64.7626	1919.22
110.028	34.0486	-313.541	638.966	-74.7626	1238.99	-73.859	1966.58
-134.177	64.724	425.413	651.299	111.543	1254.17	95.9256	2011.92
172.192	88.8589	-133.375	710.231	-60.1905	1305.88	-63.4265	2033.55
-247.956	115.354	187.468	722.902	74.3795	1329.49	122.958	2112.17
145.34	134.136	-96.0399	772.968	-22.8413	1379.81	-48.8359	2115.37
-30.5475	174.731	177.198	786.527	39.3086	1423.43	133.368	2160.48
52.282	203.036	-95.9473	847.593	-2.04123	1461.51	-104.637	2183.58
-179.551	196.168	156.583	854.076	173.93	1488.08	133.46	2235.1
58.5609	258.889	-102.073	914.871	-80.6245	1518.95	-63.1856	2227.58
-30.4177	279.206	177.36	917.121	49.8199	1553.83	75.5519	2273.5
93.8172	314.202	-178.67	905.106	-39.1588	1574.15	-52.7438	2302.01
-251.809	346.769	69.7997	975.098	188.59	1625.87	96.3288	2336.54

(Continued)

Table 3.4 EMG value of the arm signal from a Parkinson's disease affected person. (*Continued*)

Signal amplitude (UV)	Time (ms)	Signal amplitude (UV)	Time (ms)	Signal amplitude (UV)	Time (ms)	Signal amplitude (UV)	Time (ms)
213.913	349.275	-29.5604	969.489	-146.743	1613.47	-203.78	2353.34
296.737	373.849	260.259	1001.39	54.0985	1665.69	185.354	2353.54
-278.67	384.584	-112.283	1027	-59.6715	1723.78	-89.8614	2414.64
203.689	450.212	90.6044	1060.53	91.4477	1739.62	75.7373	2422.75
-185.375	505.978	-29.3751	1118.74	-49.2159	1809.41	-83.5686	2481.69
183.106	543.879	121.753	1142.04	75.0051	1833.21	82.0394	2497.26
-216.297	607.301	-122.47	1157.79	-49.1232	1884.03	-52.4426	2544.54

Table 3.5 EMG value of the foot signal from a normal person.

Signal amplitude (UV)	Time (MS)	Signal amplitude (UV)	Time (MS)	Signal amplitude (UV)	Time (MS)	Signal amplitude (UV)	Time (MS)
-6.88059	7.52394	-9.79943	404.241	-10.1827	1709.3	10.5567	2675.1
6.70283	12.9959	7.82767	445.28	13.2237	1764.02	-10.0831	2729.82
-4.97545	40.3557	-8.06829	445.28	-11.0534	1758.55	14.7701	2762.65
5.71721	54.0356	12.9124	472.64	13.9722	1805.06	-12.5716	2770.86
-9.48609	67.7155	-15.4133	500	-20.1315	1799.59	10.8315	2872.09
8.89482	75.9234	10.7129	513.68	7.72645	1846.1	-6.04473	2839.26
-6.59849	103.283	-12.5265	546.512	-11.1773	1873.46	6.37866	2899.45
8.42903	122.435	14.3521	546.512	7.31827	1895.35	-5.47065	2893.98
-9.49064	130.643	-6.63309	582.079	-12.2213	1922.71	9.3799	2962.38
7.27039	158.003	7.69921	623.119	13.6743	1928.18	-8.8276	2954.17
-15.2734	163.475	-6.75205	628.591	-11.1838	1963.75	12.8432	3030.78
24.2054	177.155	8.67989	650.479	15.6948	1963.75	-11.4333	3017.1

(Continued)

Table 3.5 EMG value of the foot signal from a normal person. (*Continued*)

Signal amplitude (UV)	Time (MS)	Signal amplitude (UV)	Time (MS)	Signal amplitude (UV)	Time (MS)	Signal amplitude (UV)	Time (MS)
-17.0114	218.194	-9.81821	664.159	-8.00795	2010.26	8.96697	3077.29
6.68642	240.082	13.3018	683.311	18.4076	2018.47	-10.2822	3085.5
-12.6797	267.442	-12.7104	691.518	-20.3207	2018.47	5.78323	3140.22
6.56686	294.802	9.53963	751.71	7.71261	2037.62	-7.68498	3140.22
-8.17342	300.274	-9.2461	746.238	-10.325	2078.66	6.64633	3194.94
9.74368	327.633	8.55499	779.07	12.2173	2092.34	-12.1398	3194.94
-10.4891	349.521	-7.80438	792.75	-7.90085	2127.91	17.338	3222.3
12.7449	390.561	9.82469	806.43	10.5933	2168.95	-14.4559	3249.66

Table 3.6 EMG value of the foot signal from a Parkinson's disease affected person.

Signal amplitude (UV)	Time (MS)	Signal amplitude (UV)	Time (MS)	Signal amplitude (UV)	Time (MS)	Signal amplitude (UV)	Time (MS)
-28.8889	-7.78425	-56.4444	663.404	53.1852	4641.67	44.2963	5600.58
21.4815	44.3263	30.3704	744.487	-32.7407	4727.41	-43.1111	5652.52
-36.2963	58.5843	-28.2963	796.929	50.2222	4763.89	36.8889	5670.74
28.8889	72.8704	49.6296	777.699	-63.8519	4848.98	-33.3333	5726.04
-29.7778	113.923	-48.1481	877.758	45.7778	4871.28	54.6667	5742.29
31.8519	136.68	18.5185	861.307	-43.1111	4969.15	-82.2222	5776.07
-52	130.797	-21.4815	871.177	51.7037	4983.72	90.2222	5836.02
65.037	166.456	18.5185	948.626	-60	5030.27	-49.6296	5862.94
-37.7778	184.235	-21.4815	958.497	39.2593	5062.72	54.6667	5894.15
24.4444	206.845	28	1010.83	-31.2593	5125.68	-46.6667	5919.15
-39.2593	260.53	-29.7778	1036.47	39.2593	5127.26	31.8519	5945.34
39.8519	278.973	39.8519	1083.83	-25.9259	5192.7	-18.5185	5988.14
-25.9259	314.188	-52	1125.48	40.7407	5195.23	42.2222	6018.71

(Continued)

Table 3.6 EMG value of the foot signal from a Parkinson's disease affected person. (*Continued*)

Signal amplitude (UV)	Time (MS)	Signal amplitude (UV)	Time (MS)	Signal amplitude (UV)	Time (MS)	Signal amplitude (UV)	Time (MS)
30.963	364.69	58.5185	1136.17	-56.4444	5276.16	-37.7778	6068.82
-30.3704	379.825	-54.0741	1213.31	39.2593	5336.07	48.7407	6085.44
45.7778	448.353	20	1221.61	-40.1481	5393.63	-57.037	6149.5
-64.4444	456.571	-25.9259	1232.94	39.8519	5423.24	39.8519	6144.58
37.7778	564.223	49.6296	1271.24	-32.7407	5486.71	-30.3704	6218.85
-40.7407	564.617	-52.5926	1307.86	32.4444	5501	39.2593	6201.67
45.7778	657.161	51.7037	1339.07	-32.7407	5562.64	-28.8889	6256.45

Table 3.7 EMG value of the thigh signal from a normal person.

Signal amplitude (UV)	Time (MS)	Signal amplitude (UV)	Time (MS)	Signal amplitude (UV)	Time (MS)	Signal amplitude (UV)	Time (MS)
-15.7432	65.3748	-4.70168	1677.11	-15.141	2396.88	-5.10444	4419.69
11.0957	79.0754	11.14122	1756.54	13.1064	2473.98	14.7709	4427.21
-7.47782	213.64	-8.47337	1778.94	-9.035	2515.58	-5.70414	4550.89
10.51497	285.177	9.52227	1861.71	13.7819	2642.4	16.0765	4584.27
-8.46863	299.968	-7.81868	1864.96	-2.01639	2738.99	-12.6393	4657.06
9.02924	416.541	15.6122	1916.75	13.4477	2822.23	13.5971	4790.72
-8.69333	412.369	-9.0683	1928.87	-2.96737	2982.61	-6.6409	4850.69
5.50881	510.833	8.0337	1981.84	10.34684	3073.75	12.3674	4933.28
-3.35627	493.767	-7.14787	2014.65	-5.06892	3181.51	-9.3639	5094.65
5.91698	623.116	6.41001	2068.29	7.87979	3328.89	11.14425	5102.05
-2.31522	605.931	-6.23624	2115.6	-7.9261	3395.52	-41.3546	5231.73
4.92144	690.719	8.08395	2180.34	7.6712	3504.96	28.6544	5267.31
-3.2899	755.927	-8.73932	2228.43	-6.84715	3657.5	-12.8152	5462.34

(Continued)

Table 3.7 EMG value of the thigh signal from a normal person. (*Continued*)

Signal amplitude (UV)	Time (MS)	Signal amplitude (UV)	Time (MS)	Signal amplitude (UV)	Time (MS)	Signal amplitude (UV)	Time (MS)
4.06574	810.729	34.9532	2313.88	9.02514	3853.02	8.47525	5559.47
-3.89624	860.909	-24.5443	2298.81	-4.254	3900.46	-8.35466	5581.35
4.98496	941.643	39.7773	2369.16	11.21486	4002.43	10.68867	5802.51
-4.75667	962.194	-51.7421	2367.57	-6.5153	3968.29	-7.0339	5798.33
2.47714	1035.75	30.5448	2400.85	32.7518	4073.3	41.1002	5927.9
-5.1127	1055.89	-46.6506	2478.98	-38.3841	4086.62	-27.4966	5970.7
3.14131	1159.22	30.9549	2520.62	10.01072	4246.1	37.9879	6134.47

Table 3.8 EMG value of the thigh signal for Parkinson's disease affected person.

Signal amplitude (UV)	Time (MS)	Signal amplitude (UV)	Time (MS)	Signal amplitude (UV)	Time (MS)	Signal amplitude (UV)	Time (MS)
-14.5432	67.6748	-3.50168	2177.11	-12.841	2696.88	-3.75444	4845.69
12.2957	81.3754	12.34122	2256.54	15.4064	2773.98	16.1209	4853.21
-6.27782	215.94	-7.27337	2278.94	-6.735	2815.58	-4.35414	4976.89
11.71497	287.477	10.72227	2361.71	16.0819	2942.4	17.4265	5010.27
-7.26863	302.268	-6.61868	2364.96	0.28361	3038.99	-11.2893	5083.06
10.22924	418.841	16.8122	2416.75	15.7477	3122.23	14.9471	5216.72
-7.49333	414.669	-7.8683	2428.87	-0.66737	3282.61	-5.2909	5276.69
6.70881	513.133	9.2337	2481.84	12.64684	3373.75	13.7174	5359.28
-2.15627	496.067	-5.94787	2514.65	-2.76892	3481.51	-8.0139	5520.65
7.11698	625.416	7.61001	2568.29	10.17979	3628.89	12.49425	5528.05
-1.11522	608.231	-5.03624	2615.6	-5.6261	3695.52	-40.0046	5657.73
6.12144	693.019	9.28395	2680.34	9.9712	3804.96	30.0044	5693.31
-2.0899	758.227	-7.53932	2728.43	-4.54715	3957.5	-11.4652	5888.34

(Continued)

Table 3.8 EMG value of the thigh signal for Parkinson's disease affected person. (*Continued*)

Signal amplitude (UV)	Time (MS)	Signal amplitude (UV)	Time (MS)	Signal amplitude (UV)	Time (MS)	Signal amplitude (UV)	Time (MS)
5.26574	813.029	36.1532	2813.88	11.32514	4153.02	9.82525	5985.47
-2.69624	863.209	-23.3443	2798.81	-1.954	4200.46	-7.00466	6007.35
6.18496	943.943	40.9773	2869.16	13.51486	4302.43	12.03867	6228.51
-3.55667	964.494	-50.5421	2867.57	-4.2153	4268.29	-5.6839	6224.33
3.67714	1038.05	31.7448	2900.85	35.0518	4373.3	42.4502	6353.9
-3.9127	1058.19	-45.4506	2978.98	-36.0841	4386.62	-26.1466	6396.7
4.34131	1161.52	32.1549	3020.62	12.31072	4546.1	39.3379	6560.47

EMG values corresponding to the arm signal of a normal person is given in Table 3.3, and Parkinson's disease affected person is shown in Table 3.4.

Similarly the EMG values from foot and thigh are recorded for normal persons and Parkinson's disease affected persons and recorded for computation. Tables 3.5 and 3.6 show the EMG values for foot of normal and Parkinson's disease affected patients, respectively, followed by EMG values of thigh for normal person and Parkinson's disease affected patient, respectively, in Tables 3.7 and 3.8.

Considering Tables 3.1–3.8, they record the bio signal amplitude level and corresponding response time of the patients compared with normal persons. On observing that the EMG data accountable for the hand

Table 3.9.1 Normal person-left leg.

Phase value	Time (S)
3.26923	-0.012845
4.71154	0.418012
3.50962	0.790517
9.08654	1.21477
1.39423	1.5759
9.51923	1.86693
1.15385	2.41376
8.55769	2.69928
2.01923	3.5654
8.94231	4.68695
1.63462	5.96704
8.84615	6.78545
3.36538	7.92682
9.13462	8.54338
5.52885	9.08837
6.58654	9.78347
6.34615	9.93431

movements and leg movements for normal persons and Parkinson's disease affected patients are varied and monitoring of nerve disorder is effectively done via sensors through classification techniques, competent rehabilitation mechanism is provided according to the decision obtained through the processor. The increase in the values of response time indicates the severity of the disease.

The results obtained by detecting the gait of normal person and Parkinson's disease affected patients are shown in Tables 3.9 and 3.10, respectively. Without considering the gravity phase and its effect, the irregularities in the gait are measured. When it comes for a normal person,

Table 3.9.2 Normal person-right leg.

Phase value	Time (S)
3.38018	0.143901
8.35832	0.356656
3.79454	0.888366
5.71429	1.31317
1.46875	1.54097
8.91516	2.30543
2.15799	2.48456
0.566579	3.96534
7.9206	4.49546
1.94294	5.38737
9.57361	6.50424
0.951024	8.15884
7.66483	8.48275
4.92663	8.81728
6.75611	9.47289
4.56644	9.93433
6.3021	10.0455

Table 3.10.1 Gait disorder-left leg.

Phase value	Time (S)	Phase value	Time (S)
5.01259	-0.042	2.96002	5.59414
5.03407	0.27522	2.32111	5.73943
4.52844	0.37879	2.73842	6.18517
3.78578	0.37565	3.26855	6.20855
1.92881	0.38894	3.74429	6.31627
1.9966	1.12918	5.88966	6.51562
2.5509	1.30066	3.62877	6.90775
3.66018	1.60133	4.26332	7.03728
3.22941	2.0012	4.07429	7.2479
2.85774	2.02077	4.23107	7.39656
3.06623	2.25421	4.12229	7.56523
2.74694	2.31628	7.61732	7.96056
1.81627	2.46034	6.73667	8.2951
2.20571	2.99053	8.19411	8.38583
3.13133	3.16358	6.5708	8.71723
3.30859	3.69287	8.42744	8.72508
2.37556	3.9849	6.64768	8.88669
2.44604	4.55603	8.5023	9.02138
4.82844	4.86208	6.98844	9.14183
4.02264	5.49293	8.04702	9.2943

the gait value is taken in terms of phase value with time period and is recorded in Tables 3.9.1 and 3.9.2.

The abnormal condition that occurs to person in course of normal walking may sometimes leads to a bent in the foot, and condition can be predicted through HMM and dynamic CNN techniques in such a way to

Table 3.10.2 Gait disorder-right leg.

Phase value	Time (S)	Phase value	Time (S)
3.65228	0.13103	2.4625	4.75821
3.59865	0.48071	3.03063	5.10917
1.13669	0.64025	2.84758	5.43801
1.08178	1.23685	1.91313	5.78588
1.96281	1.19751	2.01527	6.07416
2.22081	1.4038	2.73979	6.24026
2.09021	1.60929	4.75879	6.57363
3.28117	1.75578	4.4718	6.96399
3.15057	1.96127	2.19235	6.89757
2.94278	2.06372	1.51729	7.18425
3.14907	2.24933	3.5623	7.49709
3.40718	2.43505	5.29846	7.41836
2.26708	2.47385	3.97318	8.19753
2.03211	2.82316	4.77446	8.54897
2.26303	3.25574	5.55155	8.57115
3.09214	3.23687	6.74282	8.6559
3.45206	3.77259	8.4276	8.49476
2.51826	3.997	7.13014	8.90361
1.81857	4.03672	8.6067	8.92723
1.84213	4.48944	7.56906	9.19258

obtain the gait gesture. This information is treated at the time of rehabilitation, and the same is rectified automatically by the use of actuators placed at the bed or chapels. The gait value for the Parkinson's disease affected patients is shown in Tables 3.10.1 and 3.10.2.

3.7 Conclusion

The recent technology shows that the physical activity variations of humans can be enhanced perfectly, and the damage extremities can be restored with rehabilitation mechanism. The rehabilitation can be made with the use of the modern technology by using wearable sensors, which are placed in arms, thighs, and foot of the patient in the form of e-clothes or wearable bands. Based on the sensor values, various physical parameters are being estimated. The sensors like accelerometer and EMG provide measurements in real time, and depending on the values, the difference between normal person and the disease affected persons is easily classified through machine learning approach using dynamic CNN and HMM. The gait analysis is also done to set a protruding perception among the Parkinson's disease affected patients and the normal persons. The proposed methodology reveals better performance when compared to the state-of-the-art techniques, thereby providing efficient mechanism of rehabilitation for persons suffering from nerve disorders.

References

1. National Spinal Cord Injury Statistical Center, *Facts and Figures at a Glance*, p. 10, University of Alabama at Birmingham, Birmingham, AL, 2016.
2. Vanderborght, B. *et al.*, Variable impedance actuators: A review. *Rob. Auton. Syst.*, 61, 12, 1601–1614, 2013.
3. Cavallaro, E.E. *et al.*, Real-time myoprocessors for a neural controlled powered exoskeleton arm. *IEEE Trans. Biomed. Eng.*, 53, 11, 2387–2396, 2006.
4. Nieuwboer, A. *et al.*, Abnormalities of the spatiotemporal characteristics of gait at the onset of freezing in Parkinson's disease. *Mov. Disord.: Official Journal of the Movement Disorder Society*, 16, 6, 1066–1075, 2001.
5. Chee, R. *et al.*, Gait freezing in Parkinson's disease and the stride length sequence effect interaction. *Brain*, 132, 8, 2151–2160, 2009.
6. Gao, F., Linhong, W., Lin, T., Intelligent wearable rehabilitation robot control system based on mobile communication network. *Comput. Commun.*, 153, 286–293, 2020.
7. https://www.oefentherapie-kloostra.nl/?page_id=29&lang=en
8. Kisner, C., Colby, L.A., Borstad, J., *Therapeutic exercise: foundations and techniques*, Fa Davis, Pennsylvania, 2017.
9. Abbruzzese, G. *et al.*, Rehabilitation for Parkinson's disease: Current outlook and future challenges. *Parkinsonism Relat. Disord.*, 22, S60–S645, 2016.
10. Guzmán, C.H. *et al.*, Robust control of a hip–joint rehabilitation robot. *Biomed. Signal Process. Control*, 35, 100–1095, 2017.

11. Valdivia, C.H.G. *et al.*, Design and analysis of a new robotic mechanism for lower limbs rehabilitation. *2013 International Conference on Mechatronics, Electronics and Automotive Engineering*, IEEE, 2013.

12. Pamela, K.L. and Cynthia, C.N., Joint structure and function: a comprehensive analysis. *Shoulder Complex*, pp. 240–241, 2006.

13. Tamilarasan, A.K., Krishnadhas, S.K., Sabapathy, S. *et al.*, A novel design of Rogers RT/duroid 5880 material based two turn antenna for intracranial pressure monitoring. *Microsyst. Technol.*, pp. 1–10, 2021, https://doi.org/10.1007/s00542-020-05122-y.

14. Nordin, M. and Frankel, V.H. (Eds.), *Basic biomechanics of the musculoskeletal system*, Lippincott Williams & Wilkins, Philadelphia, 2001.

15. Kim, Y. *et al.*, Optimal Level of Assistance and Weight of Hip-joint Wearable Robot Considering Influences to the Human Body. *IFAC-PapersOnLine*, 52, 22, 13–18, 2019.

16. Guzmán-Valdivia, C.H. *et al.*, HipBot–the design, development and control of a therapeutic robot for hip rehabilitation. *Mechatronics*, 30, 55–645, 2015.

17. Guzmán, C.H. *et al.*, Robust control of a hip–joint rehabilitation robot. *Biomed. Signal Process. Control*, 35, 100–1095, 2017.

18. Sharini, H. *et al.*, Novel fMRI-Compatible Wrist Robotic Device for Brain Activation Assessment During Rehabilitation Exercise. *Med. Eng. Phys.*, 83, 112–122, 2020.

19. Manuli, A. *et al.*, Can robotic gait rehabilitation plus Virtual Reality affect cognitive and behavioural outcomes in patients with chronic stroke? A randomized controlled trial involving three different protocols. *J. Stroke Cerebrovasc. Dis.*, 29, 8, 104994, 2020.

20. Yokota, C. *et al.*, Acute stroke rehabilitation for gait training with cyborg type robot Hybrid Assistive Limb: A pilot study. *J. Neurol. Sci.*, 404, 11–15, 2019.

21. Wallard, L. *et al.*, Effect of robotic-assisted gait rehabilitation on dynamic equilibrium control in the gait of children with cerebral palsy. *Gait Posture*, 60, 55–6055, 2018.

22. Bruni, M.F. *et al.*, What does best evidence tell us about robotic gait rehabilitation in stroke patients: a systematic review and meta-analysis. *J. Clin. Neurosci.*, 48, 11–175, 2018.

23. Alias, N.A. *et al.*, The Efficacy of State-of-the-Art Overground Gait Rehabilitation Robotics: A Bird's Eye View. *Proc. Comput. Sci.*, 105, 365–370, 2017.

24. Bayon, C. *et al.*, Development and evaluation of a novel robotic platform for gait rehabilitation in patients with Cerebral Palsy: CPWalker. *Rob. Auton. Syst.*, 91, 101–1145, 2017.

25. Spildooren, J. *et al.*, Freezing of gait in Parkinson's disease: the impact of dual-tasking and turning. *Mov. Disord.*, 25, 15, 2563–2570, 2010.

26. Spildooren, J. *et al.*, Turning and unilateral cueing in Parkinson's disease patients with and without freezing of gait. *Neuroscience*, 207, 298–30655, 2012.

27. Sutskever, I., Vinyals, O., Le, Q.V., Sequence to sequence learning with neural networks. *Advances in neural information processing systems*, 2014.

28. Hochreiter, S. *et al.*, A field guide to dynamical recurrent neural networks, in: *chapter Gradient Flow in Recurrent Nets: The Difficulty of Learning Long-Term Dependencies*, pp. 237–243, Wiley-IEEE Press, Canada, 2001.

29. Schmidhuber, J. and Hochreiter, S., Long short-term memory. *Neural Comput.*, 9, 8, 1735–1780, 1997.

30. Bai, S., Zico Kolter, J., Koltun, V., An empirical evaluation of generic convolutional and recurrent networks for sequence modeling. *arXiv preprint arXiv:1803.01271*, 2018.

31. Long, J., Shelhamer, E., Darrell, T., Fully convolutional networks for semantic segmentation. *Proceedings of the IEEE conference on computer vision and pattern recognition*, 2015.

32. Vedaldi, A. and Lenc, K., Matconvnet: Convolutional neural networks for matlab. *Proceedings of the 23rd ACM international conference on Multimedia*, 2015.

33. Bouvrie, J., Notes on convolutional neural networks, 2006.

34. Chen, Y.-C. *et al.*, Effects of foot orthoses on gait patterns of flat feet patients. *Clin. Biomech.*, 25, 3, 265–270, 2010.

35. Bachlin, M. *et al.*, Wearable assistant for Parkinson's disease patients with the freezing of gait symptom. *IEEE Trans. Inf. Technol. Biomed.*, 14, 2, 436–446, 2009.

36. Belli, A. *et al.*, A treadmill ergometer for three-dimensional ground reaction forces measurement during walking. *J. Biomech.*, 34, 1, 105–112, 2001.

37. Tao, W. *et al.*, Gait analysis using wearable sensors. *Sensors*, 12, 2, 2255–2283, 2012.

38. Ayrulu-Erdem, B. and Barshan, B., Leg motion classification with artificial neural networks using wavelet-based features of gyroscope signals. *Sensors*, 11, 2, 1721–1743, 2011.

39. Tunçel, O., Altun, K., Barshan, B., Classifying human leg motions with uni-axial piezoelectric gyroscopes. *Sensors*, 9, 11, 8508–8546, 2009.

40. Takeda, R. *et al.*, Gait posture estimation using wearable acceleration and gyro sensors. *J. Biomech.*, 42, 15, 2486–2494, 2009.

41. Lloyd, D.G. and Besier, T.F., An EMG-driven musculoskeletal model to estimate muscle forces and knee joint moments in vivo. *J. Biomech.*, 36, 6, 765–776, 2003.

42. ElSayed, M. *et al.*, Ambient and wearable sensing for gait classification in pervasive healthcare environments. *The 12th IEEE International Conference on e-Health Networking, Applications and Services*, IEEE, 2010.

43. Turcot, K. *et al.*, New accelerometric method to discriminate between asymptomatic subjects and patients with medial knee osteoarthritis during 3-d gait. *IEEE Trans. Biomed. Eng.*, 55, 4, 1415–1422, 2008.

44. Baraka, A. *et al.*, Wearable Accelerometer and sEMG-Based Upper Limb BSN for Tele-Rehabilitation. *Appl. Sci.*, 9, 14, 2019, 2795.

45. Del Din, S. *et al.*, Estimating Fugl-Meyer clinical scores in stroke survivors using wearable sensors. *2011 Annual International Conference of the IEEE Engineering in Medicine and Biology Society*, IEEE, 2011.

46. Sanford, J. *et al.*, Reliability of the Fugl-Meyer assessment for testing motor performance in patients following stroke. *Phys. Ther.*, 73, 7, 447–454, 1993.

47. Badawi, A.A., Al-Kabbany, A., Shaban, H., Multimodal human activity recognition from wearable inertial sensors using machine learning. *2018 IEEE-EMBS Conference on Biomedical Engineering and Sciences (IECBES)*, IEEE, 2018.

4

Smart Sensors for Activity Recognition

Rehab A. Rayan[1]*, Imran Zafar[2], Aamna Rafique[3] and Christos Tsagkaris[4]

[1]Department of Epidemiology, High Institute of Public Health, Alexandria University, Alexandria, Egypt
[2]Department of Bioinformatics and Computational Biology, Virtual University of Pakistan, Punjab, Pakistan
[3]Department of Biochemistry, Agriculture University Faisalabad, Punjab, Pakistan
[4]Faculty of Medicine, University of Crete, Heraklion, Greece

Abstract

Nowadays, health informatics is enhancing the efficiency of healthcare via improved collecting, storing, and retrieving of vital health-related data. Smart sensors arose because of the rapidly growing information and communication technologies and wireless communications. Today, both smartphones and wearable biosensors are highly used for self-monitoring of health and well-being. Smart sensors could enable healthcare providers to monitor digitally and routinely the elderly's activities. Smart health has emerged from integrating smart wearable sensors in healthcare, while the growth in machine learning (ML) technologies enabled recognizing human activity. This chapter describes applications and limitations of a smart healthcare framework that could model and record, digitally and precisely, body movements and vital signs during daily-living human activities through ML techniques applying smartphones and wearables.

Keywords: Smart health, activity recognition, health monitoring, machine learning, biosensors

4.1 Introduction

Most of the elderly people suffer from age-related health issues like cardiovascular disorders, diabetes mellitus, osteoarthritis, dementia, and other

---

*Corresponding author: rayanr@alexu.edu.eg

Roshani Raut, Pranav Pathak, Sandeep Kautish and Pradeep N (eds.) Intelligent Systems for Rehabilitation Engineering, (95–114) © 2022 Scrivener Publishing LLC

chronic conditions. Such conditions, along with the apparent gradual decline in mental and body capabilities, limit their free-living. Recent advances in information and communication technologies (ICTs) together with innovations in ambient smart techniques, like smartphones and bio-sensors, have promoted smart settings [1]. Smart health could potentially meet the demands of such a growing elderly population via delivering smart healthcare services. For example, smart health systems could evaluate and monitor severe conditions of elderly population throughout their everyday living. The smart healthcare design could offer sustained health-care services through lowering the load over the overall health system. For adopting a smart health system, there are several limitations in many phases of the developing procedure such as distant setting monitoring, the required techniques, the needed smart processing systems, and the deliv-ering of setting-oriented services. Hence, further studies are needed [2].

Smart health monitoring systems are integrating pervasive comput-ing with ICTs, hence delivering smart healthcare services that meet indi-vidual needs. Several interventions are designed to solve many issues of such systems providing a smart context to monitor and analyze individual health status and deliver real-time smart healthcare services [2]. Figure 4.1 displays an overall structure of these systems.

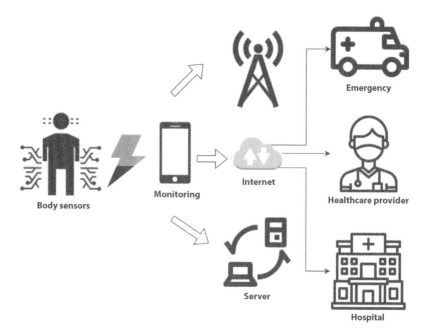

Figure 4.1 An overall structure of smart health monitoring systems.

ICT innovations have driven the wider deployment of smartphones and body sensors that could connect timely patients with healthcare providers for monitoring and analyzing health status pervasively in a smart setting, hence the rising era of smart health and mobile health monitoring platforms. This chapter highlights a smart health platform that could mainly trigger the potential of wearables and mobile-based healthcare delivery to monitor the individual health and wellbeing and offer pervasive activity recognition via machine learning (ML) techniques. Smart health is a medical health framework based on smartphones and biosensors, and it comprises deploying technologies, such as 4G systems, Global Positioning System, and Bluetooth [3].

Late advances in innovative Internet and computational technologies enabled swift connectivity among many devices [4]. The newly rising principle of smartphones and biosensors have integrated the Internet into everyday living, linking many devices and adding to the productivity of various areas like smart health systems. In smart health applications, smart biosensors involve many types of wearables allowing individuals seeking healthcare services anywhere and anytime and bringing the techniques of body sensor network, one of the highly proficient technologies in the smart health systems, where they are chiefly a mixture of lightweight and low-power wireless sensor nodes for monitoring activity recognition [5]. However, smart health should establish and evaluate the entire scope of such techniques, which justify and advance multidisciplinary smart health applications [3].

Human-activity recognition (HAR) is a promising research area for its valuable contributions in enhancing the quality of life, the safety, transportation, health in smart cities and villages, and assisting decision-makers in improving quality services [2]. HAR systems supply data on the personal behavior and activity via tracking signals from smartphones and biosensors and translating them through ML techniques, hence the ability of ongoing patient monitoring for a range of conditions [6, 7] such as everyday life activities, movements, exercise, and transportation [8]. ML techniques vary largely in quantity, speed, data frameworks like supervised and unsupervised algorithms, and using the right algorithms matching data features. Since data are yielded via multiple sources with unique types, it is vital to apply the most efficient algorithms. Furthermore, determining the precise data model is an important phase in pattern recognition and better exploration of the generated data [4]. This chapter highlights various ML for HAR applying smartphones and biosensors to explore human activity and add more precision to smart health.

The novel wireless network techniques made it possible to adopt wearables gradually for smart monitoring of everyday activities in different domains like emergency situations, cognitive assistance, and safety [9]. HAR could determine pervasively various human activities and gestures via individual motion through smartphones and biosensors. Regarding recognition of complicated activities, data-centered techniques are challenging regarding mobility, expansion, and translation; however, knowledge-centered techniques are mostly poor in handling complicated temporal data [10]. ML could minimize the vast quantities of data to reflect the whole data without circulation [11]. The sensor-driven activity recognition is turning commoner than video-driven one to safeguard privacy [12]. Wearables' gathered data could be processed via ML algorithms.

HAR is a swiftly rising research discipline with broad applications in health, assisted living, home monitoring, personal fitness, and terrorism identification. Likewise, HAR frameworks could be integrated in a smart home healthcare framework to develop and improve the patient's rehabilitation procedures [13]. Assisting elderly population proactively made the healthcare professionals apply biosensors to monitor and analyze their everyday life activities, hence helping them to live independently [14]. An activity recognition model with various wearables comprises sections for protecting and analyzing data, involving extraction and identification, categorization, and evaluation [15]. However, identifying the best ML techniques to recognize accurately human activity is needed.

4.2 Wearable Biosensors for Activity Recognition

Wearable biosensors (WBS) are gaining infinite popularity nowadays, and currently they aim to be one of the biggest inventions in the powering technology market. In WBS, a broad biosensor classification is suitable for healthcare facilities, sports-related applications, security applications, etc. Rapid growth of such devices is on track to offer benefits such as ease of use, low cost, and real-time awareness. Progress in portable health technology and WBS has been made, so that they can be considered ready for all clinical purposes. Portable biosensors are of great interest because of their ability to provide continuous, real-time physiological information through complex, non-invasive measurements of biochemical markers in bio fluids, such as sweat, tears, saliva, and interstitial fluid. Recent developments have focused on electrochemical and optical biosensors as well as advances in non-invasive testing of biomarkers including metabolites, bacteria, and hormones.

A combination of multiplexed bio-sensing, microfluidic sampling and transport systems has been developed that is integrated, miniaturized, and combined with lightweight materials to increase portability and ease of use. While the promise of portable biosensors is that a better understanding of the interactions between concentrations of blood analysis and non-invasive bio-fluids is important to improve reliability. An extended range of bio-affinity assays on the body and more sensing techniques are required to provide more biomarkers available for monitoring. Characterization techniques covering a large dataset of the development of WBS would also be needed to substantiate clinical acceptability. Precise and real-time sensing with portable biosensor technology of physiological knowledge will have a huge impact on our everyday lives.

Using portable monitoring devices or WBS that allow for continuous monitoring of physiological signals is essential for progress in both disease diagnosis and treatment. Portable systems are devices that allow physicians to overcome technology limitations and respond to the need for weeks or months of monitoring of individuals. Usually portable biosensors rely on wireless sensors found in bandages or patches or on items that can be worn. The data sets collected using these systems are then processed to detect events that predict possible deterioration of the clinical situation of the patient and are analyzed to gain access to the results of clinical interventions. The HAR aims to recognize actions performed by individuals who have been given a series of data metrics that are captured by the sensor. Successful HAR research based on understanding relatively simple behaviors as sitting or walking and their applications are mainly useful for tracking healthcare, tele-immersion, or operation. Smartphone use is one of the most open ways to understand human behavior. Biological sensors are a system in short biosensors that comprise sensors, biosensor readers, and a biological element. The environmental viewpoint here may be a cause, an inhibitor, or an antigen for nucleotides. The biological factor is designed to communicate with the measured analyte, and the sensor translates the biological responses into an electrical signal. Depending on the application, biosensors are often popularly known by names that include immuno-sensors, optrodes, biochips, glucometers, and bio-computers. Displaying the data is up to the biosensor reader system. It is known that this is the most costly part of the biosensor.

HAR is intensively studied, and a large amount of analysis shows findings from the study of all kinds of everyday human behaviors, such as traveling, sleeping, or activity generating. To this end, multiple sensors accumulate numerous bio-signals, e.g., [16] used compact trial-waist-connected axial accelerometers to differentiate between rest (sit) and active (sit-to-stand, stand-to-sit, and walk) state. In [17], five biaxial accelerometers were used to identify everyday activities such as walking, rising, and folding laundry.

The authors placed in the hands of the participants an integrated smartphone with a simple accelerometer and categorized activities such as running, climbing, sitting, standing, and bike riding [18]. In addition, accelerometers were combined with smartphones [19] to provide a simple auditory level research [20] contrasted the recognition efficiency of five machines learning classifiers (K-nearest neighbor, feedforward neural network, support vector machines, Naïve Bayes, and decision tree) and assessed the benefits and drawbacks of implementing them on a HAR laptop computer in real time.

Because of their immense potential in data modeling and customized medication therapy, advanced nursing allowed by versatile/portable devices and advanced analytics has gained considerable interest during recent years. The restricted supply of portable analytical biosensors has impeded further progress towards continued personal health monitoring. In recent years, significant advances in portable chemical sensors have been made for the study of biomarkers in tears, saliva, sweat, blood and exhalation, fabrics, applications, and device innovations. Electromyography (EMG) identified the action of muscles as another important bio-signal. It also provides the opportunity to decide the intention of a person to move before moving a joint that was being checked for causing orthosis [21]. In addition, several researchers, among them [22] and [23], used electrogoniometers to analyze films. Some new technologies in WBS innovation are Google's Smart Lens, Healthpatch Biosensor, Wearable Biosensor-Odor Diseases, QTM Sensor, Wearable Glucose Sensor, and Portable Biosensor Tattoos Monitor Sweat to Track Weight, Ring Sensor, and Smart Shirts.

4.3   Smartphones for Activity Recognition

Cellphones seem to be the most important resources in our daily lives and, with the changing technology, they are becoming more capable of fulfilling customer needs and demands every day. To make these gadgets more functional and effective, designers are adding new modules and devices to the hardware. Sensors play a major role in making smartphones more effective and environmentally conscious, so most smartphones come with numerous embedded sensors, allowing vast amounts of information to be gathered about the consumer's daily life and activities. Both the accelerometer and the gyroscope sensors are among those items.

For almost every smartphone manufacturer, the accelerometer had become a normal hardware. Since its name means velocity change in the calculation of the accelerometer, not speed itself, users could look at the microcontroller's collected data to track drastic changes. Another sensor that has become normal smartphone hardware is a gyroscope that makes use of gravity to determine the orientation. Gyroscopic-recovered signals may be analyzed to determine the device's location and orientation. Since there is a considerable difference in specifications seen between data collected from these sensors, several features may be created from those sensor data to determine the individual carrying the operation of the system. In the view of various researches, classification of mobile usage behaviors was focused on the detection of human behavior with accelerator signals [24]. Later researchers have attempted to identify movement based on several wearable gyroscopes and accelerometers [25], and after that, researchers also developed a convolutionary artificial neural network to recognize the user movement using the accelerometer sensor of smartphones [26]. Kozina *et al.* used an accelerometer to operate on autumn detection [27].

Activity analysis has gained a large portion of attention in recent decades with the world's latest developments in artificial intelligence and ML. Over the past 10 years, there has been continuous progress in this area, early research beginning with gesture spotting with body-worn inertial sensors [28], and state-of-the-art solutions for complex detection of human activity using smartphone and wrist-worn motion sensors [29]. In this section, we will look at some other user behavior detection methods.

4.3.1   Early Analysis Activity Recognition

One of the initial studies to recognize user interactions utilizing sensors has been to use body-worn sensors such as accelerometers and gyroscopes [28] to detect a wide variety of user activities, some of which included pressing a light button, shaking hands, picking up a phone, turning a phone down, opening a door, drinking, or using a spoon or eating handheld food (e.g., selecting handheld f). For this purpose, a set of sensors had been placed on the tester's arm, one end on the forearm and one end on the upper arm near the elbow. The data collected were composed of feature vector information, such as the angle at which the hand was positioned and the hand movement. It gave established outcomes using two metrics: the first was recall, calculated as the ratio of known and acceptable gestures (with obtained values of 0.87), while the second was precision, calculated as the percentage of known gestures from all collected data (attained values of 0.62).

4.3.2   Similar Approaches Activity Recognition

A very similar system used accelerometers for the cell phone to experiment with human activity detection [18]. The authors opted to use only the accelerometer sensor, since it was the only significant motion sensor used by most mobile devices at the time. In the meantime, many other sensors have reached the vast majority of smartphones. The activities that were under observation were running, jogging, sitting, standing, ascending stairs, and going downstairs. The study was broken down into three main sections: data collection, feature generation, and experiment work.

The first phase, data collection, was accomplished with the assistance of 29 users who were keeping a mobile device in their pants' pocket while doing casual activities. Even if the probability of 20-s stints was tested, each operation was ultimately performed in 10-s stints, reading sensor data every 50 ms. Not every user did the same number of attempts; the number of sets collected differed for each person and also for each operation performed. As this approach involved the use of a classification algorithm, the main objective in the next step was to form the data in such a way that it could be passed on to existing algorithms as input. At this stage, some computation was performed on each set of 10-sensor readings, called feature generation, resulting in six feature types: average, standard deviation, average absolute difference, average acceleration, peak time, and binned distribution. Playing with the extracted characteristics and three classification techniques, namely multilayer decision trees, logistic regression, and neural networks, was the final step of the functional component. The findings showed strong percentages of walking identification (92%), jogging (98%), sitting (94%), and standing (91%), which were the average values for the three methods of classification, while up and down climbing had comparatively low percentages. The last two operations averaged 49%, respectively 37% over the three classifiers, rising to 60% and 50% unless the logistic regression was taken into consideration. This eventually led to the elimination of the two operations altogether. Instead, for climbing stairs, a new activity was introduced, with an average accuracy of 77%, which is still slightly lower than what was achieved for the other four tasks, but more accurate.

4.3.3   Multi-Sensor Approaches Activity Recognition

In one of the more recent and complex studies, a solution focused on both smartphones and wrist-worn motion sensors was proposed [29]. The central concept of this approach is that the way smartphones are held by their users (for example, in the pant pocket) is not ideal for understanding human behaviors involving hand movements. That is why additional sensors are used, in addition to those from the device. Both sensor sets also included the accelerometer, gyroscope, and linear acceleration.

The data used were collected from 10 participants for 13 activities, but only 7 of those activities were performed by all participants, which are exactly the activities that the suggested solution is attempting to understand, and the mission was carried out for 3 min, with a total period of 30 min for each operation resulting in a dataset of 390 min. All data processing was conducted with two cell phones. But instead of using wrist-worn sensors, a second smartphone was mounted on the right wrist of the users. Only two elements were removed, that is, mean and standard deviation. These were chosen because of the low complexity and the logical precision shown for various activities. Results were composed of combinations of sensors. The sensor was measured separately and then in combination with the others, and the two mobile device locations were also combined. There were a few errors in distinguishing the activities using just the accelerometer and gyroscope at the wrist site; the biggest confusion was between walking and walking upstairs, with a 53% accuracy, when comparing 83% for the other activities together. The findings were improved by mixing the two test places; the overall accuracy increased to 98%. The main drawback to this solution compared to the initial solution was the use of two mobile devices, which is impracticable in real life.

4.3.4   Fitness Systems in Activity Recognition

Sports, especially fitness and running, are one area that has recently resonated greatly with activity awareness. There are numerous examples of applications that use HAR to help users track their training sessions. Samsung Health offers such a forum alongside many more, but there are other apps that concentrate specifically on running and walking, such as Nike+ and Endomondo or even cycling and swimming like Strava. Although these apps recognize a very limited range of operations, they have outstanding results, being extremely accurate in detecting the type of activity performed, giving their customers advantages such as auto pause when detecting that the user is no longer running and tailoring training patterns. In addition, there has been a drastic increase in the number of smartwatches and fitness bands such as Fitbit and Apple Watch that are able to track the number of steps, sleep cycles, inactive hours, etc. These types of devices have begun to be used as components of more complex systems that employ several sensors to perform in-depth activity detection in scenarios such as health care [30], healthy aging [31], and compelling health behavior technology [32].

4.3.5   Human–Computer Interaction Processes in Activity Recognition

The people's delight in interest and playing never vanishes, and the gaming field has undergone many changes. Recognition of action has become an integral part of playing in recent years with the advancement of technologies such as Kinect [33], PlayStation Move [34], and Nintendo Wii [35]. While some of these only recognize movement with the use of visual computing (such as Kinect), others also rely on sensors. The Nintendo Wii has a device that has a motion sensor that allows for identification of the activity. All these are used in different ways to play sports and also to develop a healthy habit. By understanding a user's emotions, the computer can understand the user and have an answer based on human reactions. Thus, human–machine interaction is possible.

4.3.6   Healthcare Monitoring in Activity Recognition

Recent research [36] showed that user activity and actions can be used to suggest human health status. Research has led medical experts to believe that there is a clear link between the amount of physical activity and the various obesity- and metabolism-related diseases. Considering the vast amount of data that can be gathered about the behavior of an individual, the concept of using these data to gather knowledge about the human health condition has evolved rapidly. While this is assumed to be a better option than a time-limited medical appointment, it is not considered a substitute, but more of an extra method.

One of the earliest attempts to tackle this issue was a Bluetooth-based accelerometer worn in three locations and RFID modules used to classify objects used daily [37]. The paper concluded that most people remain in one of the following states: sit, stand, lie, walk, and run. In addition, the aforementioned solution included a wrist-worn sensor that was used to track hand movement to improve the precision of human motion detection. This sensor also features an RFID reader to detect tags placed on certain objects. The sensor provides data when reading a nearby tag, which defines the hand movement when using that object. Several habits coupled with each state of the body were investigated for the assessment part, such as drinking while sitting, standing, or walking, and ironing, or brushing hair while standing up. The results showed a major improvement in accuracy with the use of RFID, raising the overall value from 82% to -97%. The results averaged 94%, labeling walking as the most challenging activity to identify when taking into account the recognition of body condition.

4.4   Machine Learning Techniques

The rapid developments in ICTs and wireless communication networks have resulted in the smart sensors being used. Using smart devices brings health practitioners and patients together in emerging healthcare networks for safe and automated routine tracking of older people's behaviors. Smart body sensors and tablets are used continuously for personal wellbeing monitoring and wellness. Wearable sensor technology is one of the key advances in healthcare monitoring systems with smart sensor technologies. The implementation of intelligent wearable sensors in healthcare has contributed to the advancement of smart applications, such as smart healthcare and smart healthcare monitoring systems. Figure 4.2 shows an overall framework of smart health monitoring systems. Today, health information technology is a vital area for improving healthcare quality by optimizing patient collection, storage, and retrieval of essential health information. In this context, there is a lot of optimism about advancing ML techniques, which play a crucial role in understanding human behavior.

The manner in which data are stored, interpreted, and processed has changed dramatically in the last few decades. Tremendous quantities of data are generated every second and can provide some useful insights if these data are used and analyzed effectively. Many data mining methods have advanced in analyzing the vast amount of data involved. The selection of suitable models is an important part of predictions. We developed models using several ML techniques in our exercise and compared the accuracy of different algorithms. HAR is the issue of predicting a person's actions, often indoors, based on sensor data, such as a smartphone

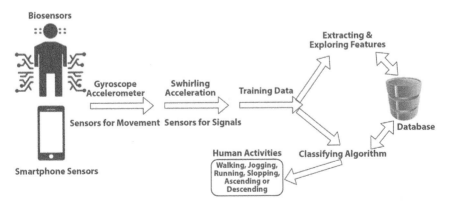

Figure 4.2 The smart health monitoring framework.

accelerometer, and sensor data streams are often split into subsequences called windows, and each window is associated with a larger process, called a sliding window approach. The convolutional neural networks and long-term memory networks are ideally suited for learning features from raw sensor data and for predicting the associated movement in deep learning, and even both together. The machine-learning algorithms are as follows.

4.4.1 Decision Trees Algorithms for Activity Reorganization

Decision trees are one of the common problem-classification algorithms, such as recognition of human behavior. The first model was developed using the decision tree C4.5 for the classification. Trees are quick to understand in a decision. However, precision will suffer if predictors and results have a nonlinear relationship.

4.4.2 Adaptive Boost Algorithms for Activity Reorganization

AdaBoost is an effectiveness-enhancing strategy. This algorithm tends to give greater importance to the wrongly categorized instances of weak learners and thus encourages weak learners to perform well. We used AdaBoost technique with 10 decision trees to improve the classification accuracy of a single deep classification tree.

4.4.3 Random Forest Algorithms for Activity Reorganization

Consequently, random forest is the algorithm aimed at putting together poor learners to increase precision. It bootstraps various predictors and produces many weak trees from bootstrapped predictors. The indicator of bootstrapping implies fewer clustered trees. And, in the end, it brings poor decision trees together to predict the result. This algorithm also provides much more accuracy when classifying decision trees.

4.4.4 Support Vector Machine (SVM) Algorithms for Activity Reorganization

It is a supervised learning algorithm in which the SVM model is used to define samples as space points and divides points based on outcome categories, with a simple dividing distance. The new group of points is determined according to which side of the distance they fall on.

4.5   Other Applications

Smart activity sensors have become more and more accessible in several fields from fashion to IT and medicine. Introducing smart biosensors in oncology in clinical trials represents a new trend with many debatable aspects [38]. The need to introduce smart sensors derives from the cost of clinical trials and the need to secure an effective collection of data. Nowadays, the cost of new anticancer treatments varies between $648 million to $2.7 billion. Only 35% of studies make it from Phase II clinical trials to Phase III clinical trials, and for those who succeed, the product will have taken about 8 years to reach the market [39]. Monitoring several factors from compliance to treatment to vital signs and patients' quality of life requires on-site visits and involves a considerable burden in terms of resources and workload. It has been estimated that more effective management of monitoring could cause a more timely screening of clinical studies that will not proceed further decreasing the cost and the time researchers and stakeholders spend [40, 41].

Recently, smart activity detecting biosensors have appeared as a promising alternative. Researchers and stakeholders have longed for a long time to connect clinical trials to eHealth and mHealth modalities [42]. According to a report published by the American Society of Clinical Oncology, novel technologies for data collection represent prime opportunities to standardize data collected across phases and to increase comparability of results [41]. Such novelties include wearable devices, smart electronic devices worn on the body as implants or accessories (including activity trackers), mobile technology, portable devices operating via wireless cellular services, biosensors, and subsystems monitoring the environment [38].

Multi-institution trials can improve their data collection methods and quantity (sample size) and quality (diversity) features of their studies. Activity biosensors can support more specific health outcome data collection via wearables and mobile technology. Wearables' tracking is categorized as clinical outcomes assessment (COA) or non-clinical outcomes assessment (non-COA) encompassing a wide variety of quantifiable factors. Quantifying individuals' physiology, mental state, or ability to complete an activity is possible as long as a key condition of requiring an activation step is involved [41].

For example, ample studies have shown the accuracy and representativeness of data collected through active sensors, mostly with sensors designed to collect a single measure [43]. Mobile-enabled blood glucose monitors, wireless pulmonary artery pressure monitors, and balance quality assessment are a few of the sensors that have been developed and validated for specific measures. The vitals of the patients reporting unseen or undermonitored incidents related to their breath pattern, cardiac function, and metabolism (glucose levels). Activity sensors placed on medicines storing boxes can monitor the patients' compliance, shedding light to bizarre patterns of efficacy and inefficacy or adverse effects. Overall, smart activity sensors in oncology can help to justify sufficient clinical benefit of a new treatment, which may increase the likelihood of proceeding to a large randomized trial. Clinical studies with poor outcomes can be ceased timely before consuming more time and resources [41].

4.6   Limitations

Introducing smart activity sensors poses several challenges. The learning curve for both researchers and patients will define their further establishment in the field. The cost is also a considerable factor. Although the funding for clinical trials in oncology is high, smart sensors will establish themselves only if they can prove their cost-effectiveness. Finally, yet importantly, despite their advantages, smart activity sensors represent an invasion in the patients' personal lives.

Although the learning curve to smart technology is small for young and educated people, many of whom are involved in clinical trials, the same does not apply to old people. Cancer becomes more prevalent with the progression of age, and most clinical trials include third age individuals. Collective or personalized training and consultation/help-center modalities can be helpful. Comparison across devices has shown that step count, for instance, is relatively accurate for most wearables for 18- to 39-year-olds but more variable in older age groups [41, 44]. However, step counting requires minimal interaction between the user and the device. In case several participants in the study cannot fully comply with the sensors' use, the collection and validation of data will be in peril. Perhaps introducing these devices to studies focusing on populations with a sufficient command of smart technology while advocating for the wider promotion of digital literacy is a prudent strategy to follow.

Access to data represents a second serious concern. This is a rather technical issue that resonates with the previous point. The documentation of the source and lineage of the data (data provenance) is usually conducted through the manufacturer's server. Tracking the specific device, where the data come from, is quite difficult and can only be resolved if each user is registered with a personal account to the server of the manufacturer [43].

Data are difficult to be collected, let alone undergo standardization from most wearable devices, unless there is specific software. The necessity of specific software increases the cost of these devices and makes most smart devices that the patient already possesses ineligible. While training patients to register themselves and use new devices they are not familiar with (rather than a new application installed in their smartphone) is a considerable burden, the regulatory consequences of such steps ought also to be taken into account [38].

4.6.1   Policy Implications and Recommendations

The regulatory infrastructure of smart activity sensors is complicated because of the disparity of legislation around the globe. In some cases, such legislation is not sufficiently developed. In other cases, for instance in Europe, that is considered the alma mater of data protection, personal data regulations may be strict enough to pose serious obstacles to the implementation of such studies. The EU Clinical Trials legislation of 2014 has no specific provisions for smart health monitoring [45], while smart sensors requirements may contradict with the legislations provisions for ethical approval of any clinical trial in Europe [46]. Similar concerns will appear in other continents, and although we cannot address all the potential scenarios in this chapter, we can hypothesize that international or intercontinental multicenter studies relying on smart activity sensors may face considerable obstacles.

4.7   Discussion

Upcoming directions in smartphones and biosensors would grow the wearables' market, where researchers could enhance wearables' frameworks for many applications. Hence, such innovations would attract applying wearables clinically and at home for health monitoring. Ongoing and accurate distant monitoring of vital medical conditions for the elderly population in everyday activities is a vital job. HAR using wearables to identify abnormal conditions, for examples falls, is a novel trend and could improve the health systems. This chapter highlighted a smart HAR applying timely biosensors to show the usability of such systems in determining activities. The system was illustrated via applications where smartphone and biosensors data could be sent to a distant server at a specific frequency, and data were analyzed timely. The system displayed practicability, precision, and efficacy in recognizing activity. The innovations in biosensors and smartphones techniques could provide critical solutions to enhance the quality of healthcare for patients suffering many disorders. This chapter shows adopting a digital, proficient, and adaptable HAR system for determining timely, serious medical status via smartphones and biosensors using gathered and kept data by ML technologies to test outcomes. HAR data recorded by biosensors might show more precision than those recorded smartphones.

4.8   Conclusion

Wearables and smartphones are growing; hence, HAR becomes interesting for several scientists to detect digitally human behavior and render validated data, for instance, in smart homes setting, healthcare monitoring applications, emergency, and transportation services. Activity recognition-centered biosensor data are quite challenging, for the various ML technologies; hence, it is vital to thoroughly explore such technologies. It is critical to expand HAR to other activities like biking or sleeping and discover further characteristics that could explore human-to-human communications and interpersonal interactions. However, despite the advances in health information technology, ML, and data mining technologies, human behavior is yet normally impulsive and a human might execute multiple or unrelated activities with variable velocities at once. Therefore, the next generation of HAR shall be developed to identify such simultaneous activities and deal with doubts in reaching better precision and enhance healthcare performance, quality, and safety.

References

1. Visvizi, A., Jussila, J., Lytras, M.D., Ijäs, M., Tweeting and mining OECD-related microcontent in the post-truth era: A cloud-based app. *Comput. Hum. Behav.*, 107, 105958, 2020, https://doi.org/10.1016/j.chb.2019.03.022.
2. Mshali, H., Lemlouma, T., Moloney, M., Magoni, D., A survey on health monitoring systems for health smart homes. *Int. J. Ind. Ergon.*, 66, 26–56, 2018, https://doi.org/10.1016/j.ergon.2018.02.002.
3. Subasi, A., Radhwan, M., Kurdi, R., Khateeb, K., IoT based mobile healthcare system for human activity recognition. *2018 15th Learn. Technol. Conf. T*, pp. 29–34, 2018, https://doi.org/10.1109/LT.2018.8368507.
4. Mahdavinejad, M.S., Rezvan, M., Barekatain, M., Adibi, P., Barnaghi, P., Sheth, A.P., Machine learning for internet of things data analysis: a

survey. *Digit. Commun. Netw.*, 4, 161–75, 2018, https://doi.org/10.1016/j. dcan.2017.10.002.

5. Gope, P. and Hwang, T., BSN-Care: A Secure IoT-based Modern Healthcare System Using Body Sensor Network. *IEEE Sens. J*, 16, 1–1, 2016.

6. Avci, A., Bosch, S., Marin-Perianu, M., Marin-Perianu, R., Havinga, P., Activity Recognition Using Inertial Sensing for Healthcare, Wellbeing and Sports Applications: A Survey. *23th Int. Conf. Archit. Comput. Syst. 2010*, pp. 1–10, 2010.

7. Clarkson, B.P., *Life patterns: structure from wearable sensors*, Thesis. Massachusetts Institute of Technology, Massachusetts, 2002.

8. Reyes-Ortiz, J.-L., Oneto, L., Samà, A., Parra, X., Anguita, D., Transition-Aware Human Activity Recognition Using Smartphones. *Neurocomputing*, 171, 754–67, 2016, https://doi.org/10.1016/j.neucom.2015.07.085.

9. Majumder, S., Aghayi, E., Noferesti, M., Memarzadeh-Tehran, H., Mondal, T., Pang, Z. *et al.*, Smart Homes for Elderly Healthcare-Recent Advances and Research Challenges. *Sensors*, p.2496, 17, 2017, https://doi.org/10.3390/s17112496.

10. Liu, L., Peng, Y., Liu, M., Huang, Z., Sensor-based human activity recognition system with a multilayered model using time series shapelets. *Knowl.-Based Syst.*, 90, 138–52, 2015, https://doi.org/10.1016/j.knosys.2015.09.024.

11. Xu, Y., Shen, Z., Zhang, X., Gao, Y., Deng, S., Wang, Y. *et al.*, Learning multi-level features for sensor-based human action recognition. *Pervasive Mob. Comput.*, 40, 324–38, 2017, https://doi.org/10.1016/j.pmcj.2017.07.001.

12. Wang Y, Fadhil A, Lange JP, Reiterer H. Towards a holistic approach to designing theory-based mobile health interventions. arXiv preprint arXiv:1712.02548. 2017 Dec 7.

13. Hassan, M.M., MdZ, Uddin, Mohamed, A., Almogren, A., A robust human activity recognition system using smartphone sensors and deep learning. *Future Gener. Comput. Syst.*, 81, 307–13, 2018, https://doi.org/10.1016/j.future.2017.11.029.

14. Liu, Y., Nie, L., Liu, L., Rosenblum, D.S., From action to activity: Sensor-based activity recognition. *Neurocomputing*, 181, 108–15, 2016, https://doi.org/10.1016/j.neucom.2015.08.096.

15. He, H., Tan, Y., Zhang, W., A wavelet tensor fuzzy clustering scheme for multi-sensor human activity recognition. *Eng. Appl. Artif. Intell.*, 70, 109–22, 2018, https://doi.org/10.1016/j.engappai.2018.01.004.

16. Mathie, M.J., Coster, A.C.F., Lovell, N.H., Celler, B.G., Detection of daily physical activities using a triaxial accelerometer. *Med. Biol. Eng. Comput.*, 41, 296–301, 2003, https://doi.org/10.1007/BF02348434.

17. Bao, L. and Intille, S.S., Activity Recognition from User-Annotated Acceleration Data, in: *Pervasive Comput.*, A. Ferscha and F. Mattern (Eds.), pp. 1–17, https://doi.org/10.1007/978-3-540-24646-6_1, Springer, Berlin, Heidelberg, 2004.

18. Kwapisz, J.R., Weiss, G.M., Moore, S.A., Activity recognition using cell phone accelerometers. *ACM SIGKDD Explor. Newsl.*, 12, 74–82, 2011, https://doi.org/10.1145/1964897.1964918.

19. Lukowicz, P., Ward, J.A., Junker, H., Stäger, M., Tröster, G., Atrash, A. *et al.*, Recognizing Workshop Activity Using Body Worn Microphones and Accelerometers, in: *Pervasive Comput.*, A. Ferscha and F. Mattern (Eds.), pp. 18–32, https://doi.org/10.1007/978-3-540-24646-6_2, Springer, Berlin, Heidelberg, 2004.

20. Leonardis, G.D., Rosati, S., Balestra, G., Agostini, V., Panero, E., Gastaldi, L. *et al.*, Human Activity Recognition by Wearable Sensors: Comparison of different classifiers for real-time applications. *2018 IEEE Int. Symp. Med. Meas. Appl. MeMeA*, pp. 1–6, 2018, https://doi.org/10.1109/MeMeA.2018.8438750.

21. Fleischer, C., Reinicke, C., Hommel, G., Predicting the intended motion with EMG signals for an exoskeleton orthosis controller. *2005 IEEERSJ Int, Conf. Intell. Robots Syst.*, 2005, https://doi.org/10.1109/IROS.2005.1545504.

22. Rowe, P.J., Myles, C.M., Walker, C., Nutton, R., Knee joint kinematics in gait and other functional activities measured using flexible electrogoniometry: how much knee motion is sufficient for normal daily life? *Gait Posture*, 12, 143–55, 2000, https://doi.org/10.1016/s0966-6362(00)00060-6.

23. Sutherland, D.H., The evolution of clinical gait analysis. Part II kinematics. *Gait Posture*, 16, 159–79, 2002, https://doi.org/10.1016/s0966-6362(02)00004-8.

24. Bayat, A., Pomplun, M., Tran, D.A., A Study on Human Activity Recognition Using Accelerometer Data from Smartphones. *Proc. Comput. Sci.*, 34, 450–7, 2014, https://doi.org/10.1016/j.procs.2014.07.009.

25. Attal, F., Mohammed, S., Dedabrishvili, M., Chamroukhi, F., Oukhellou, L., Amirat, Y., Physical Human Activity Recognition Using Wearable Sensors. *Sensors*, 15, 31314–38, 2015, https://doi.org/10.3390/s151229858.

26. Ronao, C.A. and Cho, S.-B., Human activity recognition with smartphone sensors using deep learning neural networks. *Expert Syst. Appl.*, 59, 235–44, 2016, https://doi.org/10.1016/j.eswa.2016.04.032.

27. Kozina, S., Gjoreski, H., Gams, M., Luštrek, M., Efficient Activity Recognition and Fall Detection Using Accelerometers, in: *Eval. AAL Syst. Compet. Benchmarking*, J.A. Botía, J.A. Álvarez-García, K. Fujinami, P. Barsocchi, T. Riedel (Eds.), pp. 13–23, https://doi.org/10.1007/978-3-642-41043-7_2, Springer, Berlin, Heidelberg, 2013.

28. Junker, H., Amft, O., Lukowicz, P., Tröster, G., Gesture spotting with body-worn inertial sensors to detect user activities. *Pattern Recognit.*, 41, 2010–24, 2008, https://doi.org/10.1016/j.patcog.2007.11.016.

29. Shoaib, M., Bosch, S., Incel, O.D., Scholten, H., Havinga, P.J.M., Complex Human Activity Recognition Using Smartphone and Wrist-Worn Motion Sensors. *Sensors*, 16, 426, 2016, https://doi.org/10.3390/s16040426.

30. De, D., Bharti, P., Das, S.K., Chellappan, S., Multimodal Wearable Sensing for Fine-Grained Activity Recognition in Healthcare. *IEEE Internet Comput.*, 19, 26–35, 2015, https://doi.org/10.1109/MIC.2015.72.

31. Paul, S.S., Tiedemann, A., Hassett, L.M., Ramsay, E., Kirkham, C., Chagpar, S. *et al.*, Validity of the Fitbit activity tracker for measuring steps in community-dwelling older adults. *BMJ Open Sport Exerc. Med.*, 1, e000013, 2015, https://doi.org/10.1136/bmjsem-2015-000013.

32. Fritz, T., Huang, E.M., Murphy, G.C., Zimmermann, T., Persuasive technology in the real world: a study of long-term use of activity sensing devices for fitness. *Proc. SIGCHI Conf. Hum. Factors Comput. Syst.*, Association for Computing Machinery, New York, NY, USA, pp. 487–496, 2014, https://doi.org/10.1145/2556288.2557383.

33. Han, J., Shao, L., Xu, D., Shotton, J., Enhanced Computer Vision With Microsoft Kinect Sensor: A Review. *IEEE Trans. Cybern.*, 43, 1318–34, 2013, https://doi.org/10.1109/TCYB.2013.2265378.

34. Boas Y.A. Overview of virtual reality technologies. In *Interactive Multimedia Conference*, vol. 2013, p. 4, 2013 Aug.

35. Deutsch, J.E., Brettler, A., Smith, C., Welsh, J., John, R., Guarrera-Bowlby, P. *et al.*, Nintendo wii sports and wii fit game analysis, validation, and application to stroke rehabilitation. *Top. Stroke Rehabil.*, 18, 701–19, 2011, https://doi.org/10.1310/tsr1806-701.

36. Coulston, A.M., Boushey, C.J., Ferruzzi, M., Delahanty, L. (Eds.), *Nutrition in the Prevention and Treatment of Disease*, 4th edition, Academic Press, London; San Diego, CA, 2017.

37. Hong, Y.-J., Kim, I.-J., Ahn, S.C., Kim, H.-G., Mobile health monitoring system based on activity recognition using accelerometer. *Simul. Model. Pract. Theory*, 18, 446–55, 2010, https://doi.org/10.1016/j.simpat.2009.09.002.

38. Dicker, A.P. and Jim, H.S.L., Intersection of Digital Health and Oncology. *JCO Clin. Cancer Inform.*, 2, 1–4, 2018, https://doi.org/10.1200/CCI.18.00070.

39. Galsky, M.D., Grande, E., Davis, I.D., De Santis, M., Arranz Arija, J.A., Kikuchi, E. *et al.*, IMvigor130: A randomized, phase III study evaluating first-line (1L) atezolizumab (atezo) as monotherapy and in combination with platinum-based chemotherapy (chemo) in patients (pts) with locally advanced or metastatic urothelial carcinoma (mUC). *J. Clin. Oncol.*, 36, TPS4589–TPS4589, 2018, https://doi.org/10.1200/JCO.2018.36.15_suppl. TPS4589.

40. Bai, J., Sun, Y., Schrack, J.A., Crainiceanu, C.M., Wang, M.-C., A two-stage model for wearable device data. *Biometrics*, 74, 744–52, 2018, https://doi.org/10.1111/biom.12781.

41. Cox, S.M., Lane, A., Volchenboum, S.L., Use of Wearable, Mobile, and Sensor Technology in Cancer Clinical Trials. *JCO Clin. Cancer Inform.*, 2, 1–11, 2018, https://doi.org/10.1200/CCI.17.00147.

42. Estrin, D. and Sim, I., Open mHealth Architecture: An Engine for Health Care Innovation. *Science*, 330, 759–60, 2010, https://doi.org/10.1126/science.1196187.
43. Case, M.A., Burwick, H.A., Volpp, K.G., Patel, M.S., Accuracy of Smartphone Applications and Wearable Devices for Tracking Physical Activity Data. *JAMA*, 313, 625, 2015, https://doi.org/10.1001/jama.2014.17841.
44. Miorandi, D., Sicari, S., De Pellegrini, F., Chlamtac, I., Internet of things: Vision, applications and research challenges. *Ad Hoc Netw.*, 10, 1497–516, 2012, https://doi.org/10.1016/j.adhoc.2012.02.016.
45. Petrini C. Regulation (EU) No 536/2014 on clinical trials on medicinal products for human use: an overview. Annali dell'Istituto superiore di sanità, 50, 317–21, 2014.
46. Tsimberidou A.M., Ringborg U., Schilsky R.L., Strategies to overcome clinical, regulatory, and financial challenges in the implementation of personalized medicine. American Society of Clinical Oncology Educational Book, 33, 1, 118–25, 2013.

5

Use of Assistive Techniques for the Visually Impaired People

Anuja Jadhav³*, Hirkani Padwad¹, M.B. Chandak² and Roshani Raut³

¹Bajaj Institute of Technology, Wardha, Maharashtra, India
²Ramdeobaba College of Engineering and Management, Nagpur,
Maharashtra, India
³Pimpri Chinchwad College of Engineering, Pune, Maharashtra, India

Abstract

Knowledge acquisition is not a simple task for blind people. Apart from sounds and voices, Braille is the most popular information transfer method used by blind people. There have been numerous new types of Braille created, including American Literary Braille, British Braille, computer Braille, literary Braille, music Braille, writing Braille, and so on. Conventional method used for Braille writing is slate and stylus. Other types of Braille writers and Braille computer software, such as voice recognition software, special computer keyboards, optical scanners, and radio frequency identification (RFID) based Braille character identification have been developed. A range of Smart education solutions for visually impaired people have been created, e.g., TripleTalk USB Mini Speech Synthesizer, BrailleNote Apex, TypeAbility Typing Instruction, Virtual Pencil Math Software, GeoSafari Talking Globe, IVEO Hands On Learning System, VoiceOver, BrailleTouch, List Recorder, Audible, Audio Exam Player, and Educational Chatbot, to name a few.

Keywords: Blind, Braille, learning system, visually impaired, AI, machine learning

5.1 Introduction

According to the International Agency for the Prevention of Blindness (IAPB), out of a global population of 7.3 billion people, 253 million (29%)

---

*Corresponding author: annuja.jadhav@gmail.com

Roshani Raut, Pranav Pathak, Sandeep Kautish and Pradeep N (eds.) Intelligent Systems for Rehabilitation Engineering, (115–128) © 2022 Scrivener Publishing LLC

are visually impaired, with 36 million being blind and 217 million having moderate to extreme vision impairment. At least 217 million people are severely (20/200) or moderately (20/60) impaired. Cataract, macular degeneration, and glaucoma are the most common causes of blindness worldwide; trachoma, glaucoma, and the bulk of these issues can be resolved. It is the aim of World Health Organization Initiative "Vision 2020" to decrease the worldwide blindness. From over the last century, several efforts have been made to improve the living experience for visually impaired people. Rehabilitation engineering is being used extensively for assistance and recovery of blind people. The objectives of visual rehabilitation are to enable visually impaired persons to execute maximum possible daily activities independently or with minimal aid and at the same time maintaining their security and safety alone and in societal communications. The major areas in this field include vision restorative technology, assistive technology, and enhancement technology. The emergence of artificial intelligence (AI) and machine learning (ML) has revolutionized the technological advancement towards providing independence to blind people in the activities including but not limited to routine cores, travel, safety, education, etc. This chapter provides the reader with an overview of this area in terms of its history, main concepts, major activities, and some of the current research and development projects.

People have been developing instruments to assist visually disabled and blind people for a long time, dating back to the 13th century, when spectacles were first used, followed by the invention of concave lenses. The development got a breakthrough in the year 1929 when Louis Braille published the first book of Braille code that is a series of six raised or un-raised dots that can be used by blind people or people with low vision for reading. This was accompanied by several other significant inventions, such as the blind writing machine and the white cane, which is used by blind people as a navigational aid.

The first development of electronic aid for blind people took place in early 2000, when the first mobile for visually impaired people was released. Many electronic-based aids were invented thereafter like alternative input devices and voice recognition software, which permit individuals to use keyboard and mouse substitutions. In recent years, first digital Brailler was developed that allows people with visual impairments "see" the digital world. The development of autonomous vehicles is in progress, which is going to be a revolutionary step in the independence of blind people. AI and its subfields along with Internet of Things (IoT) have unlocked a large number of possibilities to blind people providing a completely different way of experiencing the world just like normal people do. The research and development for computer-aided diagnosis as well as treatment of visually impaired people has gained momentum, and there is hope for more advancement in coming years. Many AI-based applications have been developed for computer-aided diagnostics, and efforts are being made for development of machine learning-based predictive models for better diagnosis of the reasons for visual impairment. Some of the solutions are smart televisions, smart radios, smart phones, and navigation systems, controlling the household devices, computer vision methods such as visual question answering, person and product identification, emotion detection, event detection, surrounding environment detection, safety alert and many more, AI-based lens technology, visually impaired mobility assistance, speech and text technology in the simplest of tasks like reading menus at a restaurant, and assistive interfaces.

5.2   Rehabilitation Procedure

This section gives an overview of the different rehabilitation procedures.

Vision rehabilitation is a professional field that is effective and is generally practiced as a multidisciplinary rehabilitation program.

Sensory aids for obstacle detection like laser cane, ultrasonic echolocating device, vision assistive devices for people with low vision like tele lenses, TV magnifiers, augmented vision field expansion devices, hybrid vision expansion devices, and vision multiplexing device [1] have been developed [2].

A sensor, a coupling mechanism, and a stimulator are the three components of a sensory substitution system. The sensor captures stimuli and sends them to a coupling device, which decodes them and sends them to a stimulator. Paul Bach-y-TVSS Rita's Image Substitution System [3], which transformed the image from a video camera into a tactile image and coupled it to the tactile receptors on the back of a blind person, is the oldest and most well-known type of sensory substitution devices. Several new systems have recently been developed that interface the tactile image with tactile receptors on various parts of the body, including the chest, brow, and fingers. "BlindSight," the sensory substitution technology, features devices like musical tones, vibrations, electrical stimulation of tongue, and wearable haptic actuators like vibrotactile motors, among others, to assist blind people in their navigation activity.

Prosthetic implant is an artificial device that replaces a missing body part and is expected to restore the functionality of the missing body part. The first intracranial visual prosthesis was developed and implanted in

1967 [2]. Vision restoration of the blind has always seemed to be an impossible task until recently efforts are being made in this direction, thanks to the technological advancements. Occipital cortex stimulation, retinal implants (microelectrode arrays that stimulate residual retinal cells), subretinal implants (artificial photoreceptors implant), epiretinal implants (microelectrodes are operated by electronic circuitry), and chemical neurotransmission (retinal network is chemically stimulated instead of electrically activated) are some of the visual prosthesis projects that have been undertaken [4]. Bionic Eye is a revolutionary step towards imparting slight vision to partially or completely blind persons. It is a visual device under experimental phase that is intended to restore functional vision. It works by converting images into electrical impulses, which are then transmitted to the brain through a retinal implant connected to a video camera. It works on patients facing vision loss due to degeneration of photoreceptors. Use of electrical stimulus for perception of phosphenes was proposed back in 1924 and 1929. Medical researchers have been working to overcome the problem of blindness in people with age related-degeneration by using camera-equipped eyeglasses and projecting images directly onto the nerves of the brain's visual cortex. Among several efforts, only one device has received approval so far, i.e., the Aurgus II. It is a retinal prosthesis system that comprises of external and implanted mechanisms. It has a 16 X 16 electrode array and a receiver that are surgically implanted in the eye. The outward mechanisms include a camera mounted on a glass, video processing unit (VPU), and cable. Figure 5.1 exhibits the working of Aurgus

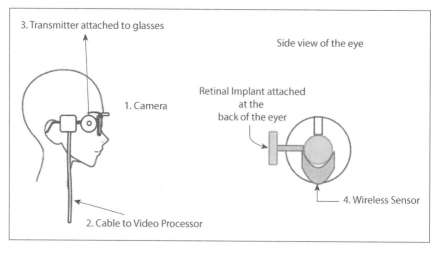

Figure 5.1 The working of Argus II Retinal Implant.

II device. The camera captures video images that are sent to the implant through the coil. The captured images are converted into stimulus commands by the VPU. These electrical signals activate the retinal cells, which deliver the signal through the optic nerve to the brain. While no cases have been identified to date, the system implant poses a risk of intraocular or orbital infection. By increasing the number of phosphenes, better performance is observed in tasks like pattern recognition [5].

Issues like lifespan of implanted electrodes, biocompatibility, and electrical safety prevail and are major challenges in vision rehabilitation [2].

Researchers have been working since at least a decade to create artificial digital retinas that when implanted can allow blind people to see again. There are many obstacles in its ongoing research, one of which is the enormous amount of heat produced by the chips as a result of the large amount of data collected by the camera, which the researchers are working hard to overcome. Image processing is being extensively used for imaging of cornea and lens that provide non-invasive diagnostic contact to significant units like retina and optic nerve. Imaging has become routine procedure in medical diagnosis as a result of which a large dataset of images is readily available, thus giving a boost to AI-based research in this filed. The application of machine learning in retina imaging is mainly done as a supervised learning task. Three use case scenarios identified are classification (Ex. assigning image to different categories based on disease stage), segmentation (Ex. identify and indicate the exact position of lesions), and prediction (ex. predict future conclusions or value of other measures like blood sugar, BP, etc.). The deep learning approach for image classification uses a convolutional neural network (CNN) model for object recognition [6]. AI has also proved to be useful in providing guidance for therapy. AI generates knowledge from large amount of data gathered from thousands of previous cases in a much more handy way than most experienced experts. Identification of patterns in datasets through machine learning techniques aids in personalized prognosis.

Optical coherence tomography (OCT) has transformed the entire ophthalmic care [7]. It is used for diagnosis and laser-assisted cataract surgery. The modern medicine relies on machines to partly perform surgery, which has paved a way to automation in ophthalmic surgery. Currently, machines are used to execute corneal incisions, lens fragmentation, etc. Researchers are working to implement robotic surgery in this range. Some of the robotic eye surgery systems are The Da Vinci robotic arm, Intraocular Robotic Interventional Surgical System (IRISS) [8], Smart instruments to assist surgeons, etc. Glaucoma is one of the causes for irreversible blindness. GAT (Goldmann Applanation Tonometry) is the standard technique used to measure introcular pressure (IOP) [7]. This method, however, cannot be used for continuous monitoring of IOP. In recent years, tonometers with latest technologies like wireless devices and implantable sensors made with microelectromechanical technology have been developed that allow for continuous monitoring of IOP. Smartphone-based imaging can be used for remote consultation and is useful for people in rural areas who do not have an easy access with a trained ophthalmologist. The smartphone camera can be converted into an ophthalmoscope using the specially developed adapters, viz. Ocular CellScope, PeekVision, D-Eye, etc. Similarly, technological development has been done for imaging in cornea and Keratoconus, refractive surgery, vitreoretinal disorders, ocular oncology, ocular drug development, etc.

Microperimetry is a widely used test used to create a retinal sensitivity map of the amount of light perceived on retina for people who have problem fixating an object or light source. The test uses scanning laser or retinal camera technology and eye tracking technology for repeated testing, which is useful for monitoring purpose.

A number of alternative approaches for vision rehabilitation have been developed, and few are under investigation phase, viz. gene therapy and stem cell transplants.

The following table summarizes the relationship between type of blindness and rehabilitation procedure [2].

	Suitable visual rehabilitation procedures			
Type of blindness	**Pre-chiasmatic prosthesis**	**Cortical prosthesis**	**Sensory substitution**	**Visual aids**
Late due to some retinopathy	Yes	Yes	Yes	Yes
Late due to peripheral cause	No	Yes	Yes	Yes
Early during development	No	Yes	Yes	Yes
Early after development	No	No	Yes	Yes

5.3   Development of Applications for Visually Impaired

The first product based on text to speech for the visually impaired was the Kurzweil Reading Machine, developed in 1976, followed by release of the first portable device, the Kurzweil-National Federation of the Blind Reader, in 2006. The KNFB Reader is now available as an app. A decent number of applications have been developed in recent years to provide a better living experience to blind people. Some of them are listed below.

Google's app "Lookout" uses computer vision to assist visually impaired and blind people. Lookout operates in five modes for different types of activities as described below.

1. Food label mode (beta version) to identify packaged food. It can also scan barcode.
2. Scan document mode reads a whole page of text. The user needs to take a snapshot of a document. The reader scans the text and it is read aloud using the screen reader.
3. Quick read mode takes superficial scan of the text and reads it aloud. It is useful for activities like sorting email.
4. Currency mode is useful to correctly identify US bank notes.
5. Explore mode, in its Beta version, gives information about objects in the surroundings. It offers native language experience to few European languages other than English.

Microsoft has developed artificial intelligence-based application "Seeing AI" for the IOS platform. It is made for people with visual impairment. It uses a device camera to identify objects and then it audibly describes the identified objects. "Seeing AI" can describe documents, text, color, people, products, light (generates an audible tone corresponding to the brightness in the surrounding), and handwriting. The app can describe age, gender, and emotional condition of a person, which it scans through a camera. It can also scan barcode and describe a product and assist a user to focus on a barcode. According to a report, the app successfully recognized people in a photograph with their names. Currency note recognition for selective currencies is also done by the app. Some functions are performed offline, whereas few complex functions like describing a scene require Internet connection.

OrCam is a company that creates a range of personal assistive devices for visually impaired people. OrCamMyEye is a voice-activated device that attaches to glasses. It can read text from a book or a smart phone or any other surface. It also recognizes faces. It works real time as well as offline. It enables visually impaired people to live an independent life. OrCamMyReader is the most advanced artificial intelligence device that read newspapers, books, menus, signs, screens, and product labels. It also responds intuitively to hand gestures. OrCam Read is another product in the range made for people with mild low vision, reading fatigue, or dyslexia. It is a handheld device that reads text from any printed surface of digital display. It can privately read the text that is chosen.

Sharing photos on Facebook is a great way for people to communicate. But the case is not the same for blind or visually impaired people who cannot enjoy the experience of viewing the news feeds. So Facebook has incorporated artificial intelligence to improve the experience of blind persons. To help the blind people understand about the happenings on the news feed, Facebook has added a feature Automatic Alternative Text, which generates a description of a photo using Object Recognition Technology such as the items in the photo, location, i.e., indoors or outdoors, etc.

Drishti (Disambiguating Real Time Insights for Supporting Human with Intelligence) is an artificial intelligence powered solution to give a better living experience to visually impaired people and to enhance their productivity in workplace, created by Accenture under its "Tech4Good" initiative through collaboration with the National Association for Blind in India. The app provides smartphone-based assistance using AI technologies like Natural Language Processing, image recognition, etc. It can recognize people in the surrounding along with their age, gender, and number. It can also read text from a book or any other document, identify currency notes, and identify obstacles like glass doors.

Envision is a popular smartphone-based app that assists blind or visually impaired people by speaking out about the surroundings. It can read text, recognize objects, find the things and people around, and use public transport independently on their own. Recently, the use of their AI-powered software in Google glasses has also been announced, taking the empowering experience for the blind and visually impaired people to another level. It is capable of recognizing text in 60 languages and provides the fastest OCR.

Samsung has developed two solutions, viz. Good vibes and Relumino, to help deaf-blind and people with low vision to communicate better. The Good vibes app aids the deaf-blind people. It uses Morse code to convert vibrations into text or voice and vice versa. It has two types of user interfaces, one that works on gestures, taps, and vibrations, and another for caregiver with standard UI. The Relumino app helps people with low vision to see images clearer by highlighting the image outline, magnifying and minimizing the image, adjusting color brightness and contrast, etc. The app was developed in association with the National Association for Blind (Delhi), which helped Samsung in testing the app.

The "VizWiz" app is an iPhone app that helps blind people to get near-real-time answers to questions about their environment. Blind people can take pictures, ask questions related to those pictures, and get answers from employees at remote locations. Use of machine learning and image recognition has now enabled to get automated reply, i.e., answers to the questions without any human intervention.

To assist visually impaired people in identifying groceries and other household products, Amazon has launched "Show and Tell." Alexa can recognize bottles, cans, and other packaged goods that are difficult to recognize only by touch.

Horus, AIServe, NavCog, Toyotas BLAID, and ESight are few other companies that are working on projects combining visual aids and artificial intelligence. According to a survey, persons with visual impairments frequently use apps for doing their daily actions and are pleased of the mobile apps and are willing to get improvements and new apps for their assistance. It is highly desirable to collaborate with blind communities and get a better understanding of their social needs and desires in order to increase their capabilities [9].

According to a survey on use of mobile applications for people who are visually blind [10], visually impaired people frequently use the apps specially designed for them to do their daily activities; they are satisfied with the apps and would like to see more apps and improvements in existing apps. Further refinement and testing is highly desirable in these kinds of apps.

5.4   Academic Research and Development for Assisting Visually Impaired

A good amount of research has been undertaken in academia since many decades towards visual rehabilitation. Many devices for assisting blind persons were proposed; however, not all could reach practical realization due to certain limitations. Few of them are mentioned below.

The researchers in [11] suggest a wearable walking guide device for blind or visually impaired people that uses an acoustic signal interface to detect obstacles. The system has a microprocessor and a PDA as a controller. Three ultrasound sensor pairs are used to obtain information about obstacle, and the obtained information is then passed to the microprocessor, which generates acoustic signal for alarm. The system also provides user with guide voice using PDA. A prototype of the system was implemented, and successful experimentation was carried out with requirement for certain modifications. A similar type of device for blind people travel aid "NavBelt" that uses mobile robot obstacle avoidance technology was proposed, but it was unable to provide guidance for fast walking. "IntelliNavi" [12] is a wearable navigation assistive system for the blind and the visually impaired people. It uses Microsoft Kinect's on-board depth sensor Speeded-Up Robust Features (SURF) and Bag-of-Visual-Words (BOVW) model to extract features. An ML-based model, viz. support vector machine classifier, is used to classify scene objects and obstacles. Devices like "GuideCane" [13] for obstacle detection, which steers around it when it senses an obstacle, are a system with electronic, mechanical, and software components, electronic mobility cane (EMC) [14], which constructs a logical map of surroundings to gather priority information and also provides features like staircase detection and non-formal distance scaling scheme, RecognizeCane, Tom Pouce, Minitact, Ultracane, K-sonar cane, etc. Recently, machine learning higher precision methods are being used for object detection and obstacle detection in navigation.

Slide-Rule [15] is an audio-based multi touch communication technique that allows blind users to access touchscreen applications. The application uses different types of touch gestures like one finger scan, two finger tap, or flick gesture to perform a variety of tasks like browsing a list, selecting an item, flipping songs, etc. A few literature works like [10] present the needs and expectations of visually impaired community from today's technological developments.

In [16], the authors propose a computer program to assist blind people who are struggling with music and music notation. The information acquisition module is responsible for understanding printed music notation and storing the data in the computer's memory. Efforts for implementation of optical music recognition using artificial neural network (ANN) [17] have been undergoing for a few decades, but practical realization is still in progress [18]. Introduces a new CAPTCHA method that can be used by blind people. Predefined patterns are used to create a mathematical problem and then converted to speech, which can then be answered by a blind user.

Electronic Travel Aids (ETA) and Electronic Orientation Aids (EOA) were invented by Rene Farcy et al. to help visually disabled people navigate in unfamiliar environments. Two devices developed by the team, an infrared proximeter and a laser telemeter, have been in use for a few years.

5.5 Conclusion

For blind people, acquiring knowledge is difficult. Apart from sounds and voices, Braille is the most popular information transfer method used by blind people. There have been numerous new types of Braille created, including American Literary Braille, British Braille, computer Braille, literary Braille, music Braille, writing Braille, and so on. Conventional method used for Braille writing is slate and stylus. Speech recognition software, special computer keyboards, optical scanners, and RFID-based Braille character identification are examples of other forms of Braille writers and Braille computer software that have been developed. A range of Smart education solutions for blind and visually impaired people have been created, e.g., TripleTalk USB Mini Speech Synthesizer, BrailleNote Apex, TypeAbility Typing Instruction, Virtual Pencil Math Software, GeoSafari Talking Globe, IVEO Hands On Learning System, VoiceOver, BrailleTouch, List Recorder, Audible, Audio Exam Player, Educational Chatbot [19], RFID, and Ontology based new Chinese Braille system, to name a few [20].

Use of AI methods such as deep learning, machine learning, and computer vision continues to be adapted and tested, so there is hope that the life of blind people will be far easier in the future.

References

1. Peli, E., Vision Multiplexing: an Engineering Approach to Vision Rehabilitation Device Development. *Optom. Vis. Sci.*, 78, 5, 304–315, May 2001.
2. Veraart, C., Duret, F., Brelén, M., Oozeer, M., Delbeke, J., Vision rehabilitation in the case of blindness. *Expert Rev. Med. Devices*, 1, 1, 139–153, 2004.
3. Bach-y-Rita, P., Collins, C.C., Saunders, F., White, B., Scadden, Vision Substitution by Tactile Image Projection. *Nature*, 221, 963–964, https://doi.org/10.1038/221963a0, 1969.
4. Weiland, J.D. and Humayun, M.S., Retinal Prosthesis. *IEEE Trans. Biomed. Eng.*, 61, 5, 1412–1424, May 2014.
5. Brelén, M.E., Duret, F., Gérard, B., Delbeke, J., Veraart, C., Creating a meaningful visual perception in blind volunteers by optic nerve stimulation. *J. Neural Eng.*, 2, 22, 2005.
6. Schmidt-Erfurth, U., Sadeghipour, A., Gerendas, B.S., Waldstein, S.M., Bogunović, H., Artificial intelligence in Retina. *Prog. Retin. Eye Res.*, 67, 1–29, https://doi.org/10.1016/j.preteyeres.2018.07.004, 2018.
7. Current Advances in Ophthalmic Technology; Ichhpujani, Parul (ed.); In Book Series: *Current Practices in Ophthalmology*, p. 1–4, 69, 84, Springer, https://doi.org/10.1007/978-981-13-9795-0, 2020

8. Chen, C.W., Lee, Y.H., Gerber, M.J., Cheng, H. *et al.*, Intraocular robotic interventional surgical system (IRISS): semi-automated OCT-guided cataract removal. *Int. J. Med. Robot. Comput. Assist. Surg.*, 14 (6): pp. 1–14, 2018.

9. Morrison, C., Cutrell, E., Dhareshwar, A., Doherty, K., Thieme, A., Taylor, A., Imagining Artificial Intelligence Applications with People with Visual Disabilities using Tactile Ideation, in: *Proceedings of the 19th International ACM SIGACCESS Conference on Computers and Accessibility*, pp. 81–90, 10.1145/3132525.3132530, 2017.

10. Griffin-Shirley, N., Banda, D.R., Ajuwon, P.M., Cheon, J., Lee, J., Park, H.R., Lyngdoh, S.N., A Survey on the Use of Mobile Applications for People Who Are Visually Impaired. *J. Vis. Impair. Blind.*, 111, 307–323, July-August 2017.

11. Kim, C.-G. *et al.*, Design of a wearable walking-guide system for the Blind. *ACM*, 2007.

12. Bhowmick, A., Prakash, S., Bhagat, R., Prasad, V., Hazarika, S., IntelliNavi: Navigation for Blind Based on Kinect and Machine Learning Multi-disciplinary Trends in Artificial Intelligence. *MIWAI '14*, vol. 8875, pp. 172–183, 10.1007/978-3-319-13365-2_16, 2014.

13. Shoval, S., Ulrich, I., Borenstein, J., Computerized Obstacle Avoidance Systems for the Blind and Visually Impaired. *J. Logic Comput. - LOGCOM*, ch14, 10.1201/9781420042122, 2001.

14. Bhatlawande, S., Mahadevappa, M., Mukherjee, J., Biswas, M., Das, D., Gupta, S., Design, Development and Clinical Evaluation of the Electronic Mobility Cane for Vision Rehabilitation. *IEEE Trans. Neural Syst. Rehabil. Eng.*, 22(6), 1148–1159, 10.1109/TNSRE.2014.2324974, 2014.

15. Kane, S., Bigham, J., Wobbrock, J., Slide Rule: Making Mobile Touch Screens Accessible to Blind people using Multi-Touch Interaction Techniques. *ASSETS'08: The 10th International ACM SIGACCESS Conference on Computers and Accessibility*, pp. 73–80, 10.1145/1414471.1414487, 2008.

16. Homenda, W., Breaking Accessibility Barriers - Computational Intelligence in Music Processing for Blind People, in: *Proceedings of the Fourth International Conference on Informatics in Control, Automation and Robotics*, vol. 1, ICINCO, pp. 32–39, 2007.

17. Macukow, B. and Homenda, W., Methods of Artificial Intelligence in Blind People Education. *International Conference on Artificial Intelligence and Soft Computing*, Springer-Verlag Berlin Heidelberg, pp. 1179–1188, 2006.

18. Shirali-Shahrezal, M. and Shirali-Shahreza, S., CAPTCHA for Blind People. *IEEE International Symposium on Signal Processing and Information Technology*, 978-1-4244-1 835-0/07, 2007.

19. Naveen Kumar, M., Linga Chandar, P.C., Prasad, V., Android Based Educational Chatbot for Visually Impaired People. *IEEE International*

Conference on Computational Intelligence and Computing Research, 10.1109/ICCIC.2016.7919664, 2016.

20. Tang, J., Using ontology and RFID to develop a new Chinese Braille learning platform for blind students. *Expert Syst. Appl.*, 40, 8, 2817–2827, https://doi.org/10.1016/j.eswa.2012.11.023, 2013.

6

IoT-Assisted Smart Device for Blind People

Roshani Raut[1], Anuja Jadhav[1]*, Swati Jaiswal[1] and Pranav Pathak[2]

[1]Pimpri Chinchwad College of Engineering Pune, Maharashtra, India
[2]MIT School of Bioengineering Sciences & Research Pune, Maharashtra, India

Abstract

Those who are blind have a lot of trouble going through their daily lives. A lot of effort has gone into making it easier for blind people to complete tasks on their own rather than relying on others. With this inspiration in mind, we proposed and created an intelligent blind stick. The smart walking stick assists visually impaired people in identifying obstacles and getting to their destination. There are a variety of walking sticks and devices that assist users in moving around both indoor and outdoor environments, but none of them include run-time autonomous navigation, object detection and identification warnings, or face and voice recognition. The stick uses IoT, echolocation, image processing, artificial intelligence, and navigation system technology to identify close and far obstacles for the user. If the blind person falls or has some other problem, then the system will send a warning to the designated person. The system uses voice recognition to recognise loved ones.

Keywords: Image processing, input/output and data communication (hardware), sensors (artificial intelligence), artificial intelligence, natural language, voice (input/output device)

6.1 Introduction

Artificial intelligence (AI) has made remarkable strides in bridging the difference between human and machine capabilities. Researchers and enthusiasts alike work on different aspects of the field to produce incredible results. The aim of this field is to allow machines to see the world in the

---

*Corresponding author: annuja.jadhav@gmail.com

Roshani Raut, Pranav Pathak, Sandeep Kautish and Pradeep N (eds.) *Intelligent Systems for Rehabilitation Engineering*, (129–150) © 2022 Scrivener Publishing LLC

same way as humans do, to see it in similar ways, and to use this knowledge for various tasks such as image and video recognition, image analysis and classification, media recreation, recommendation systems, and natural language processing (NLP). More than one basic calculation—a convolutional neural network (CNN)— has been developed and culminated over time in computer vision with deep learning [1].

The gift of sight is one of nature's most valuable gifts. Friends who are blind have a lot of trouble going through their daily lives. A lot of effort has gone into making it easier for blind people to complete tasks on their own rather than relying on others. With this inspiration in mind, a variety of inventions for visually impaired people are being created.

6.1.1   A Convolutional Neural Network

CNN is a form of neural network that employs CNNs. CNN is a television network that classifies videos. Using pretrayed CNN, the features from the input image would be extracted, and a feature vector would be created. CNN is used in the image-based model [2].

CNNs, also known as ConvNets, were first proposed by Yann LeCun, a postdoctoral computer science researcher, in the 1980s. LeCun had built on the work of Kunihiko Fukushima, a Japanese researcher who had developed the neocognitron, a fundamental image recognition neural network, only a few years before.

The first CNNs, known as LeNet (after LeCun), were capable of perceiving manually written digits. CNNs discovered a niche market reading postal codes on envelopes and digits on checks in finance and postal administrations and banking.

CNNs are similar to normal meural metworks, since they consist of weight and biassed neurons. Each neuron receives a few data sources, performs a dot product, and alternates with non-linearity. From raw image pixels on one side to class scores on the other, the entire company communicates a single differentiable score feature. They have a loss function on the last layer, which is the completely connected layer, and all of the tricks we developed for learning regular neural networks apply here as well [2].

In any case, despite their ingenuity, ConvNets remained on the periphery of computer vision and AI because they faced a difficult problem: they could not scale. CNNs required a lot of knowledge and resources to produce large-scale images effectively. The technique was only applicable to low-resolution photos at the time.

AlexNet demonstrated in 2012 that the time had come to return to deep learning, the branch of AI that employs complex neural networks. The availability of massive amounts of data, specifically the ImageNet dataset with a large number of marked images, as well as massive computer resources enabled scientists to create complex CNNs that could perform previously impossible computer vision tasks. Convolutional network architectures assume categorically that the information sources are images, allowing us to encode specific properties into the architecture. At that point, the forward work becomes more efficient to perform, and the number of parameters in the network is drastically reduced.

A CNN is a form of neural network that uses con (CNN).

A CNN is a deep learning algorithm that can take in an image as input, assign weights and biases to different objects in the image and then separate them. As compared to other classification algorithms, the amount of image pre-processing needed by a CNN is significantly less. Although primitive techniques require hand-designing channels, CNN can learn these channels/qualities with enough preparation.

The interaction of the visual cortex enlivened the engineering of a CNN, which is almost identical to the connectivity patterns of neurons in the human brain. Single neurons respond to changes in a small area of the visual field called the receptive field. A set of such fields may be used to cover the entire visual area by overlapping them.

For example, a large image, such as $400 \times 400 \times 3$, will activate neurons with weights of $400 * 400 * 3 = 480,000$. Furthermore, we would almost certainly need a few of these neurons, so the parameters will quickly add up! The network as a whole is unreliable, and the large number of parameters will lead to overfitting. CNN can be used to solve those problems.

6.1.2   CNN's Operation

CNNs are made up of several layers of artificial neurons that work together to achieve the best possible results. Artificial neurons are mathematical functions that measure the weighted number of multiple input/output activation functions and are a rough imitation of their biological counterparts [3]. The structure of artficial neuron is shown in Figure 6.1.

The question of how image recognition/deep learning recognizes artifacts in an image arises.

It functions the same way for CNNs. CNN has several layers, which allows for more accurate image classification. CNN is a feed forward network that is commonly used to analyse visible images using a grid-like topology to process data. Any CNN starts with a convolution operation. Figure 6.2 represents the structure of CNN.

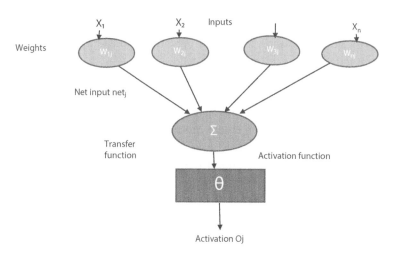

Figure 6.1 Structure of artificial neuron.

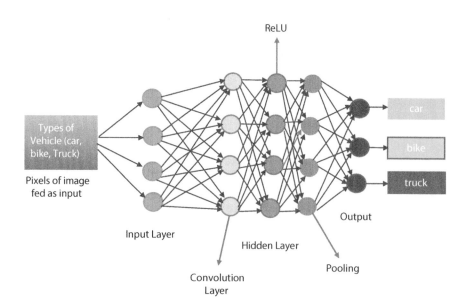

Figure 6.2 Convolution neural network.

The layers of CNN are as follows:

1. Input layer: The input layer accepts image pixels in the form of arrays as input.
2. Hidden layer: This layer performs feature extraction by circulating and manipulating data. To detect patterns in the image, this layer employs a matrix filter and a convolution operation.

Convolutional means to call or twist data around it and change it in order to identify new patterns. A convolutional layer is made up of many filters that perform convolution.

Take a look at the 5 × 5 image below, which only has pixel values of 0 and 1. Sliding the filter matrix over the image and computing the dot product to detect patterns, as shown in Figure 6.3.

The complete form of a rectified linear unit is a ReLU layer, and it essentially deals with the activation function used in CNN. After the function maps have been removed, they must be moved to a ReLU layer. For locating features, real images can have multiple convolutions and ReLU layers [3]. Figure 6.3 shows gives the various types of layers of CNN.

We do not just have one ReLU coming in, but we go through multiple feature extractions and generate multiple ReLU layers for locating the features in ReLU. We have a collection of items, such as multiple features and multiple values that will lead us to the next level.

ReLU's features include the following:

i.   Makes all negative pixels 0 pixels.
ii. It also conducts element-by-element operations.
iii. Causes the network to become non-linear.

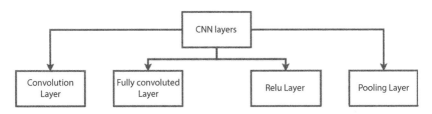

Figure 6.3 Layers of CNN.

a) Pooling layer: Detects edges, corners, leaves, stems, and other objects using several filters. The term "pooling" refers to the gathering of data. The features that have been corrected are now sent to a pooling layer. Pooling is a downsampling procedure that decreases the function map's dimensionality [4].

b) Different filters were used by the pooling layer to classify different parts of the image, such as edges, corners, leaves, stems, and roots [4].

Flattening: Flattening is a method of transforming all resulting two-dimensional arrays from pooled feature maps into one long linear vector.

Finally, a fully linked layer defines the image object. The fully linked layer uses flattened metrics from the pooling layer to identify the picture.

The image's features are extracted using a mixture of convolutional, ReLU, and pooling layers.

6.1.3   Recurrent Neural Network

A recurrent neural network (RNN) is a type of neural network that is used in machine learning. RNNs are a form of network widely used in text processing. The LSTM (Long Short-Term Memory) model will be used by the RNN for our Language-based model.

We predefine our mark and goal text before training the LSTM model.

6.1.4   Text-to-Speech Conversion

Speech synthesis is the imitation of human speech. It is the process of converting coded text into expression. The module's input is in text format, and the output is in the form of a human voice.

6.1.5   Long Short-Term Memory Network

LSTM networks are a form of repetitive neural network that can be used in sequence prediction models to learn order dependence. This is an ability that is needed in a variety of fields, including speech recognition and machine learning. Deep learning with LSTMs is a complicated area. The definition of LSTMs and how terms like bidirectional and sequence-to-sequence apply to the field can be difficult to understand. The success of LSTMs is due to their ability to transcend the failures and promises of RNNs [5]. Standard RNNs can now ignore time lags greater than 5 to 10 discrete time steps between specific input and target signals while learning. The problem raises doubts about whether standard RNNs will truly outperform window-based feedforward networks in terms of practical benefits. This problem has no effect on a modern model called "Long Short-Term Memory". By introducing consistent mistake movement through "constant error carrousels" (CECs) within special units called cells, LSTM can find out how to bind trivial delays over 1,000 discrete time steps. The LSTM solves two common network training problems: vanishing gradient and exploding gradient. The control flow of an LSTM is similar to that of an RNN. It processes data as it travels across the network. The activities within the distinctions are the cells of the LSTM. These activities help the LSTM remember or forget information [5]. The basic concept of LSTMs is the cell state and its numerous gates. The cell state served as a highway, transporting relative information across the sequence chain. It is the network's "memory", if you will. The cell state can convey critical data during the processing chain. As a result, data from earlier time steps can be progressed to later time steps, minimizing the short memory impact. As data passes through gates, it is added to or removed from the cell state. The gates are numerous neural organizations that determine which cell state data is allowed. The gates will decide which data to keep and which to delete throughout the planning process.

The sigmoid function in gates is similar to the tanh function. This is useful for updating or forgetting details since any number increased by 0 would be 0, causing esteems to disappear or be "neglected". Since any number multiplied by one equals one, the number remains the same or is "kept". The network will determine which information is unimportant and therefore can be ignored, as well as which information should be kept. Figure 6.4 represents the structure of LSTM.

The following are examples of LSTM gates:

1) Input gate: The input gate is used to refresh the cell state. To begin, we use a sigmoid capacity to transfer the hidden state and current input state. By adjusting the qualities to be anywhere between 0 and 1, this determines which values are important to change. Similarly, transfer the secret state and current state to the tanh function to help guide the network by crushing values between −1 and 1 [6]. Use the sigmoid function to multiply the tanh function. The sigmoid function will then decide the data from the tanh function is necessary to hold.

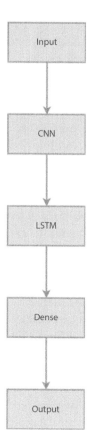

Figure 6.4 LSTM structure.

2) Forget gate: This gate determines whether data should be discarded or saved. The sigmoid ability passes data from the previous secret state as well as data from the current information. Qualities are rated between 0 and 1 on a scale of 1 to 10. The more like 0 intends to ignore and the more like 1 intends to hold, the better.

3) Cell state: The cell state is multiplied by the forget vector pointwise first. If this is duplicated by values close to 0, then the cell state's qualities which deteriorate. The output of the input gate is then used to perform a pointwise addition on the cell state, updating it to new qualities that the neural network considers essential. As a result, a new cell state has emerged.

4) Output gate: The output gate specifies the hidden state that will be revealed next. Keep in mind that the hidden state

saves data from previous inputs. The hidden condition is often used to make predictions. Second, we switch the previous hidden state and the current input using a sigmoid ability. The tanh work receives the newly changed cell state. We replicate the tanh output with the sigmoid output to determine what data the hidden state can convey. The output is the hidden state.

CNN and LSTM are two types of machine learning algorithms.

CNN LSTMs were developed to solve visual time sequence prediction problems and to generate text explanations from video/image sequences. The following sections go through the problems with action identification, image and video descriptions in particular:

- Activity Recognition: Creating a textual summary of a movement in a series of photographs.
- Video Description: Creating a text-based representation of a series of images
- Image Description: Creating a textual representation of a single image [7].

"CNN LSTMs are a type of model that is both spatially and temporally deep and can be applied to a wide range of vision tasks involving sequential inputs and outputs."

This style is used to create textual explanations of photographs. It is important to use a CNN that has been pre-trained on a difficult image classification task before being repurposed as a feature extractor to solve the subtitle generation problems. A CNN is commonly used as an image "encoder" by pre-training it for an image classification task and then contributing the final hidden layer to the RNN decoder that generates sentences. CNN-LSTM can be used to derive features from LSTM audio and textual input data for speech recognition and NLP issues [8].

This architecture is appropriate for issues such as follows:

- Input that has spatial construction, such as a 2D design of pixels in an image or a 1D design of words in a phrase, pieces, or documents.
- Involve the production of output with temporal construction, such as words in a textual depiction, or have a temporal construction in their input, such as requests for images in a video or words in text [9].

6.2 Literature Survey

Blindness is described as a state of sightlessness in which both eyes have completely lost their vision. Diabetes, macular degeneration, physical injury, infection, and glaucoma are the most common causes of impairment [10].

There are 39 million people who are blind, and another 246 million who have poor vision. The number of people who have lost their eyesight is rapidly rising. According to the Royal National Institute of Blind People (RNIB), the number of visually disabled people in the United Kingdom will exceed 2 million by 2020 [11].

The distance between the stick and the points in front of it is calculated using an ultrasonic sensor [12]. The infrared sensor is used to detect the amount. It works by reflecting an infrared beam to determine the distance to the target [13]. The image sensor's job is to detect certain obstacles with pinpoint accuracy. The image sensor is used to capture and send images to the microcontroller at regular intervals. The task at hand is to compare the captured image to the database and determine the appropriate output. Face detection and recognition, as well as street sign recognition, can be done with image processing [14]. Raspberry Pi is a single-board computer that is small and powerful. It connects to a computer, keyboard, mouse, and other peripherals. It has a fantastic learning and programming environment, as well as being used to communicate with hardware components [15]. The most available route is found using a GPS system. If he is in an emergency, then the SMS system is also used to send messages to his friends and family [16]. The Bluetooth module is used to transmit signals to the user through the module-connected cell phone [17]. Stick is only used to make smart choices, show them the right direction, and keep them away from obstacles [18]. The object's distance is measured using TOF (time of flight), the location and angle of sensors on the stick, the threshold limit of distances using ultrasonic sensors, and appropriate algorithms [19].

6.3 Smart Stick for Blind People

People who are blind tend to stick together: There are currently a large number of visually disabled people all over the world. Individuals with low site seeing to full vision loss are included in this group. They believe it is extremely difficult to cross the street or arrive at their specific destination with the help of another human. There are 50 million people in the United

States who are visually impaired and are of working age. They need independent mobility to work or walk outside, as well as to be important for the norm and to complete any remaining basic tasks. According to 2011 census results, India has 12 million people with visual impairment, the largest number of any country on the planet.

The traditional stick is incapable of distinguishing between impediments in front of you and potholes in the road. It is no longer in use. As a result, it is essential to upgrade it with current technology. With today's technology, such as the IoT and AI, it is possible to make the lives of blind people much easier and safer. Figure 6.5 gives the block diagram of hardware structure of smart stick.

The use of a white cane has considerable drawbacks because the subject must be in close proximity to the deterrent and use the tip of the white cane to feel the area of the deterrent. When using the white cane to detect obstacles, he can be struck by various obstacles. The white cane provides no detail about the nearby barrier.

The smart stick is equipped with a variety of sensors that will alert the user to various impediments that may appear in his path while walking. Clients can check their pulse rate and body temperature with this smart stick's health monitoring features. GPS and GSM modules are preprogrammed in order to monitor the user's position and transmit a warning message to another individual. The voice warning system is another important feature of this smart stick.

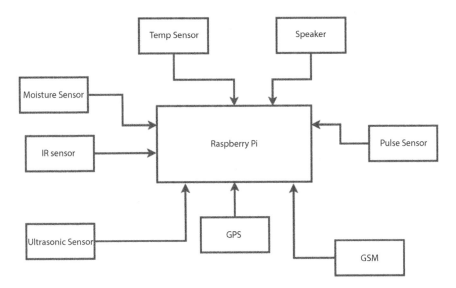

Figure 6.5 Block diagram of hardware structure of smart stick.

Deterrent, pit, wet floor, and medical issues will be communicated to the client through voice warning. This will increase the versatility of a visually disabled person because he will become more aware as a result of hearing voice alarms. Item recognition, pit detection, and water detection are some of the other notable features of this smart stick. These smart sticks are helpful in managing the mobility of elderly and visually disabled clients, as well as avoiding mishaps. This stick has a number of interconnected subsystems. Power, microcontroller, ultrasonic sensor, PIR sensor, electrodes, pulse rate sensor, temperature, speaker, and LCD are all built into the handle.

Directions in a route to follow are recommended based on this experience. The intelligent blind stick simplifies and protects the lives of blind friends. The AI-powered visually impaired stick is a novel tool designed to assist outwardly handicapped people in finding better routes and making wise decisions on which direction to follow that is free of obstacles before they cross a certain distance. Our quest space includes using three ultrasonic sensors from the front, left, and right to find the best way for a visually impaired partner who does not have an obstacle within a certain distance. These sensors detect obstacles using ultrasonic waves and direct visually impaired people to the bearing that is free of checks within a certain range. The information is gathered using three sensors that detect the distance between the obstacle and the user.

This sensor input is organized and transmitted to a blind person through an audio facility, which is then used to make a decision on which route to take that is free of obstacles. A blind man trying to cross a street was seen by George Bonham in 1930. The man wields a black stick that the motorist does not see. To prevent such occurrences, George decided to paint the stick red and white to make it more visible on the lane. Aluminum Folding Cane: This cane is inexpensive, compact, and portable. Allows blind people to use their homes more conveniently and take up less room. It can be seen at night because of the red and white colors.

Man-machine communication based on commands or text can be implemented using speech or voice recognition technologies. It is an important technology in the majority of human-machine interfaces. It is also possible to use pattern matching technology. AI plays a significant role in decision-making [10].

6.3.1   Hardware Requirements

6.3.1.1   Ultrasonic Sensor

Ultrasound waves are waves that can be heard by the human ear. They have a frequency of over 20 kHz. Ultrasonic sensors, similar to SONAR or RADAR, are used to locate objects or obstacles using these waves. The sound of waves, according to Laplace, is 343 m/s. Transducers transform electrical energy into mechanical energy in order to produce ultrasonic vibrations. The "Pulse Reflection Procedure" is used to determine the distance between two objects by measuring the transmitting and receiving pulses. The relationship between the distance to the object L and the time T can be expressed as follows:

Calculate the distance:

$$L = 0.5 * T * C$$

where L is the distance between emission and reception, T is the time between emission and reception, and C is the sonic speed (343 m/s).

6.3.1.2   IR Sensor

The infrared sensor is used to determine the existence of the object in front of you, as well as to detect short-range objects. It detects the object using infrared lights. These sensors detect objects by measuring the strength of reflected light. The sensor has a transmitter (Tx) that emits light and a receiver (Rx) that collects the object's reflected energy.

$$VO = (1 + R3/R2) \times VIN$$

When the emitter led's strength is high, more energy falls on the detector led, and the detector's resistance is low, the potential (VIN) is high. Similarly, when the amplitude is low, the detector's resistance is high, and the potential is low. A reference potential is used to equate this potential to. The performance would be 1 or 0, i.e., "ON" or "OFF", based on these compared potentials.

6.3.1.3   Image Sensor

Image sensor transforms an optical image into an electronic signal. It absorbs reflected light and transforms it to an electronic signal, which it then sends to the imaging system processor, where it is further converted into digital images.

6.3.1.4   Water Detector

A water detector senses the presence of water and warns the user. It is the famous device that uses water's electrical conductivity to reduce resistance between two contacts. When the contacts are bridged by water, however, an audible warning is given.

6.3.1.5   Global System for Mobile Communication

Global System for Mobile Communication (GSM) is a specialized communication module. It has a SIM (Subscriber Identity Module), and the GSM module works for any network provider that has a subscription. For touch and message transmission, the microcontroller is connected to a GSM module. To carry out the operations, GSM needs "Extended AT Command set" support for sending/receiving messages. The AT commands are sent to the module by the microcontroller. The module responds with an information response that includes the information needed by the AT command's action. Following that is a result code. The result code indicates whether or not the instruction was successfully executed. To send text messages, only the TXD, RXD, and GND signals of the module's serial interface can be connected to the microcontroller. This system comes with RTS.

The GSM Modem's serial port interface's CTS and RTS signals are connected. The AT+CMFG command switches the GSM module to text mode. It has two operating modes: manual and automatic. The messages are sent to the stored mobile number if the object is too near and continues to issue alerts.

6.3.1.6   Microcontroller Based on the Raspberry Pi 3

The Raspberry Pi will be used as the microcontroller; reasons for using it as a microcontroller include the following:

- Convenient, portable, and low-cost.
- Have an operating system that makes it simple to get started.
- Bluetooth and built-in Wi-Fi module.
- The 2.5 amp power source allows you to charge more complicated USB devices.
- 1 GB of memory, a 400 MHz GPU, and four USB ports
- HDMI video output with 3.5 mm port, 17 GPIO pins, and 4.1-volt Bluetooth.
- MicroUSB or GPIO header, 5V power source.
- Dimensions: 85.60 mm × 56.5mm, weight: 45 gm.

6.4   System Development Requirements

6.4.1   Captioning of Images

Picture captioning is the process of using an artificial method to translate an input image into a textual description. Converting a visual input to an audible output is a step in the process.

Essentially, it is focused on CNN and RNN, which are two internal networks.

6.4.2   YOLO (You Only Look Once) Model

The YOLO model is a single CNN that forecasts several bounding boxes and class probabilities for certain boxes at the same time. YOLO trains on complete images and increases detection accuracy in a straightforward manner. This model has a number of advantages over other object recognition methods, including: YOLO stands for "you only live once". It also comprehends the representation of generalized objects. This is possibly the best algorithm for object recognition, with results comparable to R-CNN calculations.

Figure 6.6 shows the structure of YOLO. There are two types of YOLO algorithms for object detection.

1. Classification-based algorithm: They are divided into two stages. First and foremost, they choose areas of interest in a picture. Second, they use a CNN to sort these districts. Since we need to predict each chosen sector, this arrangement can be slow. The Revolutionary Neural Network (RCNN) and its variants Fast-RCNN and Faster-RCNN, and the furthest down the line expansion to the family: Mask-RCNN is well-known examples of this form of calculation.
2. Regression-based algorithm: Instead of selecting interesting image parts, they predict classes and bounding boxes for the entire image in one calculation. The YOLO (You Only Look Once) and SSD models are the two most common models from this gathering (Single Shot Multibox Detector). They are usually used for real-time object detection, and they usually trade a little precision for a lot of speed.

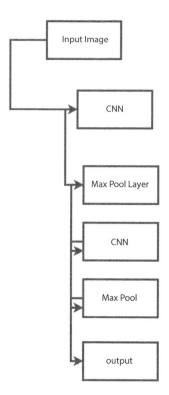

Figure 6.6 Structure of YOLO.

To understand the YOLO algorithm, you must first understand what is being expected. Finally, we want to predict an object's class and the bounding box that indicates the object's area. Four descriptors can be used to represent each bounding box:

1. bounding box center (**bxby**)
2. value **c,** which corresponds the class of object
3. width (**bw**)
4. height (**bh**)

The measures that YOLO takes to detect objects are as follows:

1. YOLO starts by taking an image as input.
2. YOLO divides the picture into a 13 by 13 cell grid: Each of these cells is in charge of anticipating five bounding boxes.

3. It uses a single neural network to process the image. This network divides the image into regions, calculating bounding boxes and probabilities for each.

4. Each grid is subjected to image classification and localization. The bounding boxes and their comparing class probabilities for objects are predicted by YOLO at that stage.

To prepare the model, we must transfer the marked information to it. Assume we have isolated the picture into a 3 × 3 structure with a total of three groups into which the elements must be arranged. Assume that the groups are cat, dog, and flamingo, respectively. As a result, the mark X for each grid cell would be an eight-dimensional vector.

YOLO's setup is completely plug-and-play, which means you can set it up to recognize any type of object. YOLO accomplishes this by using the cfg/.configuration files.

The following are the key components of these configuration files:

- Strategy for optimization
- The size of the input
- The pace of learning
- A CNN is a form of neural network that
- Containers for anchoring
- Quantity of the batch

6.5   Features of the Proposed Smart Stick

This machine is more sophisticated and shows weather conditions. Automation is accomplished in capturing weather conditions.

➢ **Assistance with reading newspapers/printed texts/books:** All of this is possible with this device because it has OCR, which translates written text into expression.

➢ **Find an object that is not where it should be:** This device will help you find an object that is not where it should be.

➢ **Alarm indicator:** An alarm indicator is included with this invention, and if the stick is not in place, then it will be indicated by a buzzer.

➢ **Provide Entertainment:** Since this invention is compatible with the Raspberry Pi, headphones can be connected to it, and since the memory of the Raspberry Pi can be expanded by connecting an external memory card, movies and songs can be uploaded.

6.6 Code

```
cam = webcam;
net = googlenet;
in_size = net.Layers(1).InputSize(1:2)
im1= snapshot(cam);
image(im1)
im1= imresize(im1,in_size);
[label,score] = classify(net,im1);
title({char(lab),num2str(max(score),2)});
h = figure;
while ishandle(h)
    im1= snapshot(cam);
    image(im1)
    im1= imresize(im,in_size);
    [lab,score] = classify(net,img1);
    title({char(lab), num2str(max(score),2)});
    drawnow
end
h = figure;
h.Position(3) = 2*h.Position(3);
p1 = subplot(1,2,1);
p2 = subplot(1,2,2);
im1= snapshot(cam);
image(a1,im1)
im1= imresize(im1,inputSize);
[label,score] = classify(net,im1);
title(p1,{char(label),num2str(max(score),2)});
[~,idx] = sort(score,'descend');
idx = idx(5:-1:1);
classes = net.Layers(end).Classes;
clnamtop = string(classes(idx));
topsc = score(idx);
barh(p2,topsc)
xlim(p2,[0 1])
```

```
title(p2, 'First 5')
xlabel(p2, 'Prob')
yticklabels(p2,clnmtop)
ax2.YAxisLocation = 'right';
p = figure;
p.Position(3) = 2*a.Position(3);
p1 = subplot(1,2,1);
p2 = subplot(1,2,2);
p2.PositionConstraint = "innerposition";
while ishandle(p)
```

% Image Classification

```
    i1= snapshot(cam);
    image(p1,i1)
    i1= imresize(im,inputSize);
    [lab,score] = classify(net,im);
    title(ax1,{char(lab),num2str(max(score),2)});
```

6.7   Results

The object detection results are shown in Figure 6.7.

The pictures and the graphs of the identified objects are shown in Figure 6.7. The probabilty of the identified object is more as compared to the other objects, like the probabilty of coffee mug is more as compared to hand towel or tissue paper.

6.8   Conclusion

Object detection helps blind people to identify the correct objects. Objects are idenfitied with the YOLO algorithm. Smart walking stick helps impaired visually recognise obstacles and reach their destination. There are a number of walking sticks and devices that help users move around indoor and outdoor environments, but none of them have autonomous navigation run-time, object detection and identification alerts, or face and voice recognition. The stick uses IoT, echolocation, image processing, AI, and navigation system technologies to locate user-friendly and far-reaching obstacles.

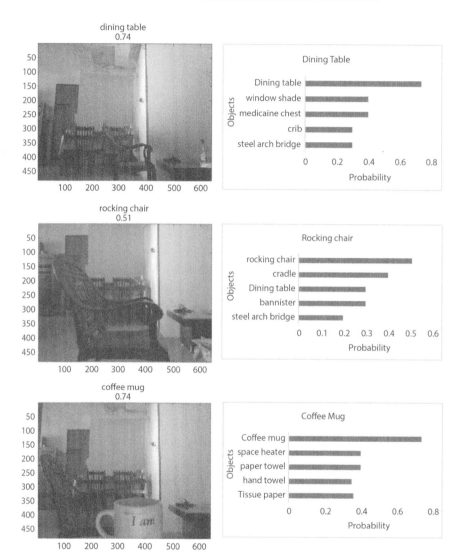

Figure 6.7 Object detection results.

References

1. Nanda, A., Chauhan, D.S., Sa, P.K., Bakshi, S., Illumination and scale invariant relevant visual features with hypergraph-based learning for multi-shot person re-identification. *Multimed. Tools Appl.*, 1–26, 2017.

2. Soomro, K., Zamir, A.R., Shah, M., UCF101: A dataset of 101 human actions classes from videos in the wild, arXiv preprint arXiv:1212.0402, Center for Research in Computer Vision University of Central Florida, Vol 1. 2012.

3. Herath, S., Harandi, M., Porikli, F., Going deeper into action recognition: A survey. *Image Vision Comput.*, 60, 4–21, 2017.

4. Nanda, A., Sa, P.K., Choudhury, S.K., Bakshi, S., Majhi, B., A Neuromorphic Person Re-Identification Framework for Video Surveillance. *IEEE Access*, 5, 6471–6482, 2017.

5. Aly, S.A., Alghamdi, T.A., Salim, M., Gutub, A.A., Data Dissemination and Collection Algorithms for Collaborative Sensor Devices Using Dynamic Cluster Heads. *Trends Appl. Sci. Res.*, 8, 55, 2013.

6. Yue-Hei Ng, J., Hausknecht, M., Vijayanarasimhan, S., Vinyals, O., Monga, R., Toderici, G., Beyond short snippets: Deep networks for video classification, in: *Proceedings of the IEEE conference on computer vision and pattern recognition*, pp. 4694–4702, 2015.

7. Schuldt, C., Laptev, I., Caputo, B., Recognizing human actions: a local SVM approach, in: *Pattern Recognition, 2004. ICPR 2004. Proceedings of the 17th International Conference on*, pp. 32–36, 2004.

8. Murthy, O.R. and Goecke, R., Ordered trajectories for human action recognition with large number of classes. *Image Vision Comput.*, 42, 22–34, 2015.

9. Lipton, Z.C., Berkowitz, J., Elkan, C., A critical review of recurrent neural networks for sequence learning, arXiv preprint arXiv:1506.00019, Vol. 1, pp. 1–38, 2015.

10. K. Greff, R. K. Srivastava, J. Koutník, B. R. Steunebrink and J. Schmidhuber, LSTM: A Search Space Odyssey, in *IEEE Transactions on Neural Networks and Learning Systems,* 28, 10, pp. 2222–2232, Oct. 2017.

11. Saaid, M.F., Mohammad, A.M., Megat Ali, M.S.A., Smart Cane with Range Notification for Blind People. *2016 IEEE International Conference on Automatic Control and Intelligent Systems (I2CACIS)*, 22 October 2016.

12. Krishnan, A., Deepakraj, G., Nishanth, N., Anandkumar, K.M., Autonomous Walking Stick For The Blind Using Echolocation And Image Processing. *2016 2nd IEEE International Conference on Contemporary Computing and Informatics (ic3i)*.

13. Swain, K.B., Patnaik, R.K., Pal, S., Rajeswari, R., Mishra, A., Dash, C., Arduino Based Automated Stick Guide for a Visually Impaired Person. *2017 IEEE International Conference on Smart Technologies and Management for Computing, Communications, Control, Energy and Materials*, 2-4 August 2017.

14. Swathi, K., Raja Ismitha, E., Subhashini, R., Smart Walking Stick Using IOT. *Int. J. Innov. Adv. Comput. Sci.* IJIACS, 6, 11, 1383–1387, November 2017.

15. Saquib, Z., Murari, V., Bhargav, S.N., BlinDar: An Invisible Eye for the Blind People. *2017 2nd IEEE International Conference On Recent Trends In Electronics Information & Communication Technology*, May 19-20, 2017.

16. Olanrewaju, R.F., Radzi, M.L.A.M., Rehab, M., iWalk: Intelligent Walking Stick for Visually Impaired Subjects. *Proc. of the 4th IEEE International Conference on Smart Instrumentation, Measurement and Applications (ICSIMA)*, 28-30 November 2017.

17. Hung, D.N., Minh-Thanh, V., Minh-Triet, N., Huy, Q.L., Cuong, V.T., Design and Implementation of Smart Cane for Visually Impaired People, in: *6th International Conference on the Development of Biomedical Engineering in Vietnam (BME6)*, T. Vo Van and *et al.* (Eds.), Springer Nature Singapore Pte Ltd, Ho Chi Minch City, Vietnam, 2018.

18. Ali, U., Javed, H., Khan, R., Jabeen, F., Akbar, N., Intelligent Stick for Blind Friends. *Int. Robot. Autom. J.*, 4, 1, pp. 68–70, 2018.

19. Chaurasia, S. and Kavitha, K.V.N., An Electronic Walking Stick for Blinds. *IEEE 2014 International Conference on Information Communication & Embedded Systems (ICICES)*, 2014.

20. J. Meng, J. Zhang and H. Zhao, Overview of the Speech Recognition Technology, *2012 Fourth International Conference on Computational and Information Sciences*, Shiyang, China, pp. 199–202, 2012.

7

Accessibility in Disability: Revolutionizing Mobile Technology

Nisarg Gandhewar[1] and Senthilkumar Mohan[2]

[1]Computer Science & Engineering, SBJITMR, Nagpur, India
[2]School of Information Technology and Engineering, Vellore Institute of Technology, Vellore, India

Abstract

Billions of population all around the world in a wide variety of diverse disabilities and desires, it's vital to be acquainted with how can we exploit today's technological advancement for the betterment of our society and overcome the disabilities. A lot of efforts have been made to assist people with disabilities to defeat physical, social, and attitudinal and many other difficulties. To avoid exclusion from many areas of life cutting edge technologies plays a vital role. In the past number of barriers, especially communication ones, may stop people with visionary, hearing, or cognitive disability from getting the messages and knowledge in a natural learning environment in a college or university. However, the situation has changed, there are multiple technological solutions developed to assist young brigade with different disabilities to acquire a proper education and subsequent benefits. Mobile technology not only transformed the process of communication however it also becoming a crucial way of education, business and rehabilitation. Impairment does not denote in capability, functionalities based on accessibility desire, should remain present in currently available mobile apps. Accessibility does not an elective one, but it is essential for many. But sometimes people with disabilities disconnect from their use. Now a day's multiple app development platforms such as android and ios have accessibility features that assist developers in building apps by using machine learning and deep learning which make the life of people with disabilities more comfortable. Various technological solutions are available in the market but every solution having its pros and cons that need to be analyzed. This analysis can be beneficial to people with disability while selecting a new solution which can address their problem up to a significant level of extent.

Corresponding author: nisarg.gandhewar@gmail.com, mosenkum@gmail.com

Roshani Raut, Pranav Pathak, Sandeep Kautish and Pradeep N (eds.) Intelligent Systems for Rehabilitation Engineering, (151–174) © 2022 Scrivener Publishing LLC

Keywords: Cutting edge technologies, mobile technology, machine learning, deep learning, android, iOS

7.1 Introduction

As per United Nations, approximately 15% of the world's populace, or nearly 1 billion people, live with disabilities [1]. As per report of World Health Organization (WHO), a disabled person is anybody who is having a problem in body function or structure, an activity limitation, has difficulty in executing a task or action; with a participation restriction". Even though the fact that disability influence roughly one out of every six persons amongst us, many of them having disability stay expelled from getting involved in various societal and economic activities because of many reasons like unavailability of proper physical environment, government services, assistive devices and technologies [2]. Disability is one of the human conditions, at particular moment in our life, each person will be temporarily or enduringly impaired, and also during old age most of person will experience rise in difficulty while functioning. Disability is complex, and the involvement to overcome the drawbacks associated with disability is numerous [3]. The number of populace experiencing any form of disability signifies a major part of the world population, from adults to children. It is also vital to emphasize the fact that a few people are multi-handicapped and have multiple disabilities. According to the WHO, nearly 1.3 billion populace are experiencing some form of visual impairment and blindness. 466 million populace suffer from deafness and hearing loss. About 200 million citizens have an intellectual disability. 75 million populace requires a wheelchair daily [4]. The different types of can affect a person's ability of hearing, vision, movement, thinking, learning, communication, interpersonal relationships, memory and mental health. Some disabilities are more noticeable openly than others. Moreover, impairment can appear at any stage in a person's life. Though a person may come across many types of disabilities, mobile technology address the following types of disabilities shown in Figure 7.1

Vision impairment: It refers to an individual who is blind or have partial vision, visually impaired person are either partly sighted, low vision, legally blind, or blind.

Hearing Impairment: It refers to an individual who are hard of hearing and might be using a variety of strategies and devices including speech, reading lips, notes writing, hearing aids, or interpreters for sign language.

Cognitive or Intellectual Disability: It refers to people with problem in mental functioning and various aspects like communication, taking care

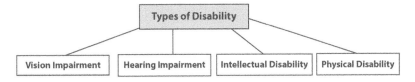

Figure 7.1 Types of disabilities.

of themselves, and social aspects. These problems will result in a child who learns and develop more slowly compared to a normal child. These people have trouble while learning in school.

Physical Disability: It refers to disability that restricts a person's mobility. Physical impairment can influence the working of limbs or the whole body. Physical impairment can restrict the accessibility of day to day activities. General physical disabilities comprises muscular dystrophy, cerebral palsy, spinal bifida, and heart defects [5, 6].

Getting access to wireless technology is essential for social and economic participation, which can be particularly challenging for people with disabilities. With millions of populace all around the world and a variety of disabilities and requirement, it's vital to know how we can utilize current technology to address various disabilities. It's universally known that there is no scarcity of mobile applications to benefit those with disabilities. Many technological giants like Android and Apple come up with easy to use artificial intelligence-enabled apps for a person with a disability.

7.2   Existing Accessibility Features for Mobile App and Devices

Smart Phones can be made reachable to an individual with different impairment by amalgamating different aspects like operating system, design of hardware and providing precise services and also through installment of third party applications like magnifiers and screen readers that can assist individual to access content and menus. Manufacturer's display information regarding accessibility enhancing features on their websites mostly. Apps provided by third party like screen readers can often gives a improved experience to users than inbuilt app available in original handset, nowadays number of manufacturers like apple are now offering high quality applications in mobile handsets.

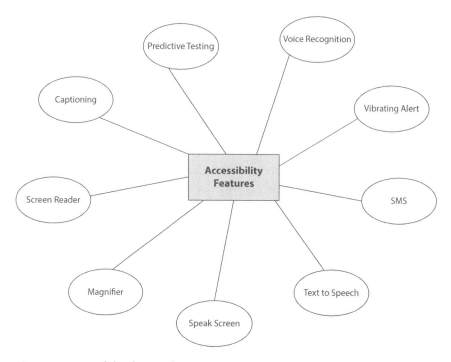

Figure 7.2 Accessibility features for mobile app.

Here we focus on the utility of Smart phones and the accessibility features mention in Figure 7.2 which are necessary to make individual with various types of disabilities accessible to special services that can be offered through mobile phones in order to achieve accessibility and quality of life [6].

7.2.1   Basic Accessibility Features and Services for Visually Impaired

Difficulty: Generally people have no idea regarding which features allows visually impaired person to utilize mobile phones, tablets, computers and other devices. Individual having low vision not able to notice screens therefore not able to utilize smart phone touch screen, contact lists to dial numbers in the address book, send and receive messages, or access the internet. **Remedy:** visually impaired person rely on computer or mobile phone's screen reader to make use of it. A screen reader is a kind of software which translates information present on the screen into speech. The latest smart phones come up with screen readers which operates based on your gesture.

This permits individual having visual disability to listen to information related to features on their handset through touch, furthermore it let them to drag and tap to manage their actions [6, 7].

In order to facilitate an individual with visual impairment to recognize, realize, navigate, interact with, and contribute to real world various features as shown in Table 7.1 need to be provided in mobile phones. Screen reader plays a very vital role by allowing visually impaired to reads the whole thing shown on the screen and converts it into speech. Whereas zoom enables an individual with low vision to magnify mobile screen to recognize objects. Similarly other accessibility features like Speak screen, Dictation, tactile feedback, Adaptable font sizes, Audible cues, Basic text to speech functionality makes life of visually impaired better.

7.2.2   Basic Accessibility Features and Services for Deaf

Difficulty: Deaf People unable to communicate by phone and interrelate socially because they are not able to listen to the caller or automated

Table 7.1 Accessibility features for visually impaired.

Sr. no.	Feature	Remark
1	Screen Reader	It reads everything showed on the screen and converts into dialogue. Voice Over and TalkBack are the screen-readers on iPhone and Android devices.
2	Zoom	It's a magnifier which allows zooming or magnifying screen to an individual with low vision. It works with third party apps and inbuilt apps, making handset fully accessible.
3	Magnifier	It allows using camera on your phone as a digitally magnifying glass, in order to amplify the size so that we can visualize the things more clearly.
4	Speak screen	It assists an individual to read emails and book also it helps to read screen when person struggle to read text.

(Continued)

Table 7.1 Accessibility features for visually impaired. (*Continued*)

Sr no	Feature	Remark
5	Display accommodations	It provides an option to invert colors, allow grey scale, reducing white point or pickup a range of filters to support a variety of colors for different levels of vision.
6	Dictation	It provides functionality to convert speech to text; therefore an individual can dictate emails, messages, tweets, facebook posts, and much more without typing it explicitly.
7	Audible or tactile feedback	It provides audio alert and feedback when button is pressed; received mail or cell phone gets turn on.
8	Adaptable font sizes	In order to satisfy user needs it helps to increase font size for better visualization.
9	Audible cues	It generates voice alert for specific services or feature like caller waiting or ending a call, low battery, adjusting the level of volume.
10	Backlit display	It makes easy to visualize specially in poor lighting, outdoors and indoors conditions.
11	Basic text to speech functionality	It is helpful while inspecting caller ID and reading text messages [7, 19].

electronic messages, like customer care of banks or airline service, additionally they are not able to avail crucial emergency services like call for medical assistance or police.

Remedy: There are multiple accessibility aspects and services provided by smart phones that makes it feasible to deaf people for making and receiving calls on a handset, ranging from basic aspect such as volume alteration and provision for video relay services [6, 7].

Today 95% of hard of hearing and deaf individuals utilize a cell phone consistently in developed nations. A lot of applications contribute to eradicate communication problem which hamper the day by day lives of millions of hard of hearing and deaf individuals around the globe. In order to assist an individual with hearing impairment to communicate freely with real world a variety of features as revealed in Table 7.2 need to be offer by smart phones. Accessibility features like Adjustable volume, vibrating alert, Text Teletypewriter, Tactile indicators for the keypad, Mono Audio, Captioning makes life of hearing impaired better.

Table 7.2 Accessibility features for deaf.

Sr. no.	Feature	Remark
1	SMS, MMS, and Email	It allows deaf people to make contact through text messages, email, SMS or MMS.
2	Adjustable volume	It helps to an individual with hearing impairment by improving the hearing aids functionality.
3	Visual or vibrating alert	This option assists to an individual by informing them about incoming messages, calls and emails.
4	Text Teletypewriter (TTY)	It's a specialized device which can be used to send text message over telephone lines.
5	Call logs	It displays missed calls that have been missed due to lack of vibration or unable to see light on screen.
6	Tactile indicators for the keypad	It helps to confirm actions being taken by highlighting keypad pressed buttons through lights or vibration.
7	Mono Audio	It helps deaf people for listening music and making calls easier by transmitting left and right side channel audio content to both ear buds of headphones.
8	Video conferencing.	It allows deaf people to communicate through face-to-face calling.
9	Captioning	It helps to understand videos and movies through captioning and subtitles [7, 19].

7.2.3   Basic Accessibility Features and Services for Cognitive Disabilities

Difficulty: Person with cognitive impairment finds it difficult to do one or more task which is carried out easily by an average individual. Based on the kind of impairment, an individual can face issue interrelated to analytical skills, memory, reading skills, attention, computational, numerical and reading comprehension and also the communication.

Table 7.3 Accessibility features for cognitive disabilities.

Sr. no.	Feature	Remark
1	Built-in calculator and schedule reminders	It helps an individual for remembering future actions and to execute tasks by using inbuilt schedule reminders and calculator through acoustic, visual, and vibrating alerts.
2	Larger display screens and formatting options	It assists to an individual by providing additional spaces among each word and highlights word in bold. Also it helps to increase brightness which makes easier and pleasurable to read.
3	Predictive Texting	It assist user while composing message in phone's text editor by predicting words which makes it easier to compose messages.
4	Auto-complete and suggestions	It can ease navigation, especially for those who have problems with memory, or for people who find decision making a trigger for anxiety.
5	Clear interactive elements	All interactive elements like links and buttons are easy to visually distinguish from the content.
6	Screen Reader	It reads everything displayed on the screen and converts into speech. Voice Over and TalkBack are the screen-readers on iPhone and Android devices [6, 7, 19].

Remedy: It's significant for person with cognitive impairment to have an apparent and easy to use user interface, and consistent UI elements for easier selection of options [7, 8].

Cognitive impairment is a collection of disabilities, conditions or issues that can go from mellow to extreme. Related indications can include: short/long haul memory troubles; regular tactile over-burden; consideration shortfall issues; slow preparing speeds; issues with critical thinking; education difficulties. Pictures, symbols and realistic substance can truly assist a client with an intellectual hindrance. Many applications with variety of features enlisted in Table 7.3 serve to eliminate interaction problem which hinder the daily activities of cognitively impaired around the world. Suggestions and auto-complete usefulness can be unbelievably valuable. Suggestions can ease route, particularly for the individuals who battle with memory, or for individuals who discover dynamic a trigger for nervousness. Auto-complete can likewise be immensely valuable for those with troubles with education and spelling. Accessibility features like schedule reminders, larger display screens and formatting options, predictive texting, auto complete and suggestions, clear interactive elements makes life of cognitive impaired better and easy.

7.2.4 Basic Accessibility Features and Services for Physically Disabled

Difficulty: It will be very difficult for an individual who is not able to make use of their hands or move their arms fingers effortlessly to physically navigate or press buttons on hand set because of impairment.

Solution: There are multiple accessibility solutions and services provided by smart phones that makes it feasible to physically disabled people to dial and attain calls on a cell phone, like voice recognition [7, 9].

Many of us are physically disabled eventually in our lives. A kid, an individual with a wrecked leg, a parent with a pram, an old individual, and so forth are totally handicapped somehow. The individuals who stay sound and physically fit for their entire lives are not many. Taking everything into account, it is significant that it should be sans obstruction and adjusted to satisfy the necessities surprisingly similarly. Truly, the requirements of the incapacitated match with the necessities of the lion's share, and all individuals are calm with them. Accordingly, getting ready for the dominant part suggests making arrangements for individuals with shifting capacities and inabilities. In order to ease physically disabled individual to carry out day to day task and contribute to real world a variety of features as shown in Table 7.4 need to be provided in

Table 7.4 Accessibility features for physically disabled.

Sr. no.	Feature	Remark
1	Voice recognition	It helps physically disabled people through voice instructions for accessing computers and cell phones for making calls, scripting and sending SMS, compose documents, opening and closing applications.
2	Auto Text	It helps to replace the specific text with preloaded texts to decrease the number of keystrokes required to prepare the message.
3	Sensitive Touch Screen	Smart Phones with sensitive touch screen assist an individual with actions limited to their fingers and answer the call by pressing any key.
4	Spoken feedback	The TalkBack function uses touch and spoken feedback to interact with their device.
5	Select to speak	It confines the spoken feedback function to only individually selected items on the screen.
6	Voice commands	It permits an individual to control their devices through spoken commands [6, 7, 19].

mobile phones. Accessibility features are intended to assist individuals with handicaps use innovation all the more without any problem. For instance, a text-to-speech highlight may recite text so anyone can hear for individuals with restricted vision, while a speech-recognition permits clients with restricted versatility to control the PC with their voice. Accessibility features like voice recognition, auto text, sensitive touch screen, spoken feedback, select to speak, Voice commands helps physically disabled a lot.

7.3 Services Offered by Wireless Service Provider

Few services provided by WSP (wireless service provider) such as Digital libraries for visual, GPS (global positioning system), relay services, living with independent, Emergency phone services, customer service as shown in Figure 7.3.

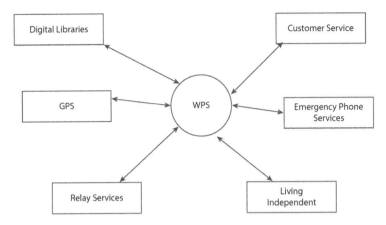

Figure 7.3 Various services offered by the wireless service provider.

7.3.1   Digital Libraries for Visual

During the downloading or finding the eBooks on the internet visually challenged users having the issue. The current/next generation mobiles with most valued features can overcome the challenges faced by the users. The users can able to access the book by using a screen reader along with talking features. This feature useful for them to read the books anywhere and at anytime without any issues. The features can download eBooks via the internet by using smart phones with many ways for visually disabled users. In advanced countries like Japan introduced smart phones for visually challenged users in the classroom to perform recording for taking class notes and work [7].

7.3.2   GPS

GPS plays a major role in the navigation of streets and overcome the barrier of information for visually disabled users. The smart phone with GPS built-in technology along with Google Maps freely available for all the users. Information is shown in the map which is accessible over the screen and performs reading based on that visually impaired.

GPS technology permits users to perform:

- Helpful to decide on travel and selection of the mode of transport available to users.
- Provide information about landmarks, nearby places which help them confirm the right direction of travel.

- During walking guidance about their destinations, path with direction.

7.3.3 Relay Services

Relay services are classified into four categories namely captioned speech relay services, Speech to speech relay services, Text relay services, and video relay services. These services are provided by human beings to conduct tasks like translation in mobile devices.

7.3.4 Living With Independent

Wireless technologies are easy to access and provide instantaneous access to physically challenged people. These people can use the services in various ways to make their lives more independent for daily routine activities. The main objective is to make the person feel comfortable and not depending on others help for services like home automation, internet browsing, reading Ebooks, text to speech, speech to text activities, emergency support, etc [7].

7.3.5 Emergency Phone Services

During the emergency the person with disabilities is able to make calls to a nearby person to get help. This has becomes very important and lifesaving. However limiting a person's capacity to communicate vital information to others is made possible by phone services.

- Listen to the message/call which fails to request assistance.
- Visually challenged person cannot give the exact location where the emergency help is needed.

7.3.6 Customer Service

Customer service is a significant part of many services offered by the service providers. Helping the visually challenged people on time without any interrupt becomes challenging and essential services. Some of the services offered orange, AT &T, NTT DoCoMo, and become success [7].

7.4 Mobile Apps for People With Disabilities

Mobile Apps acts as an interface to access various services in our day to day life for a bigger part of humankind and populace with impairment are not an exception. From the insignificant to the vital, mobile apps are serving to the requirements of people all around the world in the most dissimilar scenarios in a moment in history when almost any person, even in the extreme remote places, have access to any type of mobile device. This section list different mobile app with their features as shown in Figure 7.4 for visually disabled, speech and hearing impaired, physically disabled, and person with cognitive disabilities [19].

There are many applications as listed in Table 7.5 explicitly intended to assist individuals with visual weaknesses carry on with their best lives. Numerous mobile applications expect to help the outwardly impeded and daze distinguish fundamental items utilizing their cell phones. From perceiving colors, to perusing taxi meters and store registers, charging prepaid scratch cards and distinguishing money bills and checks it in a hurry by coordinating the versatile camera towards the chose thing. The apps like Be My Eyes, Voice Dream Reader, Learn Braille Alphabet, Light Detector, Voice Brief, List Recorder, Perfect Keyboard, Super Vision, NotNav GPS, LookTel etc makes a life of visually impaired better and easier.

As per the National Deaf Association, around 18 million individuals are estimated to be deaf especially in India. Hard of hearing individuals don't

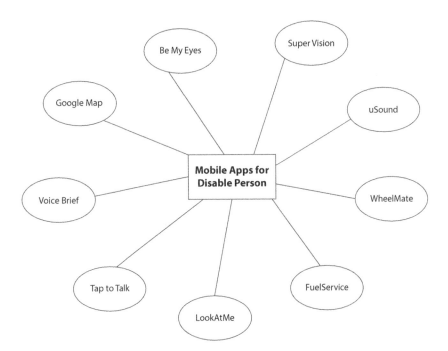

Figure 7.4 Mobile apps for person with disability.

Table 7.5 Apps for visually impaired.

Sr. no.	Mobile app	Platform	Feature
1.	Be My Eyes	iOS	It helps blind people with everyday tasks like navigation.
2.	Voice Dream Reader	iOS, Android	It provides text to speech feature for blind people.
3.	Learn Braille Alphabet	iOS, Android	It allows people to learn how to speak and listen.
4.	Light Detector	iOS	It helps to transform any form of light to sound, also can point out where the light source is.
5.	Voice Brief	iOS(paid)	It allows us to read a range of notification from your phone like calendar, Facebook, Twitter, weather, etc.
6.	List Recorder	Android	It allows us to create a to-do list, also helps to store information in audio format.
7.	Perfect Keyboard	Android	It offers a keyboard design with adjustment, which permits increase in height of key, size of text and space between rows for easier visualization.
8.	SuperVision	Android, iOS	It assists to maintain clarity in text and image at high levels; also it allows using a smart phone camera to zoom in the desired part of documents, books, and images.
9.	NotNav GPS	Android	It's a special kind of app which is developed by the blind to assist blind person while walking. It also helps to announce user's direction, nearby cross streets and nearest street address.
10.	LookTel	Android	It instantly recognizes currency and speaks the denomination of it [10, 13, 18].

have that numerous choices for speaking with a hearing individual. Deaf individuals can undoubtedly comprehend a lot what other hard of hearing individuals are stating, yet experience issues while speaking with the individuals who can hear. A sign language can assists hard of hearing and quiet individuals to converse with each other becomes unable with regards to correspondence between others. An app like WhatsApp and others as

Table 7.6 Apps for the speech and hearing impaired.

Sr. no.	Mobile app	Platform	Feature
1.	uSound	iOS, Android	It offers different sound quality and volume in a certain environment.
2.	Marlee Signs	iOS	It helps to learn American sign language, it allows typing some word and it will display how to utter that word with help of sign language.
3.	Spread the Sign	iOS, Android	It offers the biggest dictionaries of sign language in app market with around 300000 sign available.
4.	Voice Dream Reader	iOS, Android	It allows reading screen with ears.
5.	P3 mobile	iOS, Android	It enables you to make a video call, it's easy to use sleek interface.
6.	HearYouNow	iOS	It helps to understand the conversation clearly by amplifying the sound around you.
7.	Sign Smith ASL	Android	It offers near about 1200 sign. It's a better app to learn sign language.
8.	Dragon Dictation	iOS	It offers speech to text facility with remarkable accuracy and it is easy to use.
9.	Roger Voice	Android	It helps to translate what a person speaks on the phone into text on the user's screen, also it facilitates one or both of the parties who can't hear to make calls [11, 14].

listed in Table 7.6 has become a significant instrument of correspondence for the hard of hearing. A variety of apps like uSound, Marlee Signs, Spread the Sign, Voice Dream Reader, P3 mobile, HearYouNow, Sign Smith ASL, Dragon Dictation, Roger Voice acts as a bridge to interact with normal individual.

For individuals with actual incapacities, getting around in their regular daily existences can be very troublesome. Undoubtedly, for wheelchair clients a ton of obstructions can transform their outing into a horrible like checks that aren't brought down or structures with restricted doors. They need to discover business places, parking spaces or even bathrooms that are effectively available for them. In the United States, there are roughly 2.7 million individuals who utilize a wheelchair. How might they explore their way in the city and completely appreciate it? Fortunately, cell phones and applications specifically have improved their lives as it's the situation for hard of hearing and almost deaf individuals. A few applications as enlisted in Table 7.7 are accessible that help them be more self-sufficient and more tranquil in their excursions. Some were even made particularly for individuals with helpless ability or with diminished utilization of their upper appendages so they can utilize their telephones with no battle. A variety of apps like Wheelmap, It's Accessible, Wheelmate, Inclusive Britain, Assistive Touch, Google Assistant, Mouse4all Switch assist physically disabled lot to carry out their daily task.

Cognitive impairment is the point at which an individual experiences difficulty in recalling, learning new things, thinking, or settling on choices that influence their regular day to day existence. Psychological disability goes from gentle to extreme. With gentle impedance, individuals may start to see changes in intellectual capacities, yet have the option to do their regular exercises. Serious degrees of debilitation can prompt losing the capacity to comprehend the significance or significance of something and the capacity to talk or compose, bringing about the powerlessness to live autonomously. Now a day's more and more technology giants coming with innovative apps as listed in Table 7.8 to aid individual with cognitive disabilities and providing lot of accessibility features which makes life of such individual easy.

7.5   Technology Giants Providing Services

Technology giants keep on growing to satisfy humans with disabilities. Few companies like Apple, Google, and Microsoft have developed accessibility features, particularly to the physically challenged human beings.

Table 7.7 Apps for physically disabled.

Sr. no.	Mobile app	Platform	Feature
1.	Wheelmap	iOS, Android	It helps to an individual for finding places around you where wheelchair can be accessible. Here you can also put in mark for accessible places.
2.	It's Accessible	iOS	It allows sharing places like restaurants where physically disabled can visit with ease.
3.	Wheelmate	iOS, Android	It helps to locate wheelchair-accessible toilets and parking spaces. It includes 30000 locations with 45 countries.
4.	Inclusive Britain	iOS	It offers visual routes for all locations which makes it easier to find the place.
5.	Tecla Access	Android	It offers tools required to access and use cell phones without picking up your device.
6.	Assistive Touch	iOS, Android	It provides virtual buttons which permits individual to navigate a handset without touching it.
7.	FuelService	iOS, Android	It assists disabled drivers for searching and getting support for refueling their vehicles.
8.	Google Assistant	Android	It allows users to carry out numerous tasks without touching phone like making calls, opening apps and sending messages.
9.	Google Map	Android	It helps an individual for moving around more efficiently who have trouble in moving, It can also display the accessible outline of a city with availability of both wheelchair ramps and elevators.
10.	Mouse4all Switch	Android	It helps to get pleasure from mobile technology, via controlling a pointer of mouse through one or two switches [12, 15, 17].

Table 7.8 Apps for cognitive disabilities.

Sr. no.	Mobile app	Platform	Feature
1.	Miracle Modus	iOS, Android	It helps to decrease the intensity of sensory overload by make use of shapes, soft sounds and hypnotic colors.
2.	Tap To Talk	iOS	In order to make communication simple it helps to convert the phone into an augmentative and alternative communication device.
3.	Book Creator	iOS	It helps to create their own stories, support creativity.
4.	Avaz	iOS	It will be helpful for those who face difficulty while talking or who are nonverbal.
5.	Look at me	Android	It helps to improve facial recognition and make contact with others efficiently.
6.	Stepping Stones	iOS, Android	It assists individual by creating visual guides who remind them of or assist them to recognize routine task like making toast or doing the washing.
7.	JABtalk	Android	It helps to transform any Android device into an augmentative and alternative communication (AAC)device.
8.	Cough Drop	Android	It uses Augmentative and Alternative Communication (AAC) to hear the voice of any user having problems in their voice.
9.	ModMath	Android	It offers pencil-free virtual graph paper which is perfect for an individual who struggle to read their own handwriting.
10.	Autism Core Skills	Android	It provides various levels of academic learning, starting from sorting shapes and objects to basic spelling of words [7, 13, 15].

All Android mobiles with suite designed for them to perform accessibility to the screen reading those visually impaired. The first smart phone iPhone introduced features accessibility for them like Homekit, voice-over, and few of them. Artificial Intelligence-based technologies developed by Microsoft and Google. The various sectors with positive technical support provide a solution for the people. For Visually challenged people Microsoft launched a free app with AI support which results in more than 1 lakh downloaded in a short period. Microsoft developed "Be My Eyes" which is very useful for blind users. Google developed with AI for image recognition by Google Lens which is useful and gives assistance in Google Homes [7, 19].

7.5.1   Japan: NTT DoCoMo

In developed countries like Japan's rapid growth of mobile and its technologies over the last decade, according to the research survey, more than 70 % of people in the population lie I the range of 20 to 50 during the year 2004. NTT DoCoMo market shares more than 50% which is identified based on that potential to attract new customers. Based on the studies and evaluation this company identified a lack of assistance and accessibility for elderly persons. The company started developing based on the findings to adapt the design for the universal purpose of all operations and its development across the various divisions. Developing the handsets with various impairments accessible plays a major role which is offered to the customer with various disabilities [19].

7.6   Challenges and Opportunities for Technology Giants to Provide Product & Service

This section highlights the challenges and opportunities for different technology giants while providing accessible products and services for persons with disabilities like visually impaired, speech and hearing impaired, physically disabled, and persons with cognitive disabilities.

7.6.1   Higher Illiteracy Rate

According to the Economic Times survey carried out in the last month of 2019, amongst individuals with disabilities with age of 7 years and above, 52.2 percent were educated and 47.8 were still illiterate, amongst individuals with disabilities age of 15 years and above, only 19.3% had the maximum educational level as secondary and above. Literacy plays a vital role in accessing the products and services provided by many technology giants. The illiteracy rate creates challenges as well as opportunities for technology giants to launch a new product and offer service to a person with disability [16].

7.6.2   Reach out to Customers With Disabilities

People living with disabilities signify target populace, that in several cases is not represented to universal marketing campaigns or they don't think that the pros encouraged by such campaigns satisfy their requirements. This produces challenges as well as opportunities for technology giants to reach a person with a disability.

7.6.3   Higher Cost of Mobile Phones With Accessibility Features

Many assistive apps work only in high end smart phones whose cost is not affordable to several users, particularly in developing nations, the long term prospect of more powerful, cheaper smart phones creates challenge and opportunities for many companies to offer accessibility service and product to an individual with disabilities around the globe.

7.6.4   Increasing Percentage of Disability

As per United Nations, near about 15% of the world's populace, or nearly 1 billion people, live with disabilities, this will create challenges and opportunities for many companies to offer accessibility services and products to an individual with disabilities around the globe.

7.6.5   Unavailability of Assistive Technology in Regional Languages

In various countries, facilities like the text to speech or voice recognition are not offered in local languages. Especially in India, multiple regional languages are used by persons with disabilities; therefore it creates challenges and opportunities for many technology giants to offer accessibility service to an individual with disabilities around the globe [16].

7.6.6 Lack of Knowledge Concerning Assistive Solutions

In many countries various service providers offering multiple solutions but knowledge about these assistive services is missing or remains low among disabled person [7].

7.7 Good Practices for Spreading Awareness

Creating consciousness about the requirement for assimilating accessibility features into cell phone and various services for an individual with impairments amongst a variety of stakeholders, like policymakers, device manufacturers, developer's, service providing firms and standards setting organizations, will assist to promote active initiative and normal accessibility.

- Conducting communal awareness activities like installing information kiosks and traveling exhibits.
- Working with technology providers and research labs to develop universally accessible products.
- Engaging media outreach activities through advertisements and public service broadcasting that emphasizes easily used services and mobile products for a physically disabled person.
- Publish survey and reports related to the use of cell phones by an individual with disabilities.
- The government can offer monetary incentives, subsidies, and tax benefits to smaller network operators and manufacturers for adopting accessibility in services and products for disabled persons [7].
- The government can offer partnerships to companies for research and development of products and services with accessibility features.
- Governments can provide support for pilot programs through funding, partnerships, or universal service fund.
- Organizing campaigns through disabled persons to promote accessibility features among the physically disabled person.
- Encourage a review of existing easy to use mobile phones and services presented by different providers.

- Promote top handset manufacturers to propose existing easy to use products already marketed around the globe.
- Endorse opportunities to speed up the development of voice recognition and text to speech interfaces if not offered in local languages.
- Establish a practice to get feedback and recommendations on potential mobile accessibility gaps, and keep an eye on improvement made in filing these gaps by linking with different associations having individuals with many types of disabilities [7].

7.8   Conclusion

Disability is one of the key public health issues especially in developing countries like India. Accessibility is not an elective one, but it is essential for many. But sometimes people with disabilities disconnect from their use. Mobile technology has not simply transformed the pattern of communication but is also becoming an essential way for education, business and rehabilitation by providing different accessibility features for mobile app and devices. A variety of wireless service providers offer lucrative services that make life easy for a disabled person. Multiple app development platforms such as android and ios offer multiple apps that have various accessibility features that assist physically disabled to carry out multiple tasks. Implementation of good practices helps to improve the lives of the physically disabled person. Still, there are lot many challenges and opportunities are available to technology providers to serve a physically disabled person by offering innovative apps and wireless devices as a technological solution.

References

1. United Nations, Factsheet on Persons with Disabilities, Department of Economic and Social Affairs, by United Nations, Available online: https://www.un.org/development/desa/disabilities/resources/factsheet-on-persons-with-disabilities.html (16 July 2020).
2. Fu, H., Cord, L., McClain, C., A billion people experience disabilities worldwide so where data, 2019, https://blogs.worldbank.org/opendata.

3. World report on disability, by World Health Organization, DOI:10.13140/RG.2.1.4993.8644, 2011.

4. Wagner, L., Disabled people in the world in 2019 facts and figures, France, 2019, https://www.inclusivecitymaker.com.

5. https://services.anu.edu.au/human-resources/respect-inclusion/different-types-of-disabilities.

6. Holly, X., How do blind and visually impaired people use a mobile phone, 2019, https://lifeofablindgirl.com.

7. Making Mobile Phones and services accessible for Persons with disabilities. A joint report of ITU – The International Telecommunication Union and G3ict – The global initiative for inclusive ICTs, 2012.

8. Wiliams, L., Accessibility cognitive impairment, London, 2013, https://www.system-concepts.com/insights.

9. what-are-android-accessibility-features, Bureau of Internet Accessibility, East Greenwich, United States. 2017, https://www.boia.org/blog.

10. Powerful mobile apps for those with disabilities, UKS Mobility, Greater Manchester, 2015, https://www.uksmobility.co.uk/blog.

11. Top 8 mobile apps for persons with disabilities, Access2mobility, 2014, https://access2mobility.com.

12. Smartphone apps make disabled people lives easier, 2015, https://www.passionatepeople.invacare.eu.com, Invacare International GmbH, Switzerland.

13. Herzog, A., 2020, Apps-for-disabled-people, https://lifezest.co.

14. Braille Works, Top mobile apps for the blind, Braille Works, 2015, https://brailleworks.com.

15. Best android apps disabled adults, Mouse4all, 2019, https://mouse4all.com/en/articles.

16. India's 2.2 population suffering from disability nso survey for july dec 2018, https://economictimes.indiatimes.com/news/economy/indicators, Article by Economic Times, 2018, India.

17. Hindy, J., Best disabled apps and accessibility apps for android, Android Authority, 2020, https://www.androidauthority.com.

18. Best apps for visually impaired, Everyday sight, 2021, https://www.everydaysight.com.

19. Computer basics using accessibility features, by GCF Global, 2019, https://edu.gcfglobal.org/en.

8

Smart Solar Power–Assisted Wheelchairs For the Handicapped

Abhinav Bhatnagar[1]*, Sidharth Pancholi[2] and Vijay Janyani[3]

[1]Department of Electronics & Communication Engineering, Birla Institute of Applied Sciences, Bhimtal (U.K.), India
[2]Department of Electrical Engineering, Indian Institute of Technology, New Delhi, India
[3]Department of Electronics & Communication Engineering, Malaviya National Institute of Technology, Jaipur (Raj), India

Abbreviations

AI	Artificial Intelligence
CdTe	Cadmium Telluride
CIGS	Copper Indium Gallium Selenide
CNN	Coevolutionary Neural Network
EEG	Electroencephalograph
EOG	Electrooculography
EMG	Electromyography
EPW	Electric-Powered Wheelchair
FFBP	Forward and Back-Spread
GaAs	Gallium Arsenide
HMI	Human Machine Interface
ILM	Intense Learning Machine
InP	Indium Phosphide
IoT	Internet of Things
LDA	Linear Discrimination Analysis
MPPT	Maximum Power Point Tracking
MW	Manual Wheelchair
NiCd	Nickel Cadmium
NiMH	Nickel Metal Hydride

*Corresponding author: abhinavscisolar@gmail.com

Roshani Raut, Pranav Pathak, Sandeep Kautish and Pradeep N (eds.) Intelligent Systems for Rehabilitation Engineering, (175–196) © 2022 Scrivener Publishing LLC

Li-ion   Lithium ion
PPG   Pulse plethysmography
RNN   Recurrent Neural Network
RF   Radio Frequency
SPW   Solar-Powered Wheelchair
SVM   Support Vector Machine

Abstract

Mobilization for disabled people is one of the essential requirements. A standard solution to the mobility needs of individuals with a significant disability is the mechanical wheelchair. However, in a mechanical wheelchair, there is a large probability of upper limb fatigue and injury. Alternatively, electric-powered wheelchairs were developed, which helps in reducing the possibility of muscle injury and strain. The motors in any kind of electric-powered wheelchair are dependent on batteries for their power and thus have limited travel range and need frequent recharging. These limitations can be resolved by integrating a thin-film solar panel that can be fitted at the back of the wheelchair as a foldable retractable roof similar to the roof in convertible automobiles. It eliminates the use of a rigid, bulky, and heavy conventional solar panel fixed on a metal framework that cannot be dismantled. The chapter discusses the advancement and innovations in the smart solar-powered wheelchair for disabled people. The various design possibilities, electrical circuit design, and control system, emphasizing smart control through electroencephalograph (EEG) signals, smart navigation systems, and data accusation through the Internet of Things (IoT), are also discussed.

Keywords: Wheelchair, solar panel, electroencephalograph, navigation, artificial intelligence, handicapped, rehabilitation

8.1 Introduction

The evolutionary journey of wheelchairs is marked by their transformation from an ordinary chair with wheels for mobilization to a fully automated personal mobility vehicle for the handicapped. Mobilization is the primary concern for people with a severe disability, particularly disability in the lower limbs, which has initiated the need to develop limb support systems and wheelchairs. The wheelchair, in some form or other, goes back a very long way and has changed considerably over time, but the real advances in its design and technology started in the last decade. The advancements include the ergonomics of the wheelchair, ease of operation majorly, and help the handicaps move freely with the minimum efforts. Traditional manual wheelchairs (MWs), when properly used, induce a rich oxygen exchange ratio in the lungs and, hence, are beneficial to the health of the user. However, only 2% to 13.8% of the external power is converted into the metabolic power known as the mechanical efficiency of the wheelchair and greatly depends on the level of injury, the propulsion technique, the adjustments made to the seat height, ergonomic design considerations, and the intensity of the exercise undertaken [1–9]. The high physical strain and low poor mechanical efficiency may result in muscular tension, fatigue, and muscular damage in the worst-case scenario [10]. "Necessity is the mother of invention," and with the technological revolution, MWs are replaced by electric-powered wheelchairs (EPWs) that operate on rechargeable batteries, also termed as Power Wheelchair. It dramatically reduces muscular fatigue and facilitates ease of mobility [11]. However, people who use wheelchairs have mobility dependency relying on battery life, reducing the distance traveled between consecutive battery charges. Besides, recharging batteries is also time-consuming. Feasibility research has been done to overcome these limitations by fitting a solar panel on wheelchairs that could power up the batteries on the go. Fitting solar panels to an EPW minimizes the batteries' recharging time and increases the distance traveled between charges [12–15]. However, solar-powered EPW available in the market also suffers from design issues such as large physical

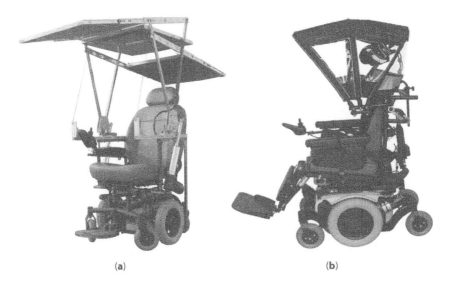

(a)   (b)

Figure 8.1 (a) Traditional solar-powered wheelchair with bulky silicon solar panel. (b) Thin-film retractable solar-powered wheelchair with lightweight, flexible, and high-efficiency CIGS photovoltaic material.

size, bulky, and lack of foldability. Current designs of the solar-powered wheelchair (SPW) include a traditional silicon solar cell roof-like panel above the wheelchair fixed firmly by the support of the metal frame (Figure 8.1a).

The metal frame, including the silicon solar cells, are bulky, heavy, and non-flexible. These limitations are greatly deciphered by the use of a retractable thin-film solar cell (TFSC) sheet (Figure 8.1b). A more advanced system comprises better and stable autonomous mobility smart wheelchairs such as a Hybrid Solar-Radio Frequency Harvesting System, capable of harvesting power from radio frequency (RF) and solar radiation [16]. Further, by embedding sensor technology and intelligent processing using microprocessors, the hardware, and software, interaction is much improved, making the next-generation smart wheelchair a reality. Conventional smart electric wheelchairs are mainly equipped with navigation control based on a joystick [17] but possess limitations for disabled and older people as they lack dexterous control of upper limbs. Improved human-machine interfaces and advanced smart controllers have been proposed, including biosignal-based controlling (EEG, EMG, or EOG), vision-based control, voice control, and navigation using hand gestures. Today, the smart wheelchair design is not only about powering it up with solar power but integrating the chair with other essential functionality making it a lot easier to maneuver, improving the user interface, and extracting medical data (blood pressure, pulse rate, etc.) from the user by developing the human-machine interface [18, 19].

8.2 Power Source

EPWs are ideal for those who cannot drive a MW or who may need to use a wheelchair for long distances or over a slope or rough terrain, resulting in muscular fatigue. Typically, to power up the wheelchair, the electric motors are fitted with rechargeable deep-cycle batteries, that provide front, center, rear-wheel drive, and all-wheel drive. Rechargeable batteries are made in various sizes and forms ranging from small button cells to large megawatt batteries which are used to power up and stabilize an electrical network. Various kinds of chemicals are commonly used in these cells, for instance, lead-acid, nickel-cadmium (Ni-Cd), nickel-metal hydride (NiMH), lithium-ion (Li-ion), and lithium-ion polymer (Li-Ion polymer). These are economical and have a minimum impact on the environment as compared to disposable batteries. Today, with the use of advance technology rapid chargers, these cells or batteries can typically be charged in 2 to 5 hours and the rate of charging relies upon the type of model, with the quickest taking as low as 15 minutes. However, most rechargeable batteries are limited to provide power for only 24-hours and thus require daily recharging.

8.2.1   Solar-Powered Wheelchair

Solar panel systems are a well-known renewable power source that converts sunlight into electrical energy. The best thing about using solar power is that it does not pollute the environment. Recently, solar energy–powered wheelchairs are being designed and developed that use solar energy as a backup to the rechargeable batteries' existing electrical energy. The solar-assisted wheelchair system's primary power circuit includes a solar panel, a hub motor, a lead-acid battery, and a boost converter or voltage regulator (Figure 8.2). The wheel hub motor, typically an electric motor (also called in-wheel motor), drives the wheels directly. The hub motors are incorporated directly into hub of wheel producing greater torque at initial startup, making them quintessential for wheelchairs as they require the maximum torque at a low speed and does not need sprockets, brackets, and drive chains. The hub motor is coupled to a speed controller which is provided to vary and control the speed of movement of the wheelchair. The most ordinarily used hub motor is the brushless DC motor, owing to its high torsion-to-weight ratio and wide constant power speed ranges [20, 21].

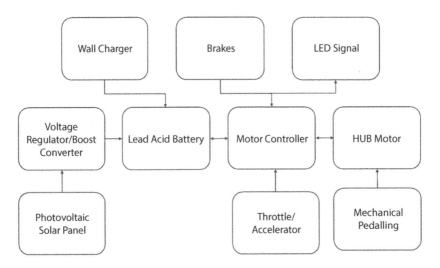

Figure 8.2 Basic block diagram of a power circuit in a solar-assisted wheelchair.

In SPWs, the solar panels are fitted above the wheelchair using a fixed or retractable support structure, which can be spread out or retracted electrically. The solar panel orientation is set to absorb maximum sunlight while acting as a shade to the individual sitting in the wheelchair from sunlight and rain. However, conventional support structures, such as canopies with a fixed metal frame or manually adjustable frame, provide no easy and accessible means for making various types of adjustments, especially for handicapped and have limited mobility for adjusting the overhead canopy. This design is improved by fitting the wheelchair with a thin-film retractable solar cell panel (Figure 8.1b). The motivation behind this design is inspired by the idea of retractable roofs of convertible automobiles. TFSCs provide numerous advantages over traditional silicon solar cells, such as low cost, high efficiency, better performance in poor irradiance conditions, flexibility, and ease of installation. New researches are being conducted to continuously improve the design and performance of TFSCs to generate more current with less material and losses [22–25]. The most common TFSCs available in the market are of Gallium Arsenide (GaAs), Indium Phosphide (InP), Cadmium Telluride (CdTe), and Copper Indium Gallium Selenide (CIGS)–based solar cells [26, 27].

8.2.2 Solar Energy Module

The solar or photovoltaic (PV) energy module comprises mainly of three parts: solar panels, Maximum Power Point Tracking (MPPT) controller, and boost converter. Solar panels are capable of converting the clean renewable energy in the form of sunlight directly into electricity which can then be used to power up various electronic devices for different applications. Depending upon the semiconductor technology, they can be classified into wafer-based and thin-film solar panels. MPPT is algorithm that is implemented in solar charge controllers and capable of extracting maximum available power from solar panel under certain conditions. Through the use of MPPT controller, the power conversion efficiency of the solar panel improves and the battery's life is extended as it protects the battery from overcharging and unwanted discharge events while the boost converter is used to meet the battery power demand by stepping up the input DC voltage level to some higher DC voltage level, required by a load.

Usually, solar array's conversion efficiency (sunlight into electric energy) is low and inapt for the specific battery charging purpose. To achieve efficient conversion, the MPPT is incorporated in the solar enery module. As illustrated in Figure 8.3, the MPPT tracks the highest power point for the

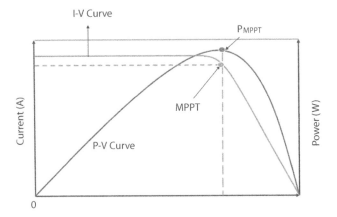

Figure 8.3 Typical characteristics of a PV module.

PV panels, providing the maximum optimal quantity of energy from the solar array to the battery bank by accommodating for differences in voltages between the solar array and the battery bank. A MPPT controller has the capability to sense the battery capacity and voltage. It then matches the required voltage needed from the solar array. Based on the theory of potential difference, the higher voltage always flows to the lower voltage between two points in an electric circuit, which is the difference between the solar array and the battery bank. During the sunny condition, harvesting voltage from the solar panels transfers into the battery. However, in the opposite cases, the power of the battery could be discharged back to the solar arrays. In this case, the MPPT works as a switch, switching off when the solar voltage is lower than the battery voltage. The MPPT can tackle this issue by preventing unnecessary discharging voltage scenarios. Moreover, the MPPT also prevents overcharging of the battery by regulating the amount of current that comes from solar panels to the battery bank.

The DC-DC boost converter is used to step up a lower DC voltage, generated by solar panels, to the higher DC voltage demanded by the wheelchair's battery. Figure 8.4 depicts the working principle of the boost converter. When the MOSFET transistor is ON (Figure 8.4a), the source's current only flows through the inductor and the MOSFET. During this period, it is isolated with the load by the reverse bias of the diode and the inductor stores the whole input source. During the switch's OFF state (Figure 8.4b), the input source flows through the inductor and the diode to the load. The output voltage (V_O) of DC-DC boost converter is much greater than the input voltage (V_S). Equation (8.1) shows the relationship between the output voltage and the source [28]:

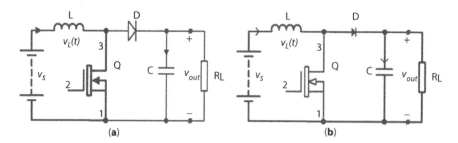

Figure 8.4 Boost converter MOSFET states, (a) when MOSFET is ON, (b) when MOSFET is OFF.

$$V_O = V_L + V_S \qquad (8.1)$$

where V_O is the output voltage of the boost converter, V_L is the inductor voltage storing during the ON state of MOSFET, and V_S is the harvesting voltage from the solar arrays. Equation (8.2) expresses the relationship between the ON and OFF modes of the MOSFET switch, where D_{on} is the ON percentage time of the MOSFET transistor and D_{off} is the OFF percentage of time of the transistor.

$$D_{off} = 1 - D_{on} \qquad (8.2)$$

On the other side, Equation (8.3) shows the direct effect of the ON and OFF time of the MOSFET transistor to the output voltage, where V_S is the source voltage, and V_O is the output voltage of the boost converter [29].

$$V_O = V_S / D_{off} \qquad (8.3)$$

Then, by using the boost converter, the output values can step up to higher levels. However, although it is above the input source, the fluctuating output voltage of such a boost converter may not be suitable for efficient charging of the battery. For this purpose a voltage regulator is used to regulate the output voltage.

8.3   Smart EMG-Based Wheelchair Control System

Electromyography is a technique to record the electric voltage produced by the skeletal muscles. As an ensuing sign of such an electrical activity, a variety of motor unit action potentials generated through muscle fibers. The EMG signal is an invaluable source of neural input that has been thoroughly researched in the fields of Human-Machine Interaction (HMI), prosthetic system creation, and various rehabilitation robots. The controlling techniques of the EMG signal-based system can be divided into on/off, proportional control, and pattern recognition-based techniques.

The classical myoelectric control method decodes the motor intent of subject through the amplitude of EMG time series acquired using surface electrodes attached to the arm muscles as conceptualized in Figure 8.5. For example, voltage for channel 1 (CH_1) is greater than the predefined threshold voltage (TH_1), and then, the corresponding action hand open (HO) is executed. Similarly, for channel 2, EMG signal voltage shows a higher amplitude than the threshold value (TH_2) then hand close (HC) is triggered. When both of the voltage values exceed the threshold amplitudes, then no action (NA) is performed using embedded programming. The HO action can be used for wheelchair forward-moving and HC for the backward motion. Nevertheless, the pattern recognition-based technique is considered as the most practical and preferred in the research community. The significant advantage of pattern recognition-based technique is its capability to mimic whole upper limb activity, including placing, lifting, grasping, reaching, and applying optimal force [20].

In the EMG-PR-based wheelchair control strategy, users voluntarily generate distinct patterns of EMG signal for different motor tasks during the training period. Subsequently, effective signal processing and suitable

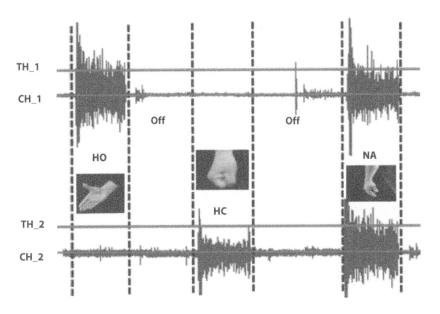

Figure 8.5 Amplitude-based myoelectric system control mechanism.

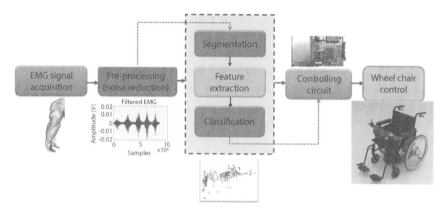

Figure 8.6 The block diagram of the EMG-based smart wheelchair control system.

machine learning techniques are applied to decode the disabled's limb intent and generate control commands for system control [30].

A typical EMG-PR–based upper system involves five main interconnected steps: (i) techniques of EMG signal collection related to amputee's limb intent, (ii) pre-processing techniques for minimizing inherent and unwanted noise and apply windowing technique, (iii) feature extraction for essential features to retain most discriminating information, and (iv) pattern recognition to predict user intent associated to user movement, (v) control wheelchair using electronic circuit as shown in Figure 8.6.

8.3.1 Techniques of EMG Signal Collection

EMG activity can be monitored and acquired using two different, widely adopted electrodes: invasive and non-invasive. Intramuscular EMG (iEMG) electrodes are introduced inside the human muscle, while in non-invasive technique, surface EMG (sEMG) electrodes are attached on the skin surface [31, 32] as shown in Figure 8.7. The use of iEMG electrodes gets the better of some severe challenges associated with sEMG, such as collecting signals from deep muscles with negligible crosstalk and electrode-skin impedance changes. Although continuous use of this method is not advisable because it needs the help of trans-cutaneous needle/wire electrodes to deliver information. The iEMG technique usually utilizes in a clinical examination such as neuromuscular disorders and muscle conduction tests [33]. In contrast to iEMG method, sEMG electrodes can collect information regarding muscular activities from several muscles, thus enabling the acquisition of appropriate and desired muscle activity signals with few

(a)

(b)

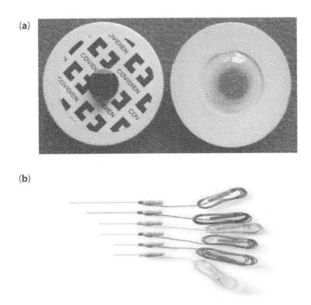

Figure 8.7 (a) Surface EMG, (b) Invasive EMG electrodes.

electrodes for smart wheelchair control. The key step in the capturing of EMG signals is to turn analog information into digital values using analog-to-digital converters (ADC). The selection of the required sampling rate is an essential consideration to prevent the undersampling and oversampling [31].

8.3.2   Pre-Possessing and Segmentation of EMG Signal

Prepossessing the raw EMG signals is an essential step toward reducing unwanted noises and confirming the appropriate examination of the signal. Therefore, several inherent interferences have been identified during EMG signal recordings.

These noises include environmental noise due to electromagnetic radiation, interference from the acquisition system, lead motion artifact produced by the movement of cables or electrode interference, and instability of the signals caused by variation in the firing rate of motor units [32–34].

Typically, the deferential mode configuration is utilized to acquire raw EMG signals. Subsequently, with the aid of digital filters (band-pass filters in the range of 10 to 20 Hz to 450 to 500 Hz), the low- and high-frequency noises are excluded, mostly distorting neural information. Also, the

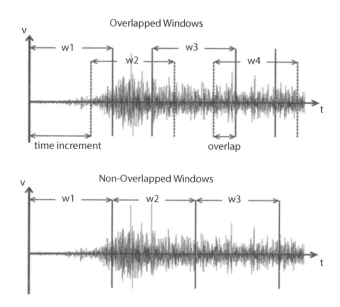

Figure 8.8 Overlapping and non-overlapping window.

power-line interference is generally removed with the aid of a notch filter (50 or 60 Hz) based on the power grid specification of the country/region. Further, EMG time series are passed through windowing (overlapping and non-overlapping) technique to segment the signal for real-time applicability, as shown in Figure 8.8. The efficiency of the collected EMG signal can be defined by the ratio of the recorded EMG signal to the undesired noise presented by external and internal factors. High-quality signals for pattern classification [23] provide more requested information. However, noise from different sources is inevitable and can reduce the efficiency of the EMG signal. For this purpose, amplifiers and different filters are used to boost the efficiency of the EMG signal or to increase the signal-to-noise.

8.3.3 Feature Extraction and Pattern Classification

After applying segmentation to the pre-processed EMG signal, a set of mathematical parameters carrying rich neural information is generally obtained from a short time window supporting the recognition of upper-limb motions. Appropriate feature extraction from the pre-processed signal would ultimately lead to a high motion recognition rate and better system control stability [35]. The high-dimensional raw pre-processed signals are mapped into low-dimensional space with mathematical or statistical models, employing a proper feature extraction technique. These mapped features help provide the signal's neural information more effectively than raw EMG signals, which may be complex and random. Due to the feature vector's comparatively smaller size, the pattern recognition technique decodes the limb motion faster [36]. Time-domain features are calculated directly from pre-processed EMG signal and the output of this is described as a function of time. These features did not require any sort of transformation and are computed directly from the amplitude. Frequency domain (FD) features are generally employed to measure muscular fatigue and analysis of force. The FD features are disadvantageous because of computational complexity, consequence in high variance and spectral leakage. Time-frequency features contain both time and frequency information of the signal and thus exhibits improvement in pattern classification performance for the dynamic and heterogeneous motions. The main advantage of these parameters is their competence to incorporate the non-stationary characteristics of the stochastic signal. It exhibits enhancement in the pattern classification rate of the myoelectric control system [36, 46].

Apart from the feature extraction method, the classification model's selection additionally impacts the overall performance of an EMG-PR–based system [30, 37]. Intelligent machine learning–based wheelchair control methods consider that the classification technique can decode input values (feature vector) provided during the training period and generate values related to their target motion in the testing phase.

Pattern classification methods offer significant improvisation in myoelectric control-based strategies along with many linear and non-linear

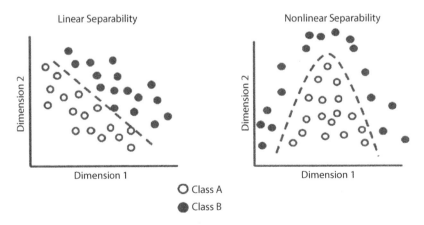

Figure 8.9 Linear and non-linear classifications.

classifiers that have been explored and investigated, as shown in Figure 8.9 [36]. A classification method should be capable of spotting EMG patterns correctly in much less time to meet the real-time constraints of the wheelchair control. Nevertheless, in the literature, only a few studies have been focused on validating classifier's potency to meet real-time control [36–39]. There are many well-known pattern classification algorithms proposed, namely, linear discriminant analysis (LDA), support vector machine (SVM), and random forest (RF). The main classification techniques are described further in this chapter.

8.3.3.1   Linear Discriminant Analysis (LDA)

This technique is commonly used as a linear classification algorithm for EMG-based pattern recognition to control the upper limb prosthetics. On the other hand, in many implementations, the LDA technique is often used for the reduction of functions. The essential advantages of using LDA are its quick computation and no parametric adjustment is needed [40, 41]. Various data sets: The most widely used LDA strategy is linear "Fishers Discrimination Analysis". In addition, many modifications were rendered in LDA using various kernels such as Quadratic Discrimination Analysis (QDA). Pattern recognition rates using the LDA classification approach varying from 80% to 90%, so there would be no risk of overfitting.

8.3.3.2   Support Vector Machine (SVM)

The most influential use of classification techniques for EMG-PR–based control strategies is the help vector machine. SVM and support vector regression (SVR) found their scope in force estimation, finger motion recognition, and hand motion recognition. The identification rate using the SVM classification is found to be higher than other linear and non-linear classifications. The SVM uses various kernels such as linear, quadratic, and radial basis function (RBF) according to feature distribution of different classes. The technique in SVM classification is to locate a hyperplane which has extreme distance from all feature group or classes [42]. The kernel-based SVM classifier is extensively analyzed and proposed for EMG-based pattern recognition applications such as least-square SVM, SVM using a linear function, and Gaussian function (RBF kernel)–based SVM. More often, SVM is playing a significant role in EMG-PR–based systems and generally achieving more classification accuracy than 80%.

8.3.3.3   Neural Network (NN)

Classification methods based on the Neural Network are becoming more common nowadays. The performance of NN-based classification methods showed a strong advantage over other counterparts. Renowned NN-based techniques include feed forward-and back-spread (FFBP), intense learning machines (ILM), coevolutionary neural network (CNN), and recurrent neural network (RNN). These techniques have received an amazing deal of prominence and achieved a higher classification accuracy of approximately 90% or more. The drawbacks of the NN-based method are the possibility of sampling overfitting to the training model. In order to prevent over-fixing, rigorous training is required, which can contribute to increased time consumption [43–47]. It is considered that the use of an instant EMG signal for a pattern recognition model is not successful for pattern classification.

8.3.3.4   Random Forest (RF)

In the RF classifier, the class selection is rendered by the number of trees allocated to a given class. It is often referred to as "ensemble learning" and is made up of various trees. It is a supervised learning system that is efficient enough to perform closed to "SVM" and "NN" classification algorithms [44]. The RF classification system has done better with higher classification rate and decreased processing time compared to ANN, MLR, and SVM. In another analysis performed by Atzori et al. [42], pattern encoding is used. A similar classification is performed via a deep convolution network as compared to the RF.

8.4   Smart Navigation Assistance

Smart navigation for wheelchair includes intelligent and autonomous maneuvers. It makes the wheelchair suitable for disabled people, especially those with severe brain injury or loss of the upper limbs. Some smart wheelchairs are developed to function just like an autonomous robot. The user feeds the information of the destination via a touch panel; the chair analyzes the path and execute the command to reach the desired goal. It is made possible by integrating the wheelchair with an autonomous robot vehicle technology [20]. The robot's computer make use of information from three lidar sensors to make a map. A localization algorithm then determines where it is on the map. The stability is provided by the six wheels of the chair, and it is designed to make sharp turns and pass through normal-sized doorframes [40]. The various decisions made during a maneuver are based on different algorithms. For instance, the collision detector avoids obstacles by detecting the possibility of frontal collisions and changes the route or stops the wheelchair. If a specific sized object is in the path of the wheelchair, then the control system prevents the motion in the direction; Path planner: it uses the visual odometer that produces an optimal approach to the specific destination. All the deviations and the upcoming turns are analyzed by the path planner using the preloaded map and the initial position estimate.

Another algorithm developed by Tomari *et al.* in 2014 [41] works well in a crowded indoor environment. The algorithm analyzes and extracts information based on the observations of people's heads, skin pigmentation, and range images. The initial estimation of the head positions, orientation, and range data help the wheelchair decide to move among humans. Jain *et al.* in 2014 [42] presented a safe docking concept. It includes the automated detection of docking locations such as rectangular or circular structures (tables, desk, etc.) using 3D point cloud data alignment information. The safe docking locations can be fed to the intelligent path planner to navigate to the desired location autonomously. Combining various algorithms, data from the sensors and visual cameras can result in smart, automated maneuvers through different terrains, and not limited to the indoor environment.

8.5   Internet of Things (IoT)–Enabled Monitoring

The rapid growth of cyberspace technology and its connectivity for physical devices and everyday objects have gained a lot of focus in the past few years. The existing techniques, such as wireless sensors, control systems, embedded systems, and machine learning, enable the IoT to be used daily. The application of IoT can be utilized for smart wheelchair applications [43]. Sensors such as pulse plethysmography (PPG), oxygen saturation (SpO_2), temperature, and heart rate monitoring can be directly utilized in a smart wheelchair for remote monitoring of human health [44]. IoT can provide an appropriate and efficient solution for a doctor to maintain a track record of patients and monitor them regularly. The framework of IoT-enabled smart wheelchair is shown in Figure 8.10. The sensor nodes are fixed on the resting arm's place of the wheelchair and can send body parameters through Bluetooth to the mobile gateway. The Wi-Fi–enabled mobile can be able to send this data in the cloud where the machine learning

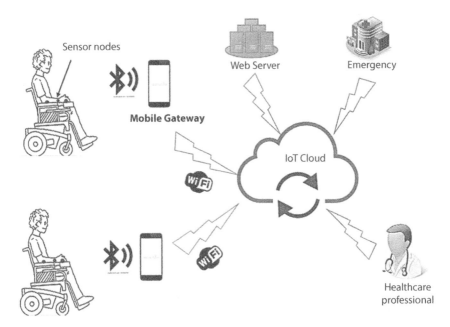

Figure 8.10 IoT-enabled wheelchair connected with different modules and central IoT cloud network.

algorithm is utilized. Further, this data can be saved in the server for future analysis purposes [45]. Through tracking the condition in real-time using a mobile medical system linked to a mobile app, connected devices can collect medical and other necessary health data and use a smartphone network link to pass the collected information to a physician.

8.6   Future Advancements in Smart Wheelchairs

Undoubtedly, smart wheelchairs cannot replace human caregivers. However, they can help disabled people to lead a better self-independent life in all environments. Overall, people are opening and adjusting to using an artificial intelligence (AI)–based robotic wheelchair to perform day-to-day tasks. Their lives could become much more comfortable now that AI could open doors to people moving their wheelchairs using facial expressions. Well, the technology to make this happen is being developed by Brazil-based company Hoobox Robotics. It has teamed up with technology company Intel to create Wheelie 7. Wheelie 7 is a kit based on AI that allows a person to move the wheelchair-using 10 facial expressions.

These expressions involve moving the eyebrows, a full smile, half-smile, blowing a kiss, sticking out the tongue, blowing cheeks, chin movement, and wrinkling the face. A user's expressions can be fed to the kit and are then linked to the wheelchair movements via an app. The kit can be installed in just seven minutes, and it is ready for use. There are many situations where only facial expressions/eyes retain movement, and the person loses control over the rest of his body. Even when the brain is functioning absolutely fine. This AI wheelchair will be a disruptive product for sure and breathe in life-giving oxygen for people who are locked forever by their disabilities [46]. However, the control will need to be improved because facial movements might not be very pointed and accurate. Also, the product needs to be scalable, so it is affordable and has the maximum reach. When a person moves, he exists. Bedridden life is tough and the wheelchair can be of immense assistance to people with spinal injuries and those with very restricted physical movements [47–49]. When it comes to old age, our old people need to be supervised for their wellbeing and welfare. They are at considerable risk of crashing due to fatigue and damaged joints [48]. Now, it is necessary to know if an older person has collapsed so that he/she can be rescued on time. People in a wheelchair also ought to be tested for fall detection [50]. We suggest a smart fall detection system for this reason. An accelerometer and a gyro-sensor to track individual motions, it can be placed on a person's hand or wheelchair for tracking. The sensor is attached to the microcontroller to continuously relay the acceleration data [51]. Now, the machine keeps track of fall detection and sudden change in movement in person.

Indeed, it is early days yet for this innovative technology but what is heartening to see is the work being done toward developing more and more accessible assistive technologies so people with disabilities can lead independent lives.

References

1. Stanfill, C.J. and Jensen, J.L., Effect of wheelchair design on wheeled mobility and propulsion efficiency in less-resourced settings. *Afr. J. Disabil.*, 6, 342, 2017.
2. Leary, M., Gruijters, J., Mazur, M., Subic, A., Burton, M., Fuss, F.K., A fundamental model of quasi-static wheelchair biomechanics. *Med. Eng. Phys.*, 34, 9, 1278–86, 2012.
3. De Groot, S., De Bruin, M., Noomen, S.P., Van Der Woude, L.H., Mechanical efficiency and propulsion technique after 7 weeks of low-intensity wheelchair training. *Clin. Biomech. (Bristol, Avon)*, 23, 4, 434–41, 2008.

4. Van der Woude, L.H., Bouw, A., Van Wegen, J., Van As, H., Veeger, D., De Groot, S., Seat height: Effects on submaximal hand rim wheelchair performance during spinal cord injury rehabilitation. *J. Rehabil. Med.*, 41, 3, 143–49, 2009.

5. Van der Woude, L.H., Hendrich, K.M., Veeger, H.E., Van Ingen Schenau, G.J., Rozendal, R.H., de Groot, G., Hollander, A.P., Manual wheelchair propulsion: Effects of power output on physiology and technique. *Med. Sci. Sports Exerc.*, 20, 1, 70–78, 1988.

6. Veeger, H.E., Van der Woude, L.H., Rozendal, R.H., Effect of handrim velocity on mechanical efficiency in wheelchair propulsion. *Med. Sci. Sports Exerc.*, 24, 1, 100–107, 1992.

7. Van der Linden, M.L., Valent, L., Veeger, H.E., Van der Woude, L.H., The effect of wheelchair handrim tube diameter on propulsion efficiency and force application (tube diameter and efficiency in wheelchairs). *IEEE Trans. Rehabil. Eng.*, 4, 3, 123–32, 1996.

8. Dallmeijer, A.J., Van der Woude, L.H., Veeger, H.E., Hollander, A.P., Effectiveness of force application in manual wheelchair propulsion in persons with spinal cord injuries. *Am. J. Phys. Med. Rehabil.*, 77, 3, 213–21, 1998.

9. Vegter, R.J., Lamoth, C.J., de Groot, S., Veeger, D.H., Van der Woude, L.H., Variability in bimanual wheelchair propulsion: Consistency of two instrumented wheels during handrim wheelchair propulsion on a motor driven treadmill. *J. Neuroeng. Rehabil.*, 10, 9, 2013.

10. Rodgers, M.M., McQuade, K.J., Rasch, E.K., Keyser, R.E., Finley, M.A., Upper-limb fatigue-related joint power shifts in experienced wheelchair users and nonwheelchair users. *J. Rehabil. Res. Dev.*, 40, 1, 27–37, 2003.

11. Mortenson, W.B., Hammell, K.W., Luts, A., Soles, C., Miller, W.C., The power of power wheelchairs: Mobility choices of community-dwelling, older adults. *Scand. J. Occup. Ther.*, 22, 5, 394–401, 2015.

12. T. Toshio, Solar assist-type electric wheelchair. Japan Patent JP2004–167022, assigned to Fujisawashi Sangyo Shinko Zaid, 2002.

13. Melanson, D., *Solar-powered wheelchair*, Engadget, New York (NY), http://www.engadget.com, 2006.

14. Messenger, S., *Man to travel 200 miles in solar-powered wheelchair*, Treehugger, Toronto (Canada), http://www.treehugger.com/cars/man-to-travel-200-miles-in-solar-powered-wheelchair.html, 2010.

15. Curram, A.M., Ramana Rao, P.S., Dontikurti, R., Solar powered wheel chair: Mobility for physically challenged. *Int. J. Curr. Eng. Technol.*, 2, 11, 211–14, 2012.

16. Nguyen, C.V. *et al.*, Hybrid Solar-RF Energy Harvesting Systems for Electric Operated Wheelchairs. *Electronics*, 9, 5, 752, 2020.

17. Fehr, L., Langbein, W.E., Skaar, S.B., Adequacy of power wheelchair control interfaces for persons with severe disabilities: a clinical survey. *J. Rehabil. Res. Dev.*, 37, 3, 353–60, 2000.

18. Hartman, A. and Nandikolla, V.K., Human Machine Interface for a Smart Wheelchair, Multiple Autonomous Robots Coordination and Navigation. *Journal of Robotics*, vol. 2019, Special Issue, 11, 2019.

19. Leaman, J. and La, H.M., A Comprehensive Review of Smart Wheelchairs: Past, Present, and Future. *IEEE Trans. Hum.-Mach. Syst.*, 47, 4, 486–499, 2017.

20. Gottipati, P., Dobzhanskyi, O., Mendrela, E.A., In-wheel brushless DC motor for a wheel chair drive. *IEEE Joint International Conference on Power Electronics, Drives and Energy Systems & 2010 Power India*, New Delhi, pp. 1–4, 2010.

21. Huang, C. *et al.*, Determination of modeling parameters for a brushless DC motor that satisfies the power performance of an electric vehicle. *Meas. Control*, 52, 765–774, 2019.

22. Bhatnagar, A. and Janyani, V., Cost Effective and High-Power Conversion Efficiency Ultra-Thin Film GaAs Solar Cell. *IEEE International Conference on Computer, Communications and Electronics (Comptelix)*, Jaipur, pp. 516–520, 2017.

23. Bhatnagar, A. and Janyani, V., Enhancing absorption in thin film organometal trihalide perovskite solar cell by photon recycling. *Adv. Mater. Lett.*, 9, 10, 721–726, 2018.

24. Zhu, R. *et al.*, Advanced materials for flexible solar cell applications. *Nanotechnol. Rev.*, 8, 1, 2191–9097, 2019.

25. Bhatnagar, A. *et al.*, Performance analysis of thin film CIGS solar cell at different values of thickness, bandgap and temperature through numerical simulation. *Proc. SPIE Nanoengineering: Fabrication, Properties, Optics, Thin Films, and Devices XVII*, San Diego, 2020.

26. Lee, T.D. and Ebong, A.U., A review of thin film solar cell technologies and challenges. *Renewable Sustainable Energy Rev.*, 70, 1286–97, 2017.

27. Bhatnagar, A. *et al.*, Photon recycling for improved absorption in thin film ITO/INP heterojunction solar cell. *J. Crit. Rev.*, 7, 19, 8836–8844, 2020.

28. Babaa, S.E., El Murr, G., Mohamed, F., Pamuri, S., Overview of boost converters for photovoltaic systems. *J. Power Energy Eng.*, 6, 16–31, 2018.

29. Hasaneen, B. and Mohammed, A.A.E., Design and simulation of DC/DC boost converter. *12th International Middle-East Power System Conference*, Aswan, Egypt, 12–15 March 2008.

30. Pancholi, S. and Joshi, A.M., Portable EMG data acquisition module for upper limb prosthesis application. *IEEE Sens. J.*, 18, 8, 3436–3443, 2018.

31. Kundu, A.S., Mazumder, O., Lenka, P.K., Bhaumik, S., Hand gesture recognition based omnidirectional wheelchair control using IMU and EMG sensors. *J. Intell. Rob. Syst.*, 91, 3–4, 529–541, 2018.

32. Pancholi, S. and Joshi, A.M., Electromyography-based hand gesture recognition system for upper limb amputees. *IEEE Sens. Lett.*, 3, 3, 1–4, 2019.

33. Kundu, A.S., Mazumder, O., Lenka, P.K., Bhaumik, S., Omnidirectional assistive wheelchair: design and control with isometric myoelectric based intention classification. *Proc. Comput. Sci.*, 105, 68–74, 2017.

34. Pancholi, S. and Joshi, A.M., Time derivative moments based feature extraction approach for recognition of upper limb motions using EMG. *IEEE Sens. Lett.*, 3, 4, 1–4, 2019.

35. Pancholi, S. and Joshi, A.M., Improved Classification Scheme using Fused Wavelet Packet Transform based Features for Intelligent Myoelectric Prostheses. *IEEE Trans. Ind. Electron.*, 67, 8517–8525, 2019.

36. Pancholi, S. and Agarwal, R., Development of low cost EMG data acquisition system for Arm Activities Recognition, in: *International Conference on Advances in Computing, Communications and Informatics (ICACCI)*, pp. 2465–2469, 2016.

37. Pancholi, S., Jain, P., Varghese, A., A Novel Time-Domain based Feature for EMG-PR Prosthetic and Rehabilitation Application, in: *2019 41st Annual International Conference of the IEEE Engineering in Medicine and Biology Society (EMBC)*, pp. 5084–5087, 2019.

38. Atzori, M., Cognolato, M., Müller, H., Deep learning with convolutional neural networks applied to electromyography data: A resource for the classification of movements for prosthetic hands. *Front. Neurorob.*, 10, 9, 20162016.

39. Pancholi, S. and Agarwal, R., Development of low cost EMG data acquisition system for Arm Activities Recognition, in: *International Conference on Advances in Computing, Communications and Informatics (ICACCI)*, pp. 2465–2469, 2016.

40. Hartman, A., Gillberg, R., Lin, C.T., Nandikolla, V.K., Design and development of an autonomous robotic wheelchair for medical mobility. *International Symposium on Medical Robotics (ISMR)*, Atlanta, GA, pp. 1–6, 2018.

41. Tomari, M., Kobayashi, Y., Kuno, Y., Enhancing Wheelchair's Control Operation of a Severe Impairment User, in: *8th International Conference on Robotic, Vision, Signal Processing & Power Applications: Innovation Excellence Towards Humanistic Technology*, Malaysia, pp. 65–72, Springer, 2014.

42. Jain, S. and Argall, B., Automated perception of safe docking locations with alignment information for assistive wheelchairs, in: *International Conference on Intelligent Robots and Systems (IROS)*, Chicago IL, USA, pp. 4997–03, 2014.

43. Rashid, Z., Melià-Seguí, J., Pous, R., Peig, E., Using Augmented Reality and Internet of Things to improve the accessibility of people with motor disabilities in the context of Smart Cities. *Future Gener. Comput. Syst.*, 76, 248–261, 2017.

44. Yang L., Li W., Ge Y., Fu X., Gravina R., Fortino G., People-Centric Service for mHealth of Wheelchair Users in Smart Cities. In: Fortino G., Trunfio P. (eds) Internet of Things Based on Smart Objects. Internet of Things (Technology, Communications and Computing). Springer, Cham, Switzerland, 2014.

45. Jagadish, B., Mishra, P.K., Kiran, M.P.R.S., Rajalakshmi, P., A real-time health 4.0 framework with novel feature extraction and classification for brain-controlled iot-enabled environments. *Neural Comput.*, 31, 10, 1915–1944, 2019.

46. Hoobox one: https://hoobox.one, 2020.

47. Pancholi, S. and Joshi, A.M., Advanced Energy Kernel-Based Feature Extraction Scheme for Improved EMG-PR-Based Prosthesis Control Against Force Variation. *IEEE Trans. Cybern.*, vol. 50, 1–10, 2020.

48. Kanani, P. and Padole, M., IoT based Eye Movement Guided Wheelchair driving control using AD8232 ECG Sensor. *Int. J. Recent Technol. Eng.*, 8, 4, 5013–5017, 2019.

49. Waheed, S.A. and Khader, P.S.A., December. A novel approach for smart and cost effective IoT based elderly fall detection system using Pi camera, in: *IEEE International Conference on Computational Intelligence and Computing Research (ICCIC)*, pp. 1–4, 2017.

50. Nayak, S.S., Gupta, P., Upasana, A.B.W., Wani, A.B., Wheel Chair with Health Monitoring System Using IoT. *Int. Res. J. Eng. Technol. (IRJET)*, 4, 05, 1063–1067, 2017.

51. Zeadally, S. and Bello, O., Harnessing the power of Internet of Things based connectivity to improve healthcare. *Internet Things*, 6, 100074, 2019.

9

Hand-Talk Assistance: An Application for Hearing and Speech Impaired People

Pradnya Borkar¹, Vijaya Balpande², Ujjwala Aher³ and Roshani Raut⁴

¹Department of Computer Science and Engineering, Jhulelal Institute of Technology, Nagpur, India
²Department of Computer Science and Engineering, Priyadarshini J.L. College of Engineering, Nagpur, India
³Department of Computer Science and Engineering, Government Polytechnic, Sakoli, India
⁴Department of Computer Science and Engineering, Pimpri Chinchwad College of Engineering, Pune, India

Abstract

In daily life, disabled persons who are deaf and mute may find it difficult to communicate in society. Some innovative technologies are needed to help mute people communicate with others. There are various technologies that may be used for hearing. The main source of communication is through hand gestures. The hearing person is unable to understand the hand gestures using sign language. Therefore, a technology is required to convert the sign language into audible voice to be understood by hearing people. This chapter describes the hand gesture hearing technology that provides how deaf people will communicate with hearing people. This technology uses the glove with special sensors. The mute person must wear the glove on his or her hand, and as the mute person does various movements by moving hand using sign language, the device intercepts the movement and smartly converts it into voice so that the hearing person can easily understand. The flex sensor pads attached in the glove are useful to sense the movements by detecting various patterns of motion and the pattern in which the curves are made by fingers. The device is designed smartly to sense every resistance and every action carried out by the hands. This chapter also describes the various applications and techniques that may be helpful for the hearing and speech impaired.

*Corresponding author: pradnyaborkar2@gmail.com

Roshani Raut, Pranav Pathak, Sandeep Kautish and Pradeep N (eds.) Intelligent Systems for Rehabilitation Engineering, (197–222) © 2022 Scrivener Publishing LLC

Keywords: Hearing and speech impaired, sign language, flex sensor, glove-based system, hand gesture, Hand-Talk assistance

9.1   Introduction

People can have a conversation with each other by exchanging thoughts and ideas. Ideas can be effectively represented through speech. For those who are unable to communicate verbally, they communicate with each other through sign language only. The downside of sign language is restricted to the limited people who are often unable to communicate verbally and, therefore, fall into the category of hearing and speech impaired people.

Individuals who are physically impaired have the privilege to choose what they want to be addressed, either as a community or personally. The persons who are unable to hear prefer to be referred to as "autistic" or "deaf" or "hearing impaired" or "dumb" [1]. Other organizations along with Deaf National Association who are dealing with deaf people use the word "deaf and hard to hear" for these people. Though there are people who use the term other than "deaf and hard to hear", it is declared as official designation in 1991 by the World Federation of the Deaf (WFD).

The following terminologies are used for hearing and speech impaired people:

- Hearing-Impaired: A term a lot of most popular by hearing folks, for the most part as a result of they read it as correctness. "Hearing-impaired" is a meaningful word that is a lot of resented by deaf and unable to hear people. Deaf and hard to hear people believe like the words "deaf" and "hard to hear" do not appear to be derogatory in any way.

  ☐ Deaf and Dumb: A legacy from the medieval English period, this may be the granddad of all misleading marks attached to deaf and hard-hearing people. The Greek philosopher and poet, Aristotle, called himself "hearing and speech impaired" as a result of his feeling that deaf people were unable to be educated, to read, and to think rationally.
  ☐ Deaf-Mute: Another derogatory word "mute" which means silent together and without a sound rises in the 18th to 19th century. This mark is scientifically incorrect, because the vocal cord of deaf and unable to hear people is working. The point is that your voice is modulated with success; you want to be able to hear your voice.

9.1.1   Sign Language

The communication language between those who are able-bodied and those that are disabled is the sign language. To promote understanding between people, language relies on sign patterns, such as visual contact, orientation, and arm movements. In all, 9.1 billion people were hearing and speech impaired all over the world. They dealt with a slew of additional contact problems in their daily lives. Speech-impaired people use language for the communication. Sign languages include a variety of signals and objects to communicate. They often represent a combination of words and symbols [2].

Sign languages have evolved and are measured at the center of native deaf cultures wherever deaf communities exist. While the deaf use linguistic communication the most, it is often used by others, such as those who can hear but cannot physically talk or have difficulty speaking due to another disability (augmentative and different communication). The vocabulary and descriptive linguistics of sign language differ from country to country. Even within the world, sign language, like spoken languages, varies from region to region.

9.1.1.1   American Sign Language (ASL)

ASL (American linguistic communication) is an intricate language which uses signs formed by hands movement in conjunction with expressions of face and body pose. This is the first language of several hearing-impaired people in North America, and it is one of the communication channels used among people who are visually impaired. The dominant sign language among deaf communities in the United States and most of Northern American hearing-impaired people is ASL. Besides the North America, ASL dialects and ASL-based creoles are spoken in a majority of countries around the world, such as West Africa and Southeast Asia. As a second language, ASL is widely practiced and being used for linguistic communication. The most highly associated marking languages are ASL and French Sign Language. It has been speculated that ASL may have been the Creole language of LSF, regardless of the fact that ASL has properties that are not found in Creole languages, such as agglutinative morphology [3].

9.1.1.2   Comparison of ASL With Verbal Language

Words are created by the use of mouth and speech to form sounds in voice communication.

However, speech sounds are also not perceived by those who are deaf (especially those who are profoundly autistic), and only a fraction of speech sounds are audible on the lips. The belief that vision is the most useful

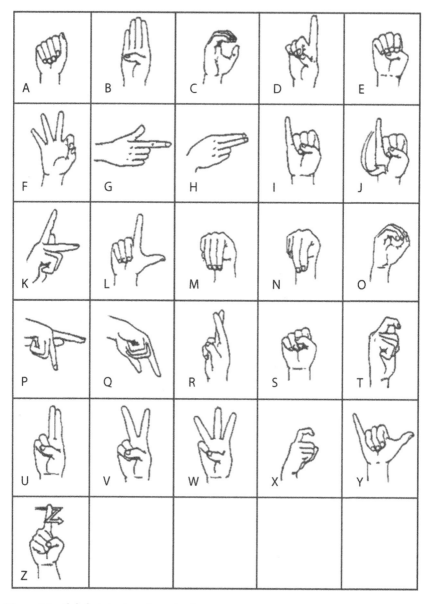

Figure 9.1 Alphabets in American sign language.

thing a person with a disability has to communicate and collect information has been reiterated.

In comparison with English, ASL is a completely new language. It observes that it have its own rules for accent, order of word, and composite grammar, as well as variety of ways of representing various functions, such as instead of an announcement, ask a question. The way this is usually done varies by language. English speakers, for example, lift their voice pitch to ask a question; Users of ASL lift their eyebrows, open their pupils, and turn their bodies forward to express their questions. Basic conduct of communicating thoughts in ASL, like alternative languages, varies as often as ASL users. In addition to voice variations in persons, ASL has regionwise pronunciation and language conversation. Regional variations in ASL singing rhythm, style, and pronunciation exist, despite the fact that bound English words are spoken differently in various parts of the world [4, 5]. Apart from origin and age, there are a slew of other variables that influence ASL use and selection. The alphabet letters in signing is depicted in Figure 9.1.

Like alphabets, gestures are defined for some actions also. Figure 9.2 shows some more combinations of actions.

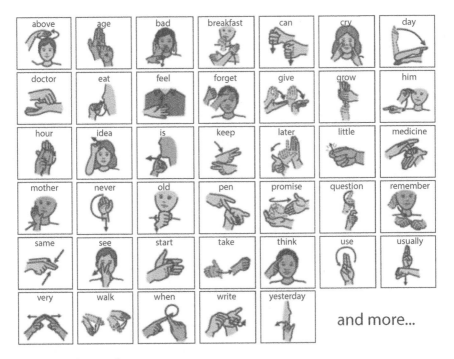

Figure 9.2 Gestures for movements.

9.1.2 Recognition of Hand Gesture

A gestural movement is described as a communicative movement of body parts. Finger curls and bends produce gestures, which are completely unique postures. Communication is done by gestures. Gestures are a basic prerequisite for developing this device as an input. Hand gestures are of two types: static and dynamic [6].

- Static: Hand gestures that are not dependent on motion and are fixed in time are known as static hand gestures.
- Dynamic: Dynamic hand movements are timed hand movements that include the movement of part of your hand. These motions involve movement that is accompanied by a mechanical phenomenon that forms the motion.

9.1.3 Different Techniques for Sign Language Detection

The invention of a system that converts sign language to speech has narrowed the gap between hearing-impaired persons and traditional or normal persons. There are two types of systems such as glove-based and vision-based used to translate sign language into speech.

9.1.3.1 Glove-Based Systems

An individual's signals during contact are passed to the computer system by wearing gloves on the hands when developing glove-based systems. The information already stored in the database, which was generated initially by storing all types of signs, is compared with the real-time sign. The information gets converted to text and sent to the sound convertor system, in which the data is processed to produce the desired sound [7].

9.1.3.2 Vision-Based Systems

In this system, mostly, a camera is used to map the person's hand gesture, and then, model matching is performed using feature extraction. It is more complicated than a glove-based system.

Hearing and speech impaired people have always found it difficult to communicate with one another, but they have devised a solution in the form of sign language. Hearing and speech impaired people have a hard time interacting with others. In order to communicate with each choice, each must be able to communicate in the target language, which is often a difficult task. Normal people may connect with hearing and speech impaired people, but it is observed that they feel it difficult to communicate since they are unfamiliar with all of the signs and terminologies [8]. A hearing or speech impaired person's natural speech speed is quicker than a normal person's when they learn sign language. In the middle, there should be a method.

9.2 Related Work

Some developers have tried to resolve the problems of hearing and speech impaired people [9] by introducing text to audio converters, interpreters for sign language, and other tools. It has been discovered that there is no single application that combines all of these functions.

Here are some of the applications that have been addressed.

1. Computerized Interpreter [10]: The aim of this application was to create a system that would improve communication quality for hearing and speech impaired people. Human-Computer Interaction and Computer-Human Interaction are two-way communication systems. The two basic processes that this system was designed to carry out are as follows.

   □ The sign language gesture is used to recognize the input voice signal and the pictorial representation that goes with it.
   □ A corresponding voice is created as an output by recording the hand gesture.

2. Hearing-Impaired Graphical Speech Training System [10]: This application addresses an advanced and Interactive graphic voice training application for hearing-impaired people that have been shown to be cost effective. In the absence of a speech therapist, this computer-based technology often assists autistic children in learning and practicing speaking skills, as well as enhancing responsiveness in deaf children, which helps them to learn and regulate muscular-based activities, which is critical to generate understandable speech for their vocal organs

3. Vision-Based Technological Approach: The gesture game is addressed in [11], which was created for deaf people and

uses Microsoft Kinect to recognize gesture commands and translate them to text. Another method, called VOM (Voice for the Mute), was developed. This method takes finger spelling as input and translates it into text. In [12], camera was used to create the finger spelling images. The finger spelling is compared to the qualified dataset after image processing and noise reduction. The corresponding text was then translated into voice.

In [13], the author explored the different forms of deaf societies, which were then discussed in [14, 15].

1. Hard-of-hearing people: These individuals are partly deaf but can hear. These individuals are also known as culturally marginalized individuals.
2. Culturally deaf people: These people can come from a deaf family and uses sign language as their mean mode of communication. It is possible that their speech clarity would be impaired.
3. Congenital or prelingual deaf people: Congenital or prelingual deafness refers to deaf people who are born deaf or who are deaf before they learn to speak. Signs may or may not be used by these people to communicate.
4. Orally educated or prelingual deaf populace: Deaf people who have been orally taught, also known as prelingual deaf people, were born deaf but gained speech skills later in life.
5. Late deafened adults: Adults who have been deaf for a long period of time, these individuals will be able to cope with their gradual hearing loss using communication strategies.

9.3 History and Motivation

Cameras, photographic, infrared, and other imaging devices have been used extensively in this field. To grasp all of these works, you will need a screen in front of you. Recognized hand gestures are another choice. Piezo-resistive sensors can now be used in the design due to technical advances. These sensors are also known as flex sensors because they measure bending. The majority of these sensors can be located in the fingertips. Two biomedical applications for these interfaces are hand prostheses and gesture vocalization. Robotic tele-operation and human-computer interaction tools will also benefit from these interfaces. As a result, an efficient technique for embedding flex sensors in a wearing glove is needed in order to improve sensor accuracy and integrity [16].

9.4   Types of Sensors

In the past, various methods to gesture recognition were used. Vision-based and glove-based methods, as well as colored marker approaches, are the most commonly used gesture recognition technologies. A laptop camera or machine camera is used as the data input device in vision-based techniques to capture information outfitted by various hand and finger movements. The correct locations of hand movements are retrieved in glove-based systems by using data gloves, since their positions are explicitly measured.

9.4.1   Flex Sensor

Flexion sensors, also known as bend sensors, counted how many deflections were caused by bending the sensing device, or sensor (from Latin flectere, "to bend"). Strain gauges1 and hall-effect sensors are two examples of ways to detect deflection [17].

The flexion sensors are of three types:

1. Ink-based conductive
2. Fiber optic
3. Polymer-based conductive

Bend sensing components have an interesting property: bending them to a certain angle at one point cannot be considered as the most helpful use of sensor. The sensor will be permanently damaged or affected if the sensing element is bent more than 90° at one point. Mixture Systems referred the parameter of sensing as "radius multiplied by flex angle". The sensing parameter was defined by Infusion Systems as "flex angle multiplied by radius".

9.4.1.1   Flex Sensor's Specification

Flex sensor is consists of basic specifications as follows:

- Deflection range
- Unit vs. bidirectional sensing
- Unit vs. bipolar sensing
- Resistance range (nominal to full-deflection)

Deflection Range: The limit or utmost deflection angle that will be evaluated is defined by the deflection range (as against the utmost sensor angle are often bent).

Unit vs. bidirectional sensing: Some of the flexion sensors raise confrontation when it is bent at any two opposite directions, but it is observed that there is no difference between measurement with orientation.

Unit vs. bipolar sensing: This bipolar flexion sensor deviates with two opposite indicators that produce different values.

Resistance range: Bend sensors may have a wide range of resistance (even within the same product) based on the difference between self-reported resistance and maximum resistance.

9.4.1.2   Flex Sensor Types

Conductive ink-based, fiber optic, and conductive fabric/thread/polymer are all examples of flex sensors.

9.4.1.2.1   Conductive Ink-Based

Such bending sensors are idle resistance tools that are usually made by placing on the lower flexible plastic a piece of opposing ink, shaped like a thin, flexible line with a length ranging from 1 to 5.

The bending sensor is defined by internal resistance and rest (when placed on the floor). The opposing elements inside it are pushed forward separately as the sensor is bent. Few neighboring particles are affected, thus increasing resistance. The automatic resistance is usually between 10k and 50k and rises to a maximum deviation by a factor of 10.

The pattern inscribed with the running ink is inside the flex sensor substrate's layers. This ink contains carbon, or silver, particles that are combined with a colored machine to make electricity. The particles of carbon are usually suspended in ink to prevent pigment from getting fade. Such ink is safe to use on paper to evade being absorbed by strings, thus altering paper structures. Most of bending sensors which are ink-based available in the market are unipolar alloys, which means that as the deviation rises on one side, the resistance increases and when curved on the other side, it is not altered.

Standing back and forth on two devices will allow bipolar measurement of deviation in both directions. Both of the levels, i.e., hysteresis as well as noise resistance are low; otherwise, they can be completely ignored.

Some flex point Sensors can be of 1", 2", and 3" long. They are provided with connectors that can be connected to standardized header's size. As soon as the length increases, the natural confrontation increases. There are also different ways to attach and cover to raise durability. Piezo-sensing sensors that work with large overlaps (angles angleshulu flex) but at high cost. An example is Bend Short v2.0 which senses bipolar deflection from −180° to +180° [18].

Features:

- High temperature and humidity tolerance
- Very low cost
- Custom (with glass, laminate equipments)

Applications:

- Vehicle applications
- Industrial applications, e.g., safety replacement, shipping, and machine control
- Medical applications (e.g., "Smart bed")
- Play equipment
- Measurement of devices
- Assistive technology
- Robots (e.g., ground map and collision detection)

9.4.1.2.2   Fiber Optic

Fiber optic bend sensors also called as optical goniometers contain a light resource (POF) fiber optical plastic with a thermal phase and photosensitive detector. The light is produced from POF on one side and is heard on another side. If the optical fiber bends, then it causes low intensity, i.e., loss of light occurs. This loss can be improved by cutting, polishing, or inserting part of POF5.

The bending sensor can also be made with fiber optic cable with LED and photodiode installed on both sides of the cable section.

Several products uses fiber-optic bend-sensing. Shape Tape, for example, creates completely localized data from the distortion and distortion of data using a series of fiber optic nerve pairs in rubber soles. Each sensor incorporates curvature and reported angular net difference (NAD).

Features:

- Mainly designed or built laboratory
- High recurrence, hysteresis is ignored
- It can bend in either direction

- Generally unit polar balancing (global flexion)
- It may be exclusive

Applications:

- Medical applications
- Educational courses

9.4.1.2.3   Conductive Fabric or Thread or Polymer-Based Sensor

Flexible fabric sensors and cord-based or polymer-based flexion sensors usually consist of double layer material with some opposing material (e.g., Velostat) in between. It is mainly wrapped in heavy layers of material, e.g., Neoprene. By bending or directly, if the pressure is applied, then the two layers of moving substance are pushed together and the sensory resistance decreases. This feeling is similar to strong emotional states. In fact, these types of nerves are pressure sensors that feel deviant, bending the sensor on a part of a solid structure causes the expansion of the nerve to the pressure of the nerve. This is a measure of pressure. Foam/polymer sensors reduce their resistance to name as the material is pressed. These nerves are characterized by abnormalities, recurrence, and hysteresis [19].

Features:

- Quasilent Equivalent Sensitive Behavior
- Low reply, due to disability (internal force)
- High hysteresis, irregularity and recurrence
- High temperature and humidity (can be used underwater)

Applications:

- Art projects

The flex sensor differs in resistance when it bends the analog values processed by the microcontroller.

Flex sensors (as shown in Figure 9.3) change resistance depending on the quantity of bending. Here is a Glove Sign Language Glove that will help those who experience any kind of communication problem using gestures, i.e., with the help of one sign language provided to you the user will perform gestures. The powerful sensor will record all movements made by the user and translate these actions into view mode using a program display, as well as audio form using a voice processor.

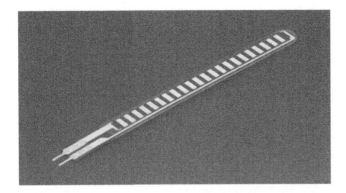

Figure 9.3 Flex sensors.

Usually, a needle and thread are used to attach with the flex sensors. They need a 5-volt input to operate and deliver output between 0 and 5 V. As the angle of bending of the sensor increases, the flexibility of the flexible sensor also increases. The sensor varies with the correct electrical power adjustment.

This change in resistance will be converted into a power conversion by connecting a flexible sensor to a separating circuit. The flex sensor is simply a resistance mechanism and its resistance depends on the width of the bend. Here is the construction of a separation network as shown in Figure 9.4 that may have two resistors. One is a flexible sensor and the other is a 10k resistor. It detects potential reductions in flexibility which means flex sensor and analog electrical power. Analog power is provided by ADC input pins for microcontroller. ADC converts the given analog value into appropriate digital values and stores in the memory of microcontroller. When the amount of electrical energy exceeds the limit value, it is known as input. Two or three sensors are attached in sequence and the sensor generates the output in analog

BASIC FLEX SENSOR CIRCUIT:

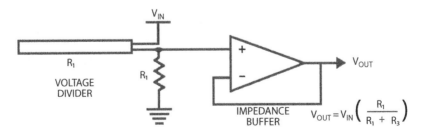

Figure 9.4 Base flex sensor circuit.

which is converted to digital using the digital converter in the controller. The results from the flexible sensors are integrated into the LM258/LM358 op-amps and used as a setup of a non-installed fashion to maximize their power. Too much bending reduces the effect [20].

In this application, glove is designed to hold the user's hand. The glove is equipped with sensors with the changing in length of each finger and thumb. Flexible sensors produce a stream of data according to the bending degree. Flex sensors will detect the bending of all fingers. Flex sensor's nerves are nerves that change resistance according to the nerve bending. They turn the transformation into an electrical resistance—the more you turn, the more resistant you are. Frequency is in line with a thin line from 1" to 5" of varying lengths of resistance. Here, the flexible sensor is used as a flexible conductor in the region that operates on the principle of a potentiometer that provides various gas energies as a separate resistant release. To measure the curvature of the fingers, flexible sensors are used.

9.4.1.2.4   Arduino Microcontroller

Arduino microcontroller as shown in Figure 9.5 controls all processes and sensory variables as well as Accelerometer.

Arduino Nano is designed for boards, which is based on ATmega328 (Arduino Nano 3.x). Almost the same applies to Arduino Duemilanove, but in somewhat different package. It simply has no DC power, and it uses Mini-B USB cable [21].

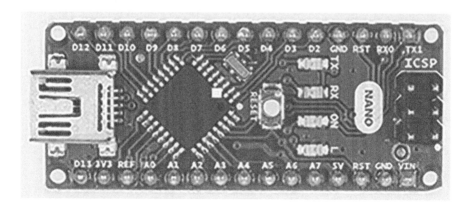

Figure 9.5 Arduino microcontroller.

9.4.1.2.4.1   Power

The Mini-B USB connector is used to power the Arduino Nano, an out-of-six controller (pin 30), or a 5-V outlet (i.e., pin 27). From the highest power source, the power source is selected.

9.4.1.2.4.2   Memory

Out of 32-KB memory of ATmega328, 2 KB is used for boot. Further, 2 KB is used for SRAM and 1 KB for EEPROM.

9.4.1.2.4.3   Installation and Removal

The input and output is carried out with help of 14 digital pins using the functions of pinMode (), digitalWrite (), and digitalRead (). It operate at 5 volts. Each pin works with a maximum of 40 mA and has an internal pulse, i.e., automatically disconnected of 20–50 kohms.

Some additional features are as follows:

- ☐ Series: [0 (RX) and 1 (TX)]: It receives (RX) and transfer (TX) TTL serial data. These pins are connected to the compatible connectors of the FTDI USB-to-TTL Serial chip.
- ☐ External disturbances: (2 and 3): These anchors can be adjusted to cause disruption of the lower value, ups and downs, or price fluctuations.
- ☐ PWM: (3, 5, 6, 9, 10, and 11): Provide 8-bit PWM output with functionality of analogWrite ().
- ☐ SPI: 10 (SS), 11 (MOSI), 12 (MISO), and 13 (SCK). These supports the SPI connection.
- ☐ LED: 13: A digital pin 13 is used to connect to the built-in LED. The LED is switched on, when the pin has high value and when the pin is FULL, LED is turned off. The total analog input pins are 8 for Nano, each of which provides 10 pieces of solution [e.g., automatically measuring from the ground up to 5 volts, but analog Reference () function can be used to change the full end of their range]. Analog anchors 6 and 7 cannot be used as a digital anchor. In addition, some anchors have special functions: I2C: 4 (SDA) and 5 (SCL). Connect the I2C (TWI) connection using the Wire library (documents on the Wiring website) I-AREF. Reliable power of analog input. Used with analog () reference. Reset. Bring this line to reset the controller. It is usually used to add a reset button to the blocking protection on the board.

9.4.1.2.4.4   COMMUNICATION

Arduino Nano has many computer connections. The serial connection is provided from ATmega328 for the UART TTL (5V), that is provided on digital pins 0 (RX) and 1 (TX).

The FTDI driver that is installed with Arduino software helps for USB communication with the help of FTDI and it provides a com port on computer software. A serial monitor allows the text data transmission to and from the Arduino board. The RX and TX LEDs on the board will light up during data transmission through FTDI chip and the USB connection to the computer.

Software Library allows serial communication on any digital Nano connector. ATmega328 also supports I2C (TWI) communication with SPI. Arduino software includes a Wire library to facilitate the use of the I2C bus. To use the SPI connection, please refer to the ATmega328 datasheet.

9.4.1.2.4.4.1   Default (Software) Reset

As an alternative of having need of material compression (reset button) previous to uploading, Arduino Nano is intended in such a means which accepts it to be reset through software executing on an associated computer. DTR of the FT232RL, one of the hardware controls is connected to the ATmega328 reset line with a 100 nanofarad capacitor. When this line is set (lowered), the reset line drops long enough to reset the chip.

Arduino software utilizes this skill to permit you to download code by just critically using the download button which is near to Arduino area. The boot loader may be short, as DTR reduction may be further intimately connected to loading start. This type of set of connections has other consequences. It resets every time a connection is complete from the software, when a Nano is associated to a computer by means of Linux or Mac OS X. In the second part, the boot loader is trying to work on the Nano.

When new code upload starts, it schedules to ignore the random data upload; once the connection is open, it starts sending the first byte of data to the board. If the drawing uses one time or another data when you start, be sure to have the interactive software wait a while before sending this data once the connection has been reopened.

In recent years, the use of Arduino has increased dramatically due to its readability and simplicity. But the point is to consider whether the use of Arduino is preferred by engineers or not. First, we will look at the benefits of Arduino, and later, we will discuss the disadvantages. Yes there could be evil in Mighty Arduino too [22].

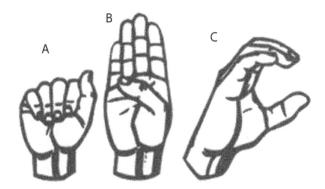

Figure 9.6 American sign language symbols.

9.5   Working of Glove

Capturing hand gestures of the user is the main motto behind the design of this glove. Flex sensors are used to fit inside the glove and this glove is designed to fit depending on the length of thumb as well as each finger. The generated output is the stream which gives the data stream as per the bend of flex sensors. The output generated from the sensors which are in analog format is then fed to the microcontroller. The conversion from analog to digital takes place by processing the signals. The recognition of gesture is carried out after this conversion and the text related to this are spotted out. The sign of particular alphabets should be known to the user. When there is introduction of new sign, it must be added in the database and supported by system.

The flex sensors are attached depends upon the length of the fingers and thumb. The finger's and thumb's bending degree generates variation in output voltage which then turned out to voice after converting the analog signals. Likewise, the gloves help speech and hearing impaired people to interact with others in the specified language.

As shown in Figure 9.6, every character and word has a predefined pattern of finger and palm combination. In this chapter, the identification of this pattern or combinations is discussed.

9.5.1   Hand Gloves

As shown in Figure 9.7, the microcontroller and flex sensors are integrated on the gloves. The jumping cables are used to attach these sensors with microcontroller.

Proposed Hardware

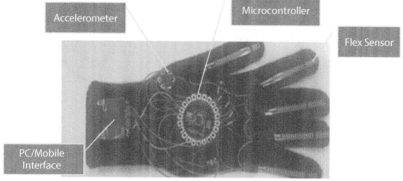

Figure 9.7 Hand gloves.

9.5.2 Implementation Details at Server Side

9.5.2.1 Training Mode

Training mode is provided for the user to interact and to update database. Flexibility of insertion of new pattern in database can be done in training mode. As shown in Figure 9.8, First, entered pattern values are checked whether it is already present in database or not. If entered value is already

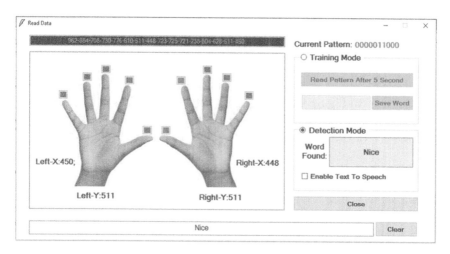

Figure 9.8 Training mode.

present, then it gives message accordingly; otherwise, it save that word in database.

As shown in Figure 9.8, initially, the color of all fingers will be green, after bending the right thumb and index finger of right hand, the color was changed and becomes red. The string appears as 0000011000. The string which is appeared on the screen is already stored in the database for the word "Nice". After identifying word, text was converted into speech. Some threshold value need to set to identity the bending of the fingers. So, the threshold is set as 750 kohms, i.e., if the threshold value of flex sensors is found to be greater than 750 kohms, then it specify that the flex sensor is not bent, but if the threshold is less than 750 kohms, then it shows bending of flex sensors and the signal turns to red.

9.5.2.2 Detection Mode

In detection mode, the pattern is used to compare to a previously saved pattern in the database by using the microcontroller's input and a combination of those inputs. If the pattern is found in the database, then it will be marked as available; otherwise, it will be marked as unavailable.

9.5.2.3 Text to Speech

After detection, the text-to-speech conversion takes place and this detected word get converted into audible format. Here, the following steps are followed.

Sign □ Word □ Speech.

Microsoft Windows operating system provides an application program interface (API) called as SAPI (Speech Application Program Interface). This API allows the speech recognition capabilities, and it allows to write the program that provides text-to-speech conversion. SAPI has the following main modules:

1. **Voice Command:** For applications, this module offers command for control speech recognition. This module facilitates to build a menu of voice commands that includes voice commands such as new file and send mail. After enabling the module, the user would be able to use the device without using a keyboard or mouse.

2. **Dictation of Voice:** This module helps a user to dictate voice through a speech recognition program. The virtual editor box receives and shows the text that the user dictates

in an application window. This module allows you to format text in a variety of ways, including converting punctuation words to punctuation marks, modifying the case of letters in the alphabet, and correcting the last word spoken or a set of words.

3. **Voice Text:** Voice Text translates text into speech that can be listened to on a device or sent over the internet. There are several different types of speech being played, each with a different accent.

4. **Voice Telephony:** This module makes use of telephony controls that are close to those used in Windows. The controls on a window are made up of keys, sliders, list boxes, and other items that can be moved around with the help of mouse or keyboard. Some other codes called as Telephony controls identifies spoken answers like Yes or No, other details such as time, date as well as phone number. Telephony controls enable the user to communicate with the device. For example, when user calls a vendor to order an item. The user want to know about several things by speaking into the telephone receiver. Instead of processing these manually, these responses are recognized by telephony controls and these responses are transferred to the processing response applications. This module also manages error conditions.

5. **Direct Speech Recognition:** This interface is somewhat same to the voice command at low level. The difference is that this module directly speaks to the speech engine.

6. **Direct Text To Speech:** This interface is similar to voice-text and it also speaks directly to search engine.

7. **Audio Objects:** Specifically, where there is audio, it is done by an audio object.

9.6   Architecture

Figure 9.9a shows the architecture of the overall system, the left and right hand glove connected with microcontroller, the microcontroller connected with server, and on other hand, server is also connected with software of pattern matching (including database).

To recognize the alphabets of sign language, the flowchart depicts the steps as shown in Figure 9.10. Once the device is switched on, the sensors are regulated and the microcontroller receives the readings from the sensors.

Depending on the values generated by bending the glove, that value is matched with the values stored in the database. If it is matched, then the related word is displayed and accordingly it is spoken out. In the training mode, the user can insert new patterns in the database, whenever that pattern is inserted, it is first checked in the database whether it is already

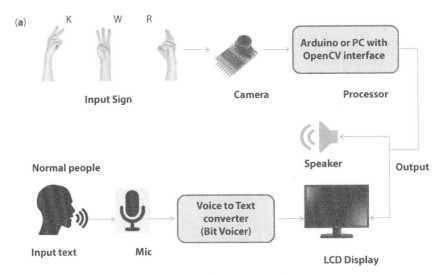

Basic block diagram of communication between
hearing and speech impaired person and normal person

Figure 9.9 (a) System architecture (basic block of communication).

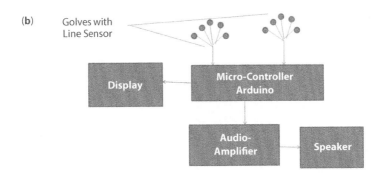

Figure 9.9 (b) System architecture (gloves interfacing with microcontroller).

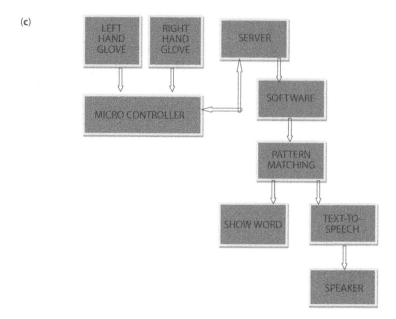

Figure 9.9 (c) System architecture (with pattern matching feature).

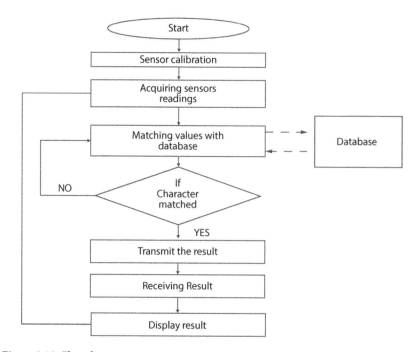

Figure 9.10 Flow diagram.

present or not, if it is not present, then it will be stored in the database otherwise discarded.

In the detection mode (Figure 9.11), the matched word is displayed but before displaying it needs to check in the database and convert it to speech, But if it is not available, then it shows "Not Available".

The values in Figure 9.12 shows the resistance value of the flex sensor and the green color indicate that finger is not bend and it sends integer value 0 in database; if the finger is bend, then the color becomes red and it sends integer value 1 in the database.

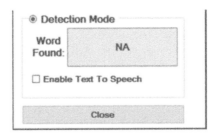

Figure 9.11 Detection mode.

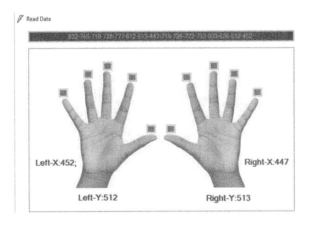

Figure 9.12 Values and signal obtained.

9.7   Advantages and Applications

Advantages

- Efficient way for mute communication.
- System is portable and flexible to users.
- It takes less power to operate the system.
- Easy to define gestures: Users can add their own gestures.
- Less time delay for conversation.
- Quick response time.
- Fully automated system.

Applications

- **Loud Venue:** A place like a pub, a building site, or a rock festival where there is so much crowd noise to have a regular conversation with people. Use ASL, it can quickly converse from a distance, no matter how much background noise there is. Users may also use earplugs to shield their ears and also talk just fine.
- **Injury Recovery or After Surgery:** Certain surgical operations (such as oral surgery) impair a person's ability to speak during recovery. People can interact with ASL without having to speak. Event Stage Squad or Teams of people employed in music, theater, or related environments benefit from being able to communicate over distances without shouting.
- **Video Production:** Working on a film collaboration alongside a few people at a big case. ASL users can chat quietly with other people from behind the camera and do not produce background conversation sounds that will interfere with video capture. Users can also communicate in a busy, noisy space without yelling.
- **Radio Station:** Users are in a radio station sound room with many people taking part in a live chat show. ASL users can connect with others on a live recording without talking or interrupting the broadcast.
- **Military Operations:** Users are delegated to special ops and required to stay fully quiet (including radio silence). Users of ASL can interact clearly with other members of the team. You can talk effectively over longer distances with binoculars.

References

1. Sharma, K. and Garg, N.K., Hand Gestures Recognition for Deaf and Dumb. *Int. J. Comput. Appl. Technol.* (s), Vol. 11, 10–13, May - 2014.
2. Shohaib Ahmed, V., MAGIC GLOVES (Hand Gesture Recognition and Voice Conversion System for Differentially Able Dumb People). *Tech Expo-The Global Summit*, London, 2012.
3. Tiwari, D. and Srivastava, S.K., A Visual Recognition of Static Hand Gestures in Indian Sign Language based on Kohonen Self-Organizing Map Algorithm. *Int. J. Eng. Adv. Technol.(IJEAT)*, 2, 165–170, Dec 2012.
4. Zhang, X., Chen, X., Li, Y., Lantz, V., Wang, K., Yang, J., A Framework for Hand Gesture Recognition Based on Accelerometer and EMG Sensors. *IEEE Trans. Syst. Man Cybern.—Part A: Syst. Hum.*, 41, 6, pp. No. 1064–1076, November 2011.
5. Heo, H., Lee, E.C., Park, K.R., Kim, C.J., Chang, M., A Realistic Game System Using MultiModal User Interfaces. *IEEE Trans. Consum. Electron.*, 56, 3, pp. 1364–1372, August 2010.
6. Alon, J., Athitsos, V., Yuan, Q., Sclaroff, S., A Unified Framework for Gesture Recognition and Spatiotemporal Gesture Segmentation. *IEEE Trans. Pattern Anal. Mach. Intell.*, 31, 9, pp. 1685–1699, September 2009.
7. Kosmidou, V.E. and Hadjileontiadis, L.J., Sign Language Recognition Using Intrinsic-Mode Sample Entropy on sEMG and Accelerometer Data. *IEEE Trans. Biomed. Eng.*, 56, 12, pp. 2879–2890, December 2009.
8. Dipietro, L., Sabatini, A.M., Dario, P., A Survey of Glove-Based Systems and Their Applications. *IEEE Trans. Syst. Man Cybern.—Part C: Appl. Rev.*, 38, 4, pp 461– 482, July 2008.
9. Advani, N., Bora, S., Bhat, A., Yerolkar, S., A Survey on Communication Gap between Hearing and Speech Impaired Persons and Normal Persons. *IJCSN Int. J. Comput. Sci. Netw.*, 2, 6, December 2013.
10. Suresh, P., Vasudevan, N., Ananthanarayanan, N., Computer-aided Interpreter for Hearing and Speech Impaired, in: *2012 Fourth International Conference on Computational Intelligence, Communication Systems and Networks*, https://www.infona.pl/resource/bwmeta1.element.ieee-pub-000006273236/tab/summary.
11. CSO-MDS-2012, *Manual on disablity statistics*, Government of India, Ministry of Statistics and Programme Implementation, New Delhi, www.mospi.gov.in, 2012.
12. Tripathy, A.K., Jadhav, D., Barreto, S.A., Rasquinha, D., Mathew, S.S., Voice for themute, in: *Proceedings of the 2015 International Conference on Technologies for Sustainable Development, ICTSD 2015*, February 2015.
13. Yousaf, K., Mehmood, Z., Saba, T. *et al.*, A Novel Technique for Speech Recognition and Visualization Based Mobile Application to Support Two-Way Communication between Deaf-Mute and Normal peoples. *Hindawi*

Wirel. Commun. Mob. Comput., Article ID 1013234, 12 Pages, 2018, https://doi.org/10.1155/2018/1013234.

14. Pray, J.L. and Jordan, I.K., The deaf community and culture at a crossroads: Issues and challenges. *J. Soc. Work Disabil. Rehabil.*, 9, 2, 168–193, 2010.

15. Barnett, S., Communication with deaf and hard-of-hearing people: A guide for medical education. *Acad. Med.: J. Assoc. Am. Med. Coll.*, 77, 7, 694–700, 2002.

16. Karlsson, N., Karlsson, B., Wide, P., A Glove Equipped with Finger Flexion Sensors as a Command Generator used in a Fuzzy Control System. *IEEE Trans. Instrum. Meas.*, 47, 5, October 1998.

17. Starner, T., Weaver, J., Pentland, A., Real-Time American Sign Language Recognition Using Desk and Wearable Computer Based Video. *IEEE Trans. Pattern Anal. Mach. Intell.*, 20, 12, 1371–1375, Dec. 1998.

18. Gujrati, A., Singh, K., Khushboo, Soral, L., Ambikapathy, Hand-talk Gloves with Flex Sensor: A Review. *Int. J. Eng. Sci. Invent.*, 2, 4, 43–46, April 2013.

19. Bretzner, L. and Lindeberg, T., Relative orientation from extended sequences of sparse point and line correspondences using the affine trifocal tensor, in: *Proc. 5th Eur. Conf. Computer Vision*, vol. 1406, Lecture Notes in Computer Science, Springer Verlag, Berlin, Germany, 1998.

20. Fels, S.S. and Hinton, G.E., — Glove-talk: A neural network interface between a data glove and a speech synthesizer. *IEEE Trans. Neural Networks*, 4, 1, 2–8, 1993.

21. Freeman, W.T. and Weissman, C.D., TV control by hand gestures. *Presented at the IEEE Int. Workshop on Automatic Face and Gesture Recognition*, Zurich, Switzerland, 1995.

22. Fu, K.S., *Syntactic Recognition in Character Recognition*, p. 112, Academic, New York, 1974, Mathematics in Science and Engineering.

10

The Effective Practice of Assistive Technology to Boom Total Communication Among Children With Hearing Impairment in Inclusive Classroom Settings

Fr. Baiju Thomas

Ramakrishna Mission Vivekananda Educational and Research Institute, Faculty of Disability Management and Special Education, Vidyalaya Campus, SRKV Post, Coimbatore, India

Abstract

It is very significant to offer accurate and applicable education for the children with hearing impairment (CwHI). The current study discovers the effective practice of Assistive Technology (AT) to gain total communication among CwHI in inclusive classroom settings. AT displays an active role in the education of CwHI in inclusive schools. This study further refer to the self-motivated benefits and motives why the practice of AT for CwHI. AT is usually determined and covers any component that increases, preserves, or improves the capabilities of a CwHI. In an inclusive classroom environment, AT devises functions to improve the total communication technique in teaching CwHI in inclusive classroom settings. Inclusive classroom settings are being measured as the best preference for CwHI and other learners with disabilities. CwHI are those students who lost their hearing both due to infections or accidents. Inclusive classroom settings can be favorable for numerous CwHI with supports and continuous bond with AT. AT is any device used to rise, sphere, or improve the communication abilities of CwHI. Through decreasing students' reliance on others, AT can endorse the outlook of elegant individuality and, thus, progress the prospect of inclusive education (IE) classroom setting. This paper discussed the model of the IE program as it marks CwHI and many trials and methods and endures facilities required for proper

Email: rtobaiju@gmail.com

Roshani Raut, Pranav Pathak, Sandeep Kautish and Pradeep N (eds.) Intelligent Systems for Rehabilitation Engineering, (223–238) © 2022 Scrivener Publishing LLC

implementation in an inclusive program for CwHI. The study confirms that AT and IE proposes beneficial recommendations to educators who target to practice AT more outstandingly in IE. AT includes products and correlated services that progress in working with CwHI. At this juncture, the author mentions some approaches to overawe the barriers by enhancing capabilities and resources to reviewing the AT to be more flexible to supply the requirements of CwHI in an inclusive classroom setting.

Keywords: Effective practice, assistive technology, boom, total communication, inclusive education, and children with hearing impairment

10.1 Introduction

It is rightly essential to offer accurate and suitable education for the hearing-impaired persons. Nowadays, it seems that spending only traditional instruction approaches is not adequate for the education of hearing-impaired persons. The usage of recent technologies marks the preparation for hearing-impaired persons more beneficial. Viewing at the literature, it is understood that there is a restricted number of studies on the broad usage of technologies used in the education of hearing-impaired persons in inclusive classroom settings. Persons with hearing impairments now have access to a variety of assistive devices that have significantly improved their educational, vocational, and recreational activities. Assistive technologies (ATs) are products or equipment that are used to advance and improve the well-made abilities of disabled people. Persons with disabilities can benefit from AT, which uses adaptive technology to help them [1]. SwHI may face a number of significant challenges in school and in their community lives [2]. Additional considerations are made when deciding on assistive devices, such as what will be the special effects of technology in shape and what will be the effects of frame on technologies [3]. "Technology has opened many educational doors for children, especially those with disabilities. In certain ways, technology-based substitute resolutions are beneficial for physical, sensory, and reasoning impairments" [4]. Children with hearing impairments (CwHIs) are more motivated to use AT than children with other disabilities. AT enables people, regardless of their disability, to overcome obstacles in their lives and become more independent in all aspects of living a useful life [5] in order to be well-protected and have equal rights. There should be no discrimination based on gender or age when it comes to AT for people with special needs [6].

The expense of AT devices for people with disabilities has been proposed to restrict their opportunity to live a self-determined life outside of school or at home [7]. AT is not a remedy for learning matters, but it can support students toil around their trials while in performance to their powers. AT aids students become more effective, creative students. At the same time, their self-assurance and individuality can develop. The suitable AT tools can be powerful in aiding students to become more effective and independent and can support students in exhausting their capabilities to toil on to learn an independent life in inclusive classroom settings.

10.2   Students With Hearing Impairment

Hearing is the capability to perceive the powered vibrations denoted to as sound. Hearing impairment is usually recognized as "deafness". It is an enclosed disability; it is difficult to identify a child with hearing impairment till relating with him/her or perceptive hearing benefits. Provisions may not be obvious as some hearing benefits are very tiny and located in or overdue the ear or have surgically fixed cochlear implants. Besides, not all persons with hearing impairments wear hearing aids. Hearing is the capability to distinguish sound. Person anguish from hearing impairment has struggle in observing or recognizing sound obviously due to hearing problems. The impairment may be independent or mutual. The sense of hearing delivers a contextual, which gives a sentiment of safety and involvement in life. It shows an acute role in the development of speech and language and nursing one's speech. Hearing-impaired persons have in common, their trouble in hearing spoken and other sounds. They also are depending on what they see which they improvement to what they hear. Students with hearing loss are labeled as "special needs" students. Hearing loss hinders the development of the developing displays, particularly language and communication. However, students with hearing impairments' speech and language abilities are critical for a detailed understanding of the depth and nature of hearing loss [8, 9]. Other issues that prevent the acquisition of social participations and limit the development of positive self-confidence include a lack of opportunities for communicating and interacting with others [10]. Hearing impairment is a broad term that refers to all degrees and types of hearing loss, as well as the condensed purpose of hearing and understanding speech and language that results from a hearing disorder [11, 12]. As a result, hearing impairment impairs students' ability to learn and participate in school and society, and deaf and hard-of-hearing students can be hampered by society's instructional structure and attitudes [13, 14]. Hearing loss and deafness are alarming to people of all ages, and they can worsen at any time, from early stages to old age. The impact of hearing loss is determined by the type, severity, and timing of the hearing loss. Some students will lose their hearing over time due to a variety of factors such as age or genetics. Others may have permanently lost their hearing due to factory noise or suffer from tinnitus, a high-pitched drumming sound in the ear. Cochlea implants or hearing aids may have enhanced, but not removed, certain people's hearing. Educators must prioritize all classrooms of pupils and, as a result, students who are deaf or hard of hearing in order to make meaningful changes to conventional teaching methods. Established approaches, on the other hand, make for a flatter difference from conventional education for both learners and educators.

10.3 The Classifications on Hearing Impairment

Hearing loss is a general term of impairment with a diversity of hereditary (existing at birth) and developed reasons. In this short-term unit, we describe some associated figures regarding hearing loss. Hearing loss that is not determined, restrictions one or more everyday actions, and/ or limits partaking, is a severe matter, mostly when it harmfully influences communication and general excellence of lifespan. Hearing loss is divided into three categories: conductive, sensorineural, and mixed. The system that mechanically transfers sound shaking into the interior ear is impaired in conductive hearing loss. The succeeding is cataloging on hearing impairments.

10.3.1 Conductive Hearing Losses

Conductive hearing losses are owed to the effects of illnesses or uncertain block in the outdoor or middle ear (the conduction paths for sound to the extent the interior ear). Conductive hearing losses normally distress all occurrences of hearing continuously and do not significance in severe losses. A person with a conductive hearing loss frequently is capable to use hearing devices well or can be aided medically or surgically. It does not upset the internal ear. In this circumstance, thus, if sound sensations can be conveyed in anyway straight to the internal ear without having to pass through the mid-ear, then the child hears. The person anguish from conductive hearing loss can be aided through procedure or over wearing bone transmission hearing aids behind the ears.

10.3.2   Sensorineural Hearing Losses

Damage to the gentle sensory hair cells of the internal ear or the nerves that supply it causes sensorineural hearing loss. Children with sensorineural hearing loss can experience difficulty hearing and speaking attentively. The severity of these hearing losses can range from mild to severe. They always interfere with a person's ability to hear secure events rather than others. Sensorineural hearing loss in young children can ensue with firm infections before birth, from a shortage of oxygen during birth or inherited disorders. Sensorineural hearing loss repeatedly cannot be treated with medicine or operation. Whereas this kind of hearing loss is perpetual, most children will advantage from hearing devices and other hearing ATs, besides with speech, language, and healing therapies.

10.3.3   Central Hearing Losses

Central hearing impairment: Cerebral cortex is the portion of the brain where the feeling of sound is formed and inferred expressively. Therefore, if there is intervention with the path through which nerve fibers continue from the brain stem to the sequential lobes of the cerebral cortex, then it outcomes to central hearing loss. In other words, a mistake in the auditory middle in the brain bases central deafness.

10.3.4   Mixed Hearing Losses

Mixed hearing losses mean to a mixture of conductive and sensorineural loss and signify that a difficult occurs in both the outdoor or mid and interior ear. Mixed hearing impairment is the grouping of conductive and sensorineural hearing loss. An individual here has exterior or middle and inner ear difficult joint. Mixed hearing deafness is often difficult to know and treat because there are problems of both broadcast and release of sound. Mixed hearing loss is obvious by a grouping of conductive injury in the external or central ear and sensorineural wound in the internal ear (cochlea) or aural nerve (Table 10.1).

Table 10.1 The relevant terms.

Deaf	Deafness	Hard of hearing
Deaf signifies to hearing impairments that eliminate effective treating of language information over audition, with or without a hearing provision. A person who is considered as "deaf" naturally has an intense hearing loss (beyond 90 dB) and is pre-lingual. In certain circumstances, deaf students may be able to speak or speech-read well.	This term refers to a profound hearing disability that greatly limits one's ability to access language knowledge exclusively by hearing, with or without the use of hearing aids. Even though they appear to be hard of hearing, students with cochlear implants are listed as mentally deaf. Deafness is not affected simply by a lack of communication skills or the need to use sign language. The inability of parents, specialists, and the general public to recognize and acknowledge the individual with this condition is the most significant issue facing a hearing-impaired child or adolescent, since deafness is often wrongly correlated with powerlessness and the need for resistance [15].	This word defines a degree of hearing loss that approves the student to process auditory information required for auditory-verbal communication, with the assist of hearing aids or assistive listening devices (ALD) when required. However, the amount of hearing loss is not a precise predictor of how one function auditorially. Hard of hearing denotes to impairment in hearing that does not completely avoid applied communication by speech. Hence, the person who is hard of hearing usually communicates by using speech. The audiologist assessment does not dependably envisage the student's capability to hear with understanding.

10.4   Inclusion of Hearing-Impaired Students in Inclusive Classrooms

The inclusion of children with disabilities in common classrooms has established the attention of extensive exploration in education. It has both academic and social well-being for all students, such as providing opportunity for communication and social relations. Inclusive education (IE) is the method of recurring to the diversity of children by enhancing participation in classrooms and reducing separation from education [16]. This change has been mentioned to variously as incorporation, straight, and, more in current times, inclusion. Inclusion denotes students with disabilities becoming a portion of the regular education classroom, getting an eloquent curriculum with essential provision, and being trained with effective approaches [17]. The notion of IE has been pinched from the human rights perception which matters that disability foundations differences in human features which may be in the procedure of sensory or physical ability, but these changes do not limit human abilities [18]. IE can be operative only if it is planned to be able to afford several stages and methods of support with both learners and educators. The source temperament is an important aspect of hearing-impaired students' inclusion in general education [19]. Starting with the awareness that many CwHIs are silently excluded from school due to a lack of support, it is critical to ensure that sufficient assets are made available [20]. In an IE system, human means are needed, and they include all people who assist hearing-impaired students in learning. Successful inclusion requires the definition of roles and obligations, teamwork, the forming of teams, and preparation [21]. A detailed prospectus is needed. Although hearing-impaired students follow the same program as their hearing peers, they are required to take additional subjects in order to participate in extra-curricular activities. Hearing-impaired students who wear hearing aids and others who have a significant hearing loss and need reserve assistance from a special educator must have their content needs addressed in inclusive classroom settings.

10.4.1   Assistive Technology

Students with disabilities can benefit from using technology to improve and increase their independence in educational and employment tasks, as well as participate in classroom debates and complete some difficult educational tasks. ATs are often recommended to colleges, parents, and educators as tools to help students with hearing impairments by offering compensatory value, resolving learning issues, and certifying individual independence. Many research projects have looked at the effectiveness of these assistive devices, mostly in terms of remediation and assistance. Students should be exposed to technical resources that can help them resolve their academic difficulties, particularly in central and unexpected schools [22]. Furthermore, if students can use a calculator but have difficulty saying numbers correctly, then they can use more specialized resources such as a speaking calculator, which can be used anytime or wherever they need it and helps students say numbers correctly [23]. Persons with disabilities have been using AT for many years, and its use in instructional, vocational, and playful activities is rapidly increasing. Following the appropriate broadcast of individual needs and technology stipulations for persons with disabilities, experts are clearing up special needs people with a variety of assistive devices and facilities [24]. Several factors are considered when selecting assistive devices, such as the impact of technology on the body and the frame's possessions on technologies [3]. The use, power, and special effects of AT on the learning of special needs students were investigated. The aim of this research is to show how useful AT can be in helping CwHIs in inclusive classrooms.

10.4.2 Assistive Technology for Hearing Impairments

ATs include a broad variety of assistive, adaptive, and rehabilitative devices for people who are deaf or hard of hearing. In the past 20 years, deafness and hearing disability assistive devices have advanced significantly. The three types of ATs are hardware-based, software-based, and prosthetic inserts. AT [25] may be a critical problem in allowing people with disabilities to engage in daily life and be a part of society. This technology has two functions: it is a tool for recognizing freedom as well as a noticeable indicator of disability [26]. When AT is treated as a tool or a method of accomplishing a desired goal, it is more likely to be incorporated into the user's life. In the other hand, technology that is viewed as a simple signal of an impairment will highlight the dishonor associated with the disability. People with a negative attitude toward technology, on the other hand, may avoid or discourage using it; they may avoid expressive acts and try to isolate themselves socially and physically [27]. In a number of environments, deaf and hard-of-hearing individuals use a variety of assistive devices to increase their user-friendliness. Most devices that have enhanced sound or alternate methods of knowledge access often provide vision and/or vibration. These technologies fall into three different categories: hearing technology, notification systems, and communication provisions. Within each key grouping, there may be subgroups based on various reasons or expected audiences when using the technology. The end aim of both of these devices is to increase information accessibility for people who use hearing aids. The illustrations that follow are meant to restore the reader's understanding of these tools' meaning, as well as when and how they could be created. Deaf and hard-of-hearing people can use ATs in particular circumstances, depending on their needs. By using intervals, these ATs can be used in parallel. Many of the approaches developed for deaf or hard of hearing people could be appropriate for people who do not have hearing loss; however, this knowledge is out of date at this time. The evidence provided is remarkable in that it is broad enough to provide the student with a common understanding of AT advanced among people who are deaf or hard of hearing. Since technology and websites for students with hearing impairments in inclusive classroom settings are constantly evolving, no computer, manufacturer, or resource can be considered dominant.

10.4.3   Hearing Technology

Hearing technology will play an important role in the education of deaf and hard-of-hearing children in inclusive classrooms. Just a few studies have looked at how these kids use technology. Hearing technology is almost indistinguishable from any other system that increases the amount of sound available to a listener. This study examines concerns surrounding children's use of and attitudes toward hearing aids, cochlear implants, teacher-worn microphones, and student-worn microphones, among other technologies. Individual amplifiers that are normally placed on the head or on the body, such as hearing aids and cochlear implants, as well as assistive listening devices that are not naturally worn on the head or on the body, such as classroom sound field amplification systems, are protected by hearing technology for deaf and hard-of-hearing citizens [28]. Despite the fact that students and educators agree that using hearing technology is self-motivated for successful inclusion [29, 30], the tools are used infrequently and ineffectively due to the stigma associated with ATs. Hearing equipment offered to deaf and hard-of-hearing students in inclusive schools has the ability to enhance teaching and learning practices in inclusive classrooms for students with hearing impairments. In inclusive classroom settings, no computer, manufacturer, or resource can have a significant influence.

10.4.4   Assistive Listening Devices

These instruments, of course, are used to increase the signal-to-noise ratio in any given situation. ALDs provide a direct connection to the sound source, reducing the special effects of contextual sound, range, and room audibility in addition to increased power. There are both individual ALDs and collective or big group ALDs. A transmitter sends a person's speech or another sound source to a headset, which distributes the sound equally in a building, such as in theaters and churches, or directly to a single person. The four key ways to transmit sound are frequency modulation (FM), infrared (light), induction loop (electromagnetic), and a straight link. Direct audio input (DAI) is a feature of some hearing aids that allows the consumer to attach directly to an FM device or an Induction Loop receiver. In many cases, a computer, television, MP3 player, or radio can be connected directly to the device. ALDs denote to several types of amplification tools intended to enhance the communication of persons with hard of hearing to improve the user-friendliness to speech indication when individual hearing devices are not appropriate. There are several types of ALDs to overawe a threesome of speech-to-sound percentage (SNR) difficulties, sound, space, and echo. ALDs contrast in their inner electronic procedures extending from simple hard-wire microphone-amplifier essentials to more fashionable broadcasting systems.

10.4.5 Personal Amplification

These devices are intended to increase a person's sound access in all situations. They are chosen because they are based on a person's interests, the diagnosis and confirmation of hearing loss, and the individual's specific characteristics. An audiologist is required to acquire and tailor this group of equipment. Although many foundations do not consider personal amplification to be AT, assistive attending devices and other auditory-based devices (MP3, TV, and computer) can be connected across these systems and explained concisely. In addition, some reserve sources say that personal intensification can be achieved by the use of AT. Students who use hearing aids or cochlear implants and are deaf or hard of hearing will be eligible to participate in AT. A teacher's voice can be transmitted directly from a wireless microphone worn by the teacher over FM radio waves to a small receiver worn by a student with hearing loss. Amplified phones have a wide range of adapted mobile phones and notification systems that can help people with varying degrees of hearing loss. Face-to-face communication systems can offer support when little, one-on-one discussions are required. Text and other adaptive telephones (TTY) can offer access for persons who cannot use amplified phones. Added choices now available contain PDAs, Blackberries, Sidekicks, and videophones. These devices amplify speech heard over the phone. They are beneficial for people who do not wear hearing aids. This technology is used fewer frequently now that texting is available over cell phones. In response to sound, notification devices show a sign. To warn the person with hearing loss that a sound has occurred, some use strobe lights, steady lights, or colorful systems.

10.4.6   Communication Supports

In inclusive classroom environments, students with hearing impairments often use a variety of ATs to improve contact with their peers. The child and family need a communication method that allows for normal, articulate, and ample exchanges. Hearing aids can help people who were born with a hearing loss or those whose hearing has deteriorated but who still have some residual hearing. Hearing aids cannot restore hearing, but they do assist in making the sounds you need to hear more audible. Certain people may benefit from cochlear implants, a surgically implanted hearing device. These are usually only recommended for people who have a severe hearing loss and are unable to use hearing aids. Smart headphones can be used for a variety of purposes, including staying in touch, searching for facts, and finding your way around. People and groups that were previously unreachable can now connect, form relationships, and connect a group thanks to social media. Videoconferencing is highly helpful because it alleviates minor possible stressors by encouraging parents to participate in their children's Individualized Education Program (IEP) resolutions in inclusive classroom environments for hearing-impaired students.

10.5   Total Communication System for Hearing Impairments

Total communication is a method in which voice, fingerspelling, and signs are all practiced [31]. In deaf educational settings, TC is the most widely used contact tool [32]. For receptive communication, newborns and small children will rely on supported residual hearing as well as visual cues from signs and lip reading. The child is strengthened to communicate sensitively using both signs and words. He went on to say that the goal is to include a variety of opportunities for children with hearing loss to learn to communicate and use speech as a social communication tool. The majority of general education teachers profit from total cooperation when it comes to resolving communication and instruction issues. The total communication system is a method for reinforcing and improving the skills required for SHI to work in a general classroom setting. Since they do not have talents, common education teachers tend to be apathetic about the use of absolute contact. Such teachers can be unconcerned about the philosophies and teaching strategies that rely on absolute contact, and as a result, they become counterproductive [33]. Furthermore, if teachers lack the necessary skills and knowledge, then a lively environment that encourages students to learn and develop their skills will not be created [34]. In educational presentations, these students may be a step behind their hearing peers [35]. In general education classrooms, teachers can also do things that are detrimental to genuine SHI teaching and learning [36]. For example, they want total communication and assistive hearing, such as hearing aids and cochlear transplants, to be continued, so that they can maximize their communication abilities [37]. Total communication is a method of educating children with hearing loss that includes all forms of communication, such as proper signs, natural movements, fingerspelling, body language, listening, lip-reading, and voice. Hearing aids or cochlear implants are worn by children on total communication channels normally.

Table 10.2 Assistive technology devices that are recommended for students with hearing impairments.

Devices	Explanations
Amplified Telephone	It builds up to ring load to vigilant those who are deaf or hard of hearing. Non-aid operators shall require getting at minimum a cell phone with amplification proficiencies.
Headphones and Headset	Headphones are a daily device for a maximum of us. Further thing to recall is that the best hearing aids have sets for "music" which proceeds into account headphones.
Personal Listeners	New device available for non-aid operators is the personal amplifier, also recognized as the personal listeners. These devices are designed as a little bigger than Mp3 players and which provides a better amplifying sound system for a hearing aid use.
Hearing Aids	A hearing aid is a battery-powered electronic device aimed to improve your hearing. A BTE hearing aid is the best frequently used variety of aid with children.

(Continued)

Table 10.2 Assistive technology devices that are recommended for students with hearing impairments. (*Continued*)

Devices	Explanations
Cochlear Implants Processors	Cochlear implants are surgically implanted electric devices that restore hearing to people who are profoundly deaf or hard of hearing in both ears.
Blee	Blee is a wearable band for deaf and hard of hearing persons. In daily life, deaf persons false step on several occasions, occasionally even emergency notifications for the reason that they cannot respond to sound.
Personal FM System	An FM module is a type of hearing aid that improves the speech-to-noise ratio by using a distant microphone that can be rented near the sound source.
Automatic Speech Recognition	Automatic Speech Recognition (ASR) is the procedure of stemming the transcript of a sound, given the speech waveform. Speech understanding goes one phase more and gathers the sense of the sound to transport the speaker's command.
Voice Carry-Over	Voice Carry-Over (VCO) treaties persons with a hearing loss endure to use their voice on the telephone. VCO, a technology established by Ultratec, lets persons to speak straight to the person they are calling, then read that person's reply on their CapTel, TTY, or IPhone show.
T-Mobile Sidekick	This text-based communication standard, along with on-device email and a full QWERTY keyboard, made it general with the deaf community, providing a telecommunication tool for use both intimate and outdoor the home.
Real-Time Captioning	Distant real-time captions are designed at a distant area and then sent to the spot where the program is taking place.
Screen Readers	A screen reader is a software application that empowers persons with deaf and hard of hearing to use a computer. The software provides manuscript documents and even the names of programs on headlines on the screen.
Caption Call	This phone interprets the voice to manuscript. This works on the internet [38].

In inclusive classroom environments, the aim is to support language learning in whatever way is most active for each child (Table 10.2).

10.6   Conclusion

The CwHI are capable of making the best of teaching and learning results together with their normal-hearing equals in an inclusive educational setting if presumed a proper learning atmosphere with satisfactory provisions of concerned expert staff, devices, tools, and resources that will improve the execution of the inclusion platform for CwHI. Learning is a procedure that occurs in obvious and ideal conditions, according to studies, to the point where circumstances in which students are engaged deliberately or then have great special effects on them. It also discusses educator attitudes toward the inclusion of hearing-impaired students, stating that doing so is always dangerous and fraught with conflicts and discrepancies. Finally, teacher skills, learner needs, and the availability of ATs for enhancing complete contact between hearing-impaired and their normal-hearing peers in inclusive classroom settings have played a role in enabling the inclusion of hearing-impaired students.

References

1. UNESCO. ICTs in education for people with special needs. Institute for Information Technologies in Education Specialized Training course, Moscow, 2006.
2. Akçamete, G., Kış, A., Gürgür, H., *Özel gereksinimli öğrenciler için kaynaştırma modeli geliştirme projesi, Ankara Üniversitesi bilimsel araştırma projesi kesin raporu*, 2009.
3. Hersh, M.A. and Johnson, M.A., Anatomy and physiology of hearing, hearing impairment and treatment, in: *Assistive technology for the hearing impaired, deaf and deafblind*, M.A. Hersh and M.A. Johnson (Eds.), pp. 1–39, Springer, London, 2003.
4. Dede, C., *Learning with Technology. 1998 ASCD Yearbook*, Association for Supervision and Curriculum Development, 1250 N. Pitt St., Alexandria, VA 22314–1453 (Stock No. 198000; $15.95, member; $18.59, non-member), 1998.
5. Bouck, E.C., Shurr, J.C., Tom, K., Jasper, A.D., Bassette, L., Miller, B., Flanagan, S.M., Fix it with TAPE: Repurposing technology to be assistive technology for students with high-incidence disabilities. *Prev. Sch. Fail.: Alternative Education for Children and Youth*, 56, 2, 121–128, 2012 Jan 1.

6. Borg, J., Larsson, S., Östergren, P.O., The right to assistive technology: For whom, for what, and by whom? *Disabil. Soc.*, 26, 2, 151–167, 2011 Mar 1.

7. Harris, F., Sprigle, S., Sonenblum, S.E., Maurer, C.L., The participation and activity measurement system: an example application among people who use wheeled mobility devices. *Disabil. Rehabil.: Assist. Technol.*, 5, 1, 48–57, 2010 Jan 1.

8. Gilliam, M.L. Gonadotrophin-releasing hormone antagonists for assisted reproductive technology. *Obstet. Gynecol.*, 118, 3, 706–707, 2011.

9. English, M.A. and Mastrean, M.B., Congestive heart failure: Public and private burden. *Crit. Care Nurs. Q.*, 18, 1, 1–6, 1995.

10. Stotz, K.E., Itoi, M., Konrad, M., Alber-Morgan, S.R., Effects of self-graphing on written expression of fourth grade students with high-incidence disabilities. *J. Behav. Educ.*, 17, 2, 172–186, 2008.

11. Balciuniene, J., Dahl, N., Jalonen, P., Verhoeven, K., Van Camp, G., Borg, E., Jazin, E.E. Alpha-tectorin involvement in hearing disabilities: One gene–two phenotypes. *Hum Genet.*, 105, 3, 211–216, 1999.

12. Stach, B.A. and Ramachandran, V., Hearing aids: Strategies of amplification. *Cumming otolaryngology-head and neck surgery*, 5th ed., pp. 2265–2275, Mosby Elsevier, Philadelphia, 2010.

13. Paul, P.V. and Whitelaw, G.M., *Hearing and deafness: An introduction for health and education professionals*, Jones & Bartlett Publishers, 2010.

14. Zhu, J., Yamane, H., Paul, W.E., Differentiation of effector CD4 T cell populations. *Ann. Rev. Immunol.*, 28, 445–489, 2009.

15. Adoyo, P.O. and Maina, E.N., Practices and Challenges in Deaf Education in Kenya. *Deaf Education Beyond the Western World: Context, Challenges, and Prospects*, pp. 73–86, 2019.

16. UNESCO. *World conference on special needs education: Access and equality. Salamanca, Spain.* Paris, Author, 1994.

17. Attewell, J. and Savill-Smith, C., Mobile learning and social inclusion: Focusing on learners and learning. In *Learning with Mobile Devices: Research and Development*, pp. 3–11, 2004.

18. Cober, E.R., Rioux, S., Rajcan, I., Donaldson, P.A., Simmonds, D.H., Partial resistance to white mold in a transgenic soybean line. *Crop Sci.*, 43, 1, 92–95, 2003.

19. Chimedza, R. and Peters, S., Disabled people's quest for social justice in Zimbabwe, in: *Disability, human rights, and education: Cross-cultural perspectives*, pp. 7–23, 1999.

20. Chakuchichi, D.D., Chimedza, R.M., Chiinze, M.M., Kaputa, T.M., Including the excluded issues in disability and inclusion. Zimbabwe Open University, Harare, 2003.

21. Ainscow, M., Education for all: Making it happen. Keynote address, in: *International Special Education Congress*, Birmingham, 1995.

22. Mull, C.A. and Sitlington, P.L., The role of technology in the transition to postsecondary education of students with learning disabilities: A review of the literature. *J. Spec. Educ.*, 37, 1, 26–32, 2003 May.

23. Lankutis, T., Special Needs Technologies: An Administrator's Guide. *Technol. Learn.*, 25, 2, 30, 2004 Sep 1.

24. Cook, A.M. and Hussey, S., *Assistive Technologies: Principles and Practice,* Mosby, St. Louis, MO, 2002.

25. Schneidert, M., Hurst, R., Miller, J., Üstün, B., The role of environment in the International Classification of Functioning, Disability and Health (ICF). *Disabil. Rehabil.*, 25, 11–12, 588–595, 2003 Jan 1.

26. Jutai, J.W., Fuhrer, M.J., Demers, L., Scherer, M.J., DeRuyter, F., Toward a taxonomy of assistive technology device outcomes. *Am. J. Phys. Med. Rehabil.*, 84, 4, 294–302, 2005.

27. Lu, Y., Luo, X., Polgar, M., Cao, Y., Social network analysis of a criminal hacker community. *J. Comput. Inform. Syst.*, 51, 2, 31–41, 2010.

28. Dillon, H., Hearing aid technology and the future, in: *Presentation at the Acoustical Society of American conference,* Honolulu, HI, 2006.

29. Eriks-Brophy, A., Durieux-Smith, A., Olds, J., Fitzpatrick, E., Facilitators and barriers to the inclusion of orally educated children and youth with hearing loss in schools: Promoting partnerships to support inclusion. *Volta Rev.*, 106, 1, 53, 2006 Apr 1.

30. Luckner, J.L. and Muir, S., Successful students who are deaf in general education settings. *Am. Ann. Deaf,* 435–446, 2001.

31. Olawole, G., *Total quality management in Nigerian SME companies: a case study of Rolling Technologies communication limited,* 2010.

32. GRI. *Sustainability reporting guidelines.* GRI, Boston, MA, 2002.

33. Raji, A., Seely, E.W., Bekins, S.A., Williams, G.H., Simonson, D.C., Rosiglitazone improves insulin sensitivity and lowers blood pressure in hypertensive patients. *Diabetes Care,* 26, 1, 172–178, 2003 Jan 1.

34. Adaka, A. and Ugwuanyi, L.T., Using total communication technique in teaching students with hearing impairment in inclusive classrooms in Enugu State-Nigeria: Teachers' perspectives and difficulties. *Aust. J. Basic Appl. Sci.,* 11, 5, 100–107, 2017.

35. Esplugas, S., Bila, D.M., Krause, L.G.T., Dezotti, M., Ozonation and advanced oxidation technologies to remove endocrine disrupting chemicals (EDCs) and pharmaceuticals and personal care products (PPCPs) in water effluents. *J. Hazard. Mater.,* 149, 3, 631–642, 2007.

36. Kolo, J., Information and communication technology transformation in the Middle East: issues and initiatives from the sustainability prism, in: *Technological Transformation and Competitiveness in the Middle East,* Inderscience, Enterprises Ltd, London, UK, 2007.

37. Marschark, M., Lang, H.G., Albertini, J.A. Reading, writing, and literacy. In *Educating Deaf Students.* Oxford University Press, New York, 2002.

38. Thomas, F.B., The significance of assistive technology in inclusive education: Creating scope for persons with disabilities. *Int. J. Adv. Res. Ideas Innov. Technol.*, 5, 1, 721–727, 2019.

Index

Printed and bound by CPI Group (UK) Ltd, Croydon, CR0 4YY